ADAPTATION AND SYMBOLISM

Sir Raymond Firth, 1974. Photograph by Hugh Firth.

ADAPTATION AND SYMBOLISM: ESSAYS ON SOCIAL ORGANIZATION

Presented to
Sir Raymond Firth
by His Students in the United States and Canada
1968–1974

Edited by
Karen Ann Watson-Gegeo and S. Lee Seaton

🌾 AN EAST-WEST CENTER BOOK
From The East-West Culture Learning Institute

Published for the East-West Center
by The University Press of Hawaii

Library of Congress Cataloging in Publication Data
Main entry under title:

Adaptation and symbolism.

  Includes bibliographies and index.
  CONTENTS: Watson-Gegeo, K. A. Introduction.—
Feinberg, R. Rank and authority on Anuta Island.—
Ryan, D. Cliques, factions, and leadership among the
Toaripi of Papua. [etc.]
  1. Social structure—Addresses, essays, lectures.
2. Ethnology—Addresses, essays, lectures. 3. Firth,
Raymond William, 1901–   —Addresses, essays, lectures.
I. Firth, Raymond William, 1901–   II. Watson-
Gegeo, Karen Ann, 1942–   III. Seaton, S. Lee,
1943–
GN478.A3   301.4   78–3815
ISBN 0-8248-0559-3

Frontispiece photograph by Hugh Firth

Contents

Preface

A good teacher is one whose knowledge is both broad and deep, who is committed to a perspective and yet is familiar with and open to a variety of ideas and approaches, whose keen ability at analysis is joined to an exciting talent for synthesis. A good teacher is one who, like the mythic guide, unveils to students worlds they never dreamed of.

A great teacher is one who does all these so skillfully that students come to master the creative process themselves. Sir Raymond Firth is such a teacher, a fact well known to the several generations of students who have had the privilege of studying with him.

For those of us attending graduate schools of anthropology and sociology in the United States and Canada since his retirement from the London School of Economics, the privilege of studying with Professor Firth has been especially appreciated. We are a generation of students who arrived at the time when British social anthropology and American cultural anthropology were moving beyond détente to mutual synthesis: synthesizing perspectives on human behavior, exchanging techniques of analysis and arriving at new ones jointly, evolving toward a humanistic and scientific anthropology capable of dealing with both an urbanizing world and a rural world. All this without forfeiting the uniqueness of approach which characterizes each school.

And so Professor Firth's sojourn through universities of the United States and Canada since the late 1960s—Hawaii (1968-1969), British Columbia (1969), Cornell (1970), Chicago (1970-1971), Graduate School of the City University of New York (1971), California (Davis 1974)—was more than a set of guest seminars by a distinguished scholar. It was, rather, a genuine infusion of alternative ways of looking at human behavior and human institutions gained less through reading the major works of anthropology than through the dynamics of the seminar. It was understanding gained from face-to-face talk with the man who is perhaps the greatest living teacher of anthropology today.

For Professor Firth's reputation is based not only on his writings, which have been undeniably profound, exacting, and prolific, and always bring a special emphasis when he is mentioned as The Ethnographer. Professor Firth's reputation is also based on the many students who have taken his ideas and built on them to make contributions of their own.

In this lies the genius of Raymond Firth as teacher and seminar leader. He takes an active role as catalyst and arbiter rather than as instructor and director. Yet his hand is subtly there in the form of the discourse to give the process direction, and he makes his statements through the students by guiding the seminar in such a way that realizations and ideas are drawn out of them. His seminars are genuine examples of learning as transaction. If anything aptly illustrates one of Professor Firth's important theoretical contributions to anthropology—the concept of social organization—it is how he conducts his own seminars.

Even so, as brilliant a scholar and teacher as he is, the fundamental quality of Raymond Firth is his humanity. And here it is impossible to express the spirit of knowing him as a person. To try to do so is to speak in the complex semiparadoxes of human character, where gentleness, humor, and receptivity are balanced with strength, sincerity, and commitment. To try to do so brings one at last to words and qualities unfashionable these days—grace, charity, sensitivity, wisdom, a giver of light.

The essays in this volume are as widely ranging as Professor Firth's own interests, and they share with each other a synthesis of Firthian perspectives with those of other theoretical schools. They also share a concern with process and organization of human behavior.

We, his students from universities in Canada and the United States, present these essays in his honor to Professor Firth with our love and deep appreciation.

Honolulu, Hawaii   KAREN ANN WATSON-GEGEO
                                                      S. LEE SEATON

Introduction

KAREN ANN WATSON-GEGEO

In his paper "The Meaning of Social Anthropology," first read as a Josiah Mason Lecture in 1947, Raymond Firth distinguishes social anthropology from the other social sciences on the basis of three characteristic features.[1] The first of these is intensive, detailed, and systematic observation of people's behavior in groups. The second is the holistic implication of anthropology inquiry: the study of any particular aspect of a society is always considered in terms of its relation to the whole society, and thus there must be an emphasis on contextualization. Third, social anthropology aims at comparison among different societies, "with the object of establishing types and seeing variants from them" (1961:17–18). In summary, then (ibid.:19):

> The intensive character of anthropological observation gives reality to the data; the science deals with the behavior of real people. The relational character gives the aim of looking at social life as process, of finding meaning in effects and not simply in appearances. The comparative character gives generalizations which apply to human beings in many different kinds of circumstances over the globe. Social anthropology aims therefore at being truly a science of Man, and not simply a science of ourselves.

Inherent in Firth's view of social anthropology is a respect for cultural variation understood within the context of the systematic nature of society. His books and essays, written at a time when overt forms of colonialism were coming to an end in Asia and the Pacific, include some strongly worded appeals to the West that the values and traditions of nonindustrialized societies be understood and respected, that the same standard of human rights be accorded to all, and that the impact of Westernization on non-Western communities be recognized.

Firth's reputation as anthropologist and ethnographer rests on his prolific writings that delve into the implications of all three characteristic features of social anthropology. His work has been eclectic in methodology, for he always realized that the social sciences are interrelated. His work has also been eclectic in content, for no aspect of human behavior has escaped his notice, and his research has taken him into the field among the Maori, the Malay, and the Tikopia.

It is generally recognized that Firth's most significant contribution to anthropological theory is his concept of *social organization,* described in 1947 as "social process, the arrangement of action in sequences in conformity with selected social ends," "the exercise of choice, the making of decisions," and "the allocation of resources" (ibid.:36). These elements of social organization lead to recognition of others: time, magnitude, representation, responsibility (ibid.:37–38). The study of social relations from the perspective of social organization directs the ethnographer's attention to everyday life, with the assumption that variation, adaptation, and social change are normal to the human condition: societies are dynamic, not static.

The essays in this volume range almost as widely across anthropology as Firth's own writings. Nevertheless, they fall into two groups. The first five essays—by Feinberg, Ryan, Peoples, Boggs, and Wu—analyze organization principles as they are worked out in the course of social interaction, emphasizing the situational nature of behavior and decision-making. These essays are also concerned with patterns of adaptation and social change, particularly those changes precipitated by external forces. All five authors draw on oral tradition and on observed episodes in everyday life, echoing Firth's own descriptive and analytic style in, for instance, *We, The Tikopia* (1957).

Richard Feinberg's "Rank and Authority on Anuta Island" is a detailed and illuminating account of kin groups, rank, and chieftainship on Anuta, a Polynesian outlier in the Solomon Islands. Anuta language, culture, and society are closely related to those of nearby Tikopia. Thus Feinberg's analysis invites comparison with Firth's "Authority and Public Opinion in Tikopia," "Succession to Chieftainship in Tikopia," and "Some Principles of Social Organization" (all reprinted in Firth 1964). Feinberg notes, for example, that the rules of succession to chieftainship on Anuta are temporarily set aside much more frequently than they are on Tikopia, in order to guarantee a present and competent chief. At the same time, in contrast to the Tikopia, the Anuta are willing to appoint a regent for a child of the chiefly line until he reaches the proper age to assume full chieftainship.

A major difference between Anuta and Tikopia is the role of the Christian church. When Firth originally went to Tikopia in 1929, the church played a small though in some ways significant role in Tikopian life. When he returned to Tikopia in 1955, he found that the influence of the church had grown, but that it was not yet a dominating factor in Tikopian society. Feinberg's study of Anuta in the early 1970s reveals that on Anuta the church is the "central institution," and the four *pakaako* or catechists are regarded as having *manuu* (*mana* or power) equal to that of the two traditional *ariki* (chief). The *pakaako* are assisted by a voluntary lay group, the Companions, who are also believed to have *manuu* because of their association with the church. The adaptation of the *ariki* system to these new social entities, the church's use of traditional Anutan principles in its own ranking system, and the potential competition for political authority is interestingly documented by Feinberg.

Dawn Ryan's "Cliques, Factions, and Leadership Among the Toaripi" and James Peoples' "From Cargo to Politics: The Transformation of the Yali Cult" are both concerned with politics and leadership in New Guinea societies. Beyond that, they are steps toward the realization of what Firth argued was the object of "dynamic theory," taken here as the criteria for dynamic analysis: the identification and assessment of the general magnitude of changes in social form, the forces responsible for such change, and the direction or trend of events (Firth 1964:9).

Ryan's essay challenges the assumption that traditional leadership in Melanesia was necessarily of the "Big Man" type. She begins by sketching what is known about the nature of leadership prior to 1920 among the Toaripi, a people on the south coast of New Guinea. Traditionally, peace-keeping and leadership were exercised through patrilineal men's houses, each of which was headed by a number of *pukari*. The *pukari*'s leadership was backed by supernatural sanction, but any single *pukari*'s influence was situational. Ryan argues that the "inheritance of knowledge which sustained [the *pukaris*'] positions of authority marked off a catchment of people who competed to exercise actual leadership, but there was no provision for the emergence of a Big Man of the kind so frequently described in the literature."

The traditional *pukari* form of leadership was destroyed as a result of the Vailala Madness, a cargo cult movement in 1919. To prevent further cargo cult activities, the colonial government set up a village constable system. The village constables, along with Christian missionaries, exercised leadership from 1920 to 1960. Among Toaripi today there is a diffuse pattern of leadership without supernatural support. "Leadership among the Toaripi emerges from the successful manipulation of interests served by membership of cliques and factions." Ryan's engrossing account of the social organization of these cliques, their inherent factionalism, and the reasons why a clique leader can never become a "Big Man" as that term is usually meant is an excellent illustration of "continuity and adaptation of organizational principles to meet changing circumstances."

While Ryan concentrates on post-cargo cult leadership in New Guinea, Peoples is concerned with the cult phenomenon itself. In an excellent reanalysis of the cargo cult led by Yali in New Guinea's Madang district during the 1940s, Peoples rejects ideological explanations of cargo cults such as that offered for the Yali cult by Peter Lawrence. Peoples argues that ideological explanations fail to account for why cargo cults "became a force for action in the context and structure of the colonial situation." Moreover, cargo cultism was not the only ideological alternative available to Melanesians who sought to obtain wealth like that displayed by the Europeans during World War II. Thus Peoples sets out to show that cargo cults are better understood through a social organizational approach that examines the goals of the actors, the means available to them, and the factors influencing their choices.

Peoples combines an incisive critique of Lawrence's analysis with a careful historical reconstruction of Yali's activities and the circumstances and events that led to the emergence of the cult. He maintains that Yali resisted cultism, but finally accepted the role of a cargo cult prophet on situational grounds as "a pragmatic political act—an act intended to consolidate and legitimate his status and power with the Madang people." In contrast to the view that cultism formed the basis of the first panregional (multivillage) organization in Melanesia, therefore, Peoples shows that Yali's efforts were actually a reaction against cultism.

Ultimately, as Peoples concludes, it is not the ideology of a movement that is important in judging whether the movement is a positive or negative force for economic and political development, since a leader will adopt the ideology that justifies his or her status and builds popular support. In his essay "Social Change in Peasant Communities" (1961:203), Firth had called cargo cults "creative attempts of the people to re-form their own institutions, to meet new demands or withstand new pressures." Peoples goes further to assert that cults may be more effective in achieving social unity than "functionally specific" political organizations which actually serve the interests of economically and politically powerful groups in a community, rather than the broader needs and interests of subordinate groups.

Anthropologists have always regarded kin relations as the core of human society. Firth's own writings on kinship have been seminal and prolific. The subtitle of *We, The Tikopia* itself is "A Sociological Study of Kinship in Primitive Polynesia." At the beginning of his essay, "From the Mouths of Babes: Reflections of Social Structure in the Verbal Interaction of Part-Hawaiian Children," Stephen T. Boggs cites Firth's remark that the apparently trivial incidents of everyday life "in reality form the substance of the kinship pattern" (Firth 1957:138; see also in the same volume his chapter on "Personal Relations in the Family"). Since 1966 Boggs has been recording what Hawaiian children say to one another, to members of their families, and to him as an interviewer, as well as conducting participant observation among children and their families. His aim has been to find out how children themselves understand Hawaiian kinship, how they interact with parents, siblings, and peers, and the process of socialization through which they come to share the adult values of the Hawaiian community.

Previous studies of personality development among Polynesians have emphasized a "rejection hypothesis": that infants are indulged by their parents, but after infancy any intrusive demands they make on their parents are punished. This hypothesis has suggested that children might wish to return to the "happy condition of the infant." When Hawaiian children were interviewed, however, Boggs found that they expressed a strong desire to be older, and that the age-graded sibling hierarchy in the family encourages the desire of young children to be older, to be given more responsibility, and to reap the benefits of prestige and authority.

Boggs traces the socialization experience for children aged 3 to 12, showing that socialization and interactional patterns in the Hawaiian family are still similar to those in other Polynesian societies: babies are indulged, older children direct the activities of younger children, age is used as a principle for ordering relationships among siblings, there is a strong norm against acting older than one's age, and techniques of conflict resolution are learned during adolescence. By the time a Hawaiian has reached young adulthood, the values of humility and nonassertiveness have been thoroughly instilled.

What makes Boggs' essay such fascinating (and often humorous) reading is his inclusion of what children themselves report directly and indirectly about behavior in the family, social organization among siblings, and their own experiences in social interaction. Verbal routines and verbal play—especially the hazing of younger boys by older boys through which humility and nonassertiveness are learned—are highly significant in Hawaiian socialization. Boggs has analyzed the structure of conversational routines and the social rules governing verbal play among Hawaiian children elsewhere (see especially Boggs 1972, Boggs and Watson-

Gegeo 1976, and Watson-Gegeo and Boggs 1977). The finding that Hawaiian socialization patterns continue to bear a close resemblance to those of other Polynesian groups, despite the virtual destruction of traditional Hawaiian culture a century ago, suggests that socialization of young children may be one area of behavior most resistant to rapid social change.

That the persistence of child-rearing patterns may have a positive effect on adaptation to a new social situation is supported by David Wu's "The Chinese in New Guinea: The Adaptation of an Immigrant Population." Wu's essay is an insightful examination of how immigrant Chinese came to occupy a specialized "social niche" in the socioeconomic structure of Papua New Guinea. He approaches the history and adaptation of immigrant Chinese from two perspectives: the outsider or European perspective (reconstructed from records of the colonial administration and other European writings), and the insider or Chinese perspective (from in-depth interviews and participant-observation in the community). By integrating these two perspectives, Wu shows that from the late nineteenth century until World War II, the Chinese occupied a social niche indispensable to both Europeans and the native population: they were the artisans and traders who serviced the other two groups.

The adaptability of the Chinese is manifest in their willingness to take any opportunity available, including changing from one job to the next—from carpenter to plantation manager to sailor to storekeeper—and their willingness to convert to Christianity. On the other hand, many traditional Chinese social institutions, especially the voluntary associations based on clan, hometown, dialect, and guild, proved very useful in adjusting to the new environment. Wu attributes the commercial success of the immigrant working-class Chinese to four factors: (1) traditional cultural values emphasized in child-rearing, especially nonaggressiveness, patience, endurance, frugality, austerity, temperance, and hard work (for a description of Chinese socialization, see Wu 1974); (2) the corporate bond within the Chinese family; (3) kinship ties beyond the family, especially the associations which were essential to building capital; and (4) the recognition by immigrant Chinese of the need for their children to acquire secondary or higher education. (Wu is currently preparing a book on Chinese commercial development in Papua New Guinea. See also Wu 1974a, 1975.) The adaptive strategies followed by Chinese immigrants are good illustrations of the organizational principles of responsibility, accommodation, and economy of effort (Firth 1964:69, 74, 80; compare also Firth, et al. 1957).

The last four essays in this volume—by Prattis, Cove, Attinasi, and

Seaton and Watson-Gegeo—tackle theoretical issues related to Firth's work in economics, symbolism, language, and anthropological (culture) theory itself. All four essays are synthetic and pragmatic in approach.

The first of these is J. I. Prattis' penetrating essay, "Competing Paradigms and False Polemics in Economic Anthropology." The debate—or more accurately, the series of debates—over which paradigm should govern economic analyses in anthropology is recounted in Ronald Frankenberg's "Economic Anthropology: One Anthropologist's View" and Percy S. Cohen's "Economic Analysis and Economic Man" (both in Firth 1967). Essentially the issues have revolved around whether classical economic theory is applicable to nonindustrialized societies, and if not, then what alternative paradigm should be adopted. Firth early took an active role in economic anthropology, pointing out, for example, that classical economic theory is based on the money market system typical of capitalistic economies, and that it has ignored social context as relevant to economic behavior (1961:122–154).[2]

Prattis addresses the "new polemic" between exchange theorists and production theorists (both of whom reject classical economics) as to whether exchange or production should have "primacy as the explanatory paradigm in economic anthropology." Exchange theorists maintain that social and economic processes can be generalized from interpersonal exchange among individuals, the basic model of which is reciprocity. Production theorists contend that exchange relations are "simply observations of specific social relations already defined at the productive level" and therefore are incapable of explaining structural constraints, which arise out of factors of production. Thus both sides of the debate make their case on epistemological grounds.

To clarify the positions taken by both sides, Prattis reviews and critiques the arguments made by exchange theorists from Malinowski and Mauss to Barth and Blau, and the response to these arguments by such production theorists as Berthoud, Cook, and Godelier. Prattis shows that ultimately the dispute is nothing more than polemic because the issue at stake is not an epistemological issue at all. That is, exchange theorists and production theorists are arguing on different *ontological* levels rather than on different *epistemological* levels.

To resolve the debate, Prattis puts forth the thesis that "both exchange and production theory can be conceptualized in terms of an equilibrium model applied at different levels—exchange theory at the level of the actor and production theory at the level of social structure." The remainder of Prattis' essay is an explication of equilibrium theory and its application to both exchange and production theory. Prattis ends his essay by calling for the development of a theory that "bridges the gap between levels served by exchange and production theory," suggesting that the answer may lie in a synthesis between the two.

Symbolism is another area of anthropological study in which there has been strong debate over analytic paradigms. The most intriguing paradigm to emerge in this century is structuralism, usually identified with its leading proponent in French *sociologie,* Claude Lévi-Strauss. As John J. Cove points out in his essay, "Ecology, Structuralism, and Fishing Taboos," the dilemma facing the structuralist school is the difficulty of evaluating the results of its analyses, and the impossibility of predicting social behavior from them. This dilemma arises from the stance taken by structuralists, that structural analysis aims at understanding the internal organization of a symbolic system, and not the relationship of that system or its elements to anything external (such as social structure or everyday life).

Structuralism's supporters concede these points to their critics. Thus, Edmund Leach shrugs off the question of whether a structural analysis should be able empirically to justify its selection or interpretation of elements in a symbolic system, explaining that structural analysis "is more like literary or dramatic criticism" (Leach 1967:xviii). In fact, to divorce his paradigm from empirical test and to stress that it applies to cognitive rather than social behavior, Lévi-Strauss claims that natural species singled out in totemism, for instance, are chosen "not because they are 'good to eat' but because they are 'good to think'" (1964:89).

Cove believes that the way out of the dilemma is to synthesize structuralism with another approach that can relate the phenomenon of study (in this case, fishing taboos) to behavioral phenomena external to it. The approach Cove advocates is an ecological one. His essay is a study of fishing taboos in two societies, eastern Cornwall of the nineteenth and early twentieth centuries, and Nootka, a Northwest Coast Indian tribe in North America. He demonstrates that "the items prohibited [by the respective taboo systems] are ecologically correct symbols for the activity and that the relationship between those items can be understood by the ecological stressing of certain oppositions."

Firth's treatment of taboo, such as his explanation of taboos associated with sago extraction, relates the magico-religious dimensions of taboo to social organization and behavior (1967:273–274; see also Firth 1957, 1973). Cove follows Malinowski in seeing both magic and taboo as strategies for ensuring fishing success in cases of uncertainty. Other strategies include fishing agreements, lookouts, and so forth. "Taboos are strategy rules concerned with avoiding the worst possible conditions or outcomes. They are more likely to occur in contexts where these conditions and outcomes can vary and individuals have little or no information for determining what will happen." Cove then goes on to dramatize his ecological-structuralist synthesis with a revealing analysis of Cornwall and Nootka fishing taboos to show that the elements under taboo are directly related both to ecological conditions and to social organization in the two societies.

John J. Attinasi's "Structural Analysis of Chol Mayan Pronouns" also uses a structural approach, this time borrowed from linguistics, to analyze the Chol Mayan pronoun system. Attinasi takes the position that grammatical categories are "meaningless if viewed in isolation. It is only the internal structure—the number, nature, and contrast of oppositions within the category—which gives grammatical meaning. And it is the internal structure which provides the link between . . . the grammatical system and the extensional reference to extralinguistic reality."

The ability to speak well in a variety of situations governed by complex social rules is a value central to Chol culture, one around which all else seems to revolve. In fact, as Attinasi indicates, the Chol view their *social* activity as speaking, and especially not merely "saying something," but "speaking to someone." Attinasi's painstaking structural analysis identifies clusion, address, and number as the significant distinctions of pronoun contrast. The pronoun system supports a world view that emphasizes "immediacy in all experience," "the supreme value of the speech event," and a deeply held interest in "abstract principles and comprehensive symbolizations." The key triangle marked by pronouns consists of speaker, hearer, and omniperson, which are those most frequently used in speech. Thus a structural analysis of the pronoun system is congruent with observed behavior and stated social norms.

In his introduction to *Social Anthropology and Language* (1971:xiii–xiv), Ardener states that the relevance of linguistics to anthropology may be viewed on three levels: the technical, the pragmatic, and the explanatory. Raymond Firth's study of language data has been primarily on the pragmatic level. That is, he has analyzed language to "seek what help, if any, linguistic data can give in the interpretation of anthropological data" (ibid.:xiii; see, for example, Firth 1926, 1957, 1966a).

Attinasi would seem to be working between the pragmatic and the explanatory level, which Ardener describes as seeking "the relevance, if any, of theories *about* language . . . to theories *about* society, or about culture . . ." (1971:xiv). Although not fully developed in this essay, the implications of Attinasi's work have to do with how a purely structural analysis of grammar can suggest or help to confirm hypotheses about social (speech) behavior.

The final essay, Seaton and Watson-Gegeo's "Meta-anthropology:

The Elementary Forms of Ethnological Thought," moves to a level of abstraction above theory: metatheory. Metatheory is the "enterprise of theorizing about theory." Meta-anthropology, therefore, is "the study of ethnological theory and hence the study of theories of culture"— taking "culture" to mean socioculture.

Seaton and Watson-Gegeo borrow their architectonic for meta-anthropology from the philosopher Stephen Pepper. Pepper's concept of world hypothesis is adapted to refer to a general theory of culture (one which claims to be a comprehensive approach to the ethnology of a total culture). Each world hypothesis is governed by an underlying root metaphor to which the criteria of scope and precision can be applied when comparing one world hypothesis with another. Thus Pepper's architectonic allows the metatheorist to compare theories of culture, examining the operational consequences of selecting one theory over another, from a perspective other than that of traditional divisions in anthropology (for example, American, British, French schools, and so forth).

Pepper distinguishes between inadequate world hypotheses (animism and mysticism) and adequate world hypotheses (formism, contextualism, organicism, mechanism). When the authors arrange theories of culture (including Firth's social organization) into the four adequate categories according to the root metaphor of each, there are some surprises. The basis on which the arrangement is made is given as a brief sketch of the culture theory, and is meant to be indicative rather than exhaustive.

This final paper should be read as a heuristic exercise aimed at helping anthropologists take note of where they have ventured and where they have not ventured in general culture theory. For comparing the strengths and weaknesses of culture theories, it offers a reasonably objective model unconstrained by the ideology of any particular culture theory. It is a way of stepping back to see where anthropological theorists have been and pausing to consider where they might go through theoretical refinement and synthesis.

NOTES

1.   Where interpretations of Sir Raymond's work occur in this introduction, I assume full responsibility for any errors, omissions, or misconceptions. It should also be mentioned that he has not had the opportunity to review or comment on the book prior to its publication.

2.   Sir Raymond studied economics in New Zealand before arriving at the London School of Economics as a postgraduate student in 1924. At LSE he intended to continue in economics and to "do anthropology as a hobby," as he is quoted by Freedman (1967). Thus it should come as no surprise that his contribution to economic study goes beyond that of the essay cited in the text ("The Social Framework of Economic Organization"). See also Firth 1939, 1959, 1964a, and 1966.

REFERENCES CITED

Ardener, Edwin, ed.
1971   *Social anthropology and language.* London: Tavistock.

Boggs, Stephen T.
1972   The meaning of questions and narratives to Hawaiian children. In *Functions of language in the classroom,* ed. Courtney B. Cazden, Vera P. John, and Dell Hymes. New York: Teachers College Press.

Boggs, Stephen T. and Karen Ann Watson-Gegeo
1976   Interweaving routines: strategies for encompassing a social situation. Paper presented at the 74th annual meeting of the American Anthropological Association, December, San Francisco. In press, *Language in Society.*

Firth, Raymond
1926   Proverbs in native life, with particular reference to those of the Maori. *Folk-lore* 37:134–153, 245–270.
1939   *Primitive Polynesian economy.* London: Routledge.
1957   *We, the Tikopia.* Boston: Beacon Press (original 1936).
1959   *Economics of the New Zealand Maori.* 2nd edition. Wellington, N.Z.: University of Wellington.
1961   *Elements of social organization.* Boston: Beacon Press (original 1951).
1964   *Essays on social organization and values.* London: Athlone Press.
1964a   Capital, saving and credit in peasant societies: a viewpoint from economic anthropology. In *Capital, saving and credit in peasant societies,* ed. Raymond Firth and B. S. Yamey. Chicago: Aldine.
1966   *Malay fishermen, their peasant economy.* Hamden, Conn.: Archon Books (original 1946).
1966a   The meaning of *pali* in Tikopia. In *In memory of J. R. Firth,* ed. C. E. Bazell et al. London: Longmans.
1967   Economics and ritual in sago extraction. In *Tikopia ritual and belief,* by Raymond Firth. Boston: Beacon Press (essay originally published in 1950).
1973   *Symbols: public and private.* Ithaca, N.Y.: Cornell University Press.

Firth, Raymond, et al.
1957   Factions in Indian and overseas Indian societies. *British Journal of Sociology* 8:291–342.

Freedman, Maurice, ed.
1967   *Social organization: essays presented to Raymond Firth.* Chicago: Aldine.

Leach, Edmund, ed.
1967   *The structural study of myth and totemism.* London: Tavistock.

Lévi-Strauss, Claude
1964   *Totemism.* London: Merlin Press.

Watson-Gegeo, Karen Ann and Stephen T. Boggs
1977   From verbal play to talk story: the role of routines in speech events among Hawaiian children. In *Child discourse,* ed. Susan Ervin-Tripp and Claudia Mitchell-Kernan. New York: Academic Press.

Wu, David
1974   An immigrant minority: the adaptation of Chinese in Papua New Guinea. Ph.D. dissertation, Australian National University.
1974a   To kill three birds with one stone: the rotating credit associations of the Papua New Guinea Chinese. *American Ethnologist* 1:656–684.
1975   Overseas Chinese entrepreneurship and kinship transformation: an example of Papua New Guinea. *Bulletin of the Institute of Ethnology,* Academica Sinica, no. 39:85–105 (Taiwan).

Rank and Authority on Anuta Island

RICHARD FEINBERG

Anuta Island is a small Polynesian outlier in the eastern part of the Solomon Islands. This essay is concerned with the positions of ritual honor and political authority which an Anutan may hold, the roles which persons holding these positions are expected to play, and the principles according to which these positions are attained. Also to be examined is the interlocking set of principles according to which hierarchical relationships are established. We shall observe how these principles interact as partially independent variables, forming a number of distinct but interrelated subsystems of Anutan rank. And finally we shall consider some key concepts that permeate Anutan culture, in terms of which the ranking system must be understood. First, however, let us turn to positions of rank in Anutan culture.

CHIEFS

From an honorific point of view, and with some qualifications also from a political point of view, the two chiefs sit at the apex of the Anutan ranking system.

There are on Anuta four major "descent" groups called *kainanga*.[1] The *kainanga* are ranked on the basis of genealogical seniority: the Kainanga i Mua is descended from Tearakura, a former chief who ruled about eight generations ago and became the island's premier deity after his death; the Kainanga i Tepuko is descended from Tearakura's younger brother, Pu Tepuko, who also served for a time as chief; the Kainanga i

Pangatau is descended from Tearakura's two sisters, Nau Ariki (she was the eldest of the siblings and known as *te ariki papine,* "the female chief"),[2] and Nau Pangatau, both of whom were married to one Pu Pangatau;[3] and the Kainanga i Rotomua is descended from the youngest of the siblings, Tearakura's brother, Tauvakatai (see Figure 1). The two chiefs are genealogically the most senior males in the two leading *kainanga.* The first chief, the Ariki i Mua or Tui Anuta, is at the head of the Kainanga i Mua and a direct descendant of Tearakura; the second chief, known as the Ariki i Muri, the Ariki Tepuko, or Tui Kainanga, is at the head of the Kainanga i Tepuko and a direct descendant of its founder Pu Tepuko (see Figure 2).

Succession to Chieftainship

Succession is patrilateral and based on a principle of primogeniture. A chief is normally his predecessor's eldest direct descendant in the male line, which means in most cases his eldest son. If the eldest son has died, is away from the island and not expected to return, or is incompetent to hold the job, he may be passed over in favor of his eldest available brother.

Many chiefs have attained their positions due to the deaths of their elder brothers, the most recent being the present Ariki Tepuko, whose elder brother was lost at sea many years ago. On the other hand, oral traditions attest to only one case of an elder brother who was passed over strictly because of unsuitable behavior. Tearakura's great-grandfather Toroaki had three sons: Pu Ratu, the eldest, Pu Rongomai, the second, and Pu Pongi, the third. Pu Rongomai was a troublemaker and challenged Pu Ratu to fight to the death, partly over control of a garden and partly just to prove that he was the greater warrior. Pu Ratu refused to fight his brother, and when he left the island some time later on a voyage

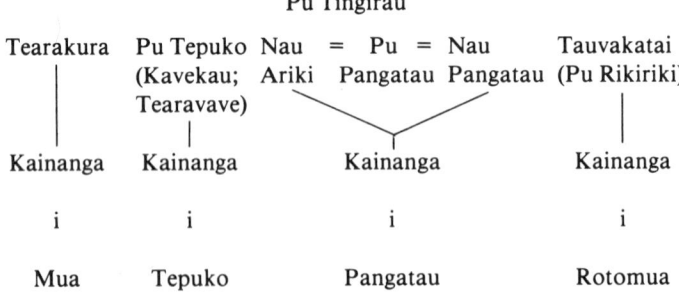

FIGURE 1.   Founders of the Four Anutan *Kainanga*

which brought him to Tikopia and then to Tonga he announced his desire that Pu Pongi (his youngest brother) should take his place, succeeding to the chieftainship when their father died. Pu Rongomai should be passed over because of his unfraternal behavior and disobedience toward his elder brother.

Once more Pu Rongomai disobeyed his brother's instructions, and when their father died he succeeded to the chieftainship. No one attempted to prevent his succession, but shortly after asssuming office he became severely ill. The illness was interpreted as resulting from his disobedience, and upon this realization he abdicated, deciding that his holding the chiefly office was not worth the price. The short time he held the position is considered to have been usurped, and therefore his name is not included in chiefly genealogies as they are recited at the present time.

Firth notes that on Tikopia there is but a single aberrant case of a dying chief announcing his successor. On Anuta overt decisions to contravene the normal succession patterns are not nearly so rare. We have already discussed the case of Pu Ratu. Tearakura before the end of his life proclaimed that his brother Pu Tepuko, rather than Kavataurua, his son and the proper successor, should succeed to his position—and other than a few mild protests by Pu Tepuko himself, no one suggested that there was anything improper in this decision. In the next generation the chieftainship was returned to the senior line in the person of Kavataurua, but after his death a conscious decision was made to divide the office so that Pu Tepuko's line would be assured of a chiefly title to complement that held by the descendants of Tearakura. And a few generations later it was at the suggestion of the dying chief Pu Koroatu (Matakiapo)[4] that Pu Mapai of an entirely different line became *ariki* ("chief") since no one in the chiefly line was in a position to take office at that time. In the following generation the title reverted to the chiefly line, but had Pu Mapai's sons objected there would have been room for debate. In short, the provision for overriding genealogical ties on the basis of overt agreement and appropriate behavior, which is central to many aspects of Anutan culture,[5] provides an element of voluntarism and flexibility to the system of succession to chiefly office as well.

The case of Pu Mapai brings out the problems in determining a proper successor when the deceased chief has no son or no son of sufficient age to hold office.

If a chief has a direct patrilineal male descendant (that is, a son or a grandson who has survived his father) who is too young to assume office, the Anutans are usually perfectly happy, unlike the Tikopians, to appoint a regent and wait for many years if necessary for the child to reach the age of responsibility. To my query as to what would happen should

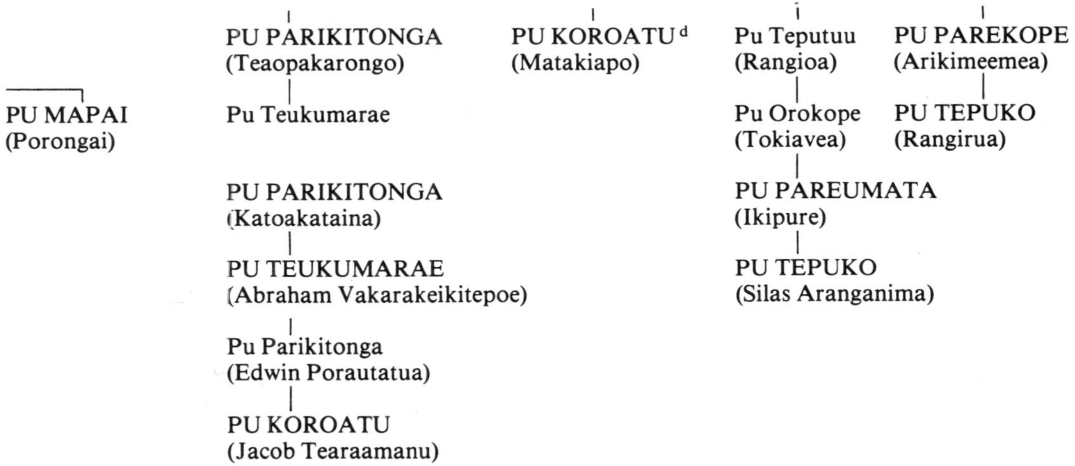

PU MAPAI
(Porongai)

PU PARIKITONGA
(Teaopakarongo)

PU KOROATU [d]
(Matakiapo)

Pu Teputuu
(Rangioa)

PU PAREKOPE
(Arikimeemea)

Pu Teukumarae

Pu Orokope
(Tokiavea)

PU TEPUKO
(Rangirua)

PU PARIKITONGA
(Katoakataina)

PU PAREUMATA
(Ikipure)

PU TEUKUMARAE
(Abraham Vakarakeikitepoe)

PU TEPUKO
(Silas Aranganima)

Pu Parikitonga
(Edwin Porautatua)

PU KOROATU
(Jacob Tearaamanu)

FIGURE 2. Genealogy of the Anutan Chiefs

[a] Chiefs appear in capital letters, nonchiefs in lowercase.
[b] Pu Taupare was an Uvean who arrived at Anuta around the same time as Pu Kaurave's arrival in a Tongan canoe.
[c] Pu Neo was Pu Tauraro's paternal half-brother.
[d] Pu Koroatu was the only chief who never married; known as *te ariki tamaaroa*.

he die in the near future, the present Tui Anuta replied that his brother would not become chief, but he would "watch the island" until his son was old enough to assume the chieftainship. And when Pu Parikitonga, the great-grandfather of the present chief, died in early 1900s, Pu Raropuko, the leading *maru* ("noble"), "watched the island" for many years until Pu Teukumarae was ready to take over. In fact, in contrast to Tikopia it seems to be considered somewhat improper for a man to succeed to the chieftainship too soon after the death of his predecessor. Two or three years elapsed between the death of Pu Teukumarae and the succession to his office of his grandson Pu Koroatu, the present chief, although the latter was in his twenties at the time. And the present Ariki Tepuko took office more than a year after his father's death despite his obvious qualification and more than forty years of age.

If a chief has no patrilineal male descendants there is more of a problem. In this case the title should generally go to his eldest surviving brother or the eldest son of the eldest brother to have male offspring. Pragmatic considerations like the respective ages of the persons involved in such a case would enter the final decision. And as illustrated by the case of Pu Mapai, it is possible for the chieftainship to pass out of the chiefly line altogether under certain circumstances. If, however, the office has passed to a junior line because the deceased chief's descendants were unavailable or not of age—as in the time of Pu Mapai—rather than because he did not have any male descendants, in the following generation the title is normally expected to revert to the senior line. This reversion of title is illustrated by the passage of the chiefly title from Tearakura to Pu Tepuko and back to Kavataurua, and from Pu Koroatu to Pu Mapai and then back to Pu Koroatu's elder brother's son, Pu Parikitonga (Katoakataina). The most recent example of such a succession pattern begins with Pu Teputuu (Rangioa), the great-grandfather of the present Ariki Tepuko. Pu Teputuu was the eldest son and in line to become chief, but while still a young man he traveled to Tikopia and never returned, thus forfeiting his right of succession to his younger brother Pu Parekope (Arikimeemea). On Pu Parekope's death he was followed by his son Pu Tepuko (Rangirua), but while he dwelt in the chiefly office Pu Teputuu's son Pu Orokope returned from Tikopia, and in the following generation the chieftainship was returned to the senior line in the person of Pu Orokope's son Pu Pareumata (Ikipure), father of the present *ariki*.

In cases like this, however, nothing can be taken for granted. Pu Pareumata had no trouble obtaining the chieftainship because Pu Tepuko had no sons to contest it. But if he had they could well have put up an argument as to why the office should have remained in their line, and it is not at all certain which way the outcome would have gone. After a lapse of only one generation, if the senior contender is qualified he will probably get the job. As the number of generations increases, however, the claim of the junior line becomes increasingly strong. Ultimately it is a matter of divergent claims carrying varying degrees of strength and validity. There are no hard and fast rules by which a definitive decision can invariably be reached.

Means of Installment

No chief was installed in office during my stay on Anuta, and I was unable to elicit the kind of detailed account I would have liked of the actual procedure by which this feat is accomplished. I did get some data, however, especially with respect to one incident which sheds considerable light on some of the principles involved.

Unlike Tikopia, where a new chief is installed by the leading men of the other *kainanga,* on Anuta a chief is installed by men from his own *kainanga* but from a different *patongia*.[6] Pu Pareumata, the former Ariki Tepuko, died in the early 1960s. At that time the only other *patongia* in the Kainanga i Tepuko, that of Pu Rongovaru, had already split and joined forces with the Kainanga i Pangatau because of a conflict with the old chief's son. They were not about to install in office the man who had driven them from their natal *kainanga*.[7] Hence it seemed that there was no one to perform the service, and people were saying that there could never again be another Ariki Tepuko—from that time on Anuta would go back to having just one chief. The leading men from the Kainanga i Mua objected to this idea, however, and Pu Tokerau along with Pu Teaokena (the two brothers of Ariki i Mua) took the matter into their own hands by deciding to elevate Pu Tepuko to his chiefly status. This was not procedurally correct, as was generally recognized, but the legitimacy of Pu Tepuko's claim on the office, the authority of Pu Tokerau and the Kainanga i Mua, the strength with which the tradition of having two chiefs was inculcated into the Anutans' scheme of values, and a recognition of the exigencies of an extraordinary situation were such that no one objected to the new *ariki*'s manner of installment or refused to recognize his position as rightful chief.

This incident does not inform us about the actual procedures involved in the installment ceremony itself, but it does indicate a good deal about the underlying sociocultural factors involved in the installment of a new chief. Moreover, it illustrates very plainly the degree of flexibility which the Anutan cultural system can permit when the exigencies of practical social life make it impossible to conform with ideal standards in every case.

The Role of the Chiefs: Political Authority and Ritual Honor

From an honorific point of view the two chiefs are clearly at the top of the Anutan social hierarchy. There is no chiefly language as in Tonga, Samoa, and other Polynesian cultures, but everyone must show the greatest deference in other respects. No one may stand in the *ariki*'s presence if the chief is seated. No one may touch any part of his body, especially not his head, except on his direct instructions. Shouting or even raising one's voice in the chief's presence and playing in the vicinity of his house are forbidden. Should anyone meet one of the chiefs while walking on a path he or she is expected to step aside until the *ariki* has passed. When a distribution of vegetables or fish takes place, in addition to the one pile or basket for each of the island's nineteen *patongia* there is a special portion called the *pakaariki* which is set aside for each of the chiefs. If some especially desirable fish is caught, it may be given to one or both chiefs as a special present he may keep for himself and his *patongia* or give to someone toward whom he happens to be feeling particularly sympathetic at the time. These are all situations which constantly arise in the course of everyday life, and these rules are all scrupulously followed.

There are many types of feast and ceremony in which one or both chiefs are singled out for special honor, and no general feast may start until both chiefs are present.[8] Those immediately around the chief at a meal should not begin to eat before he does, or at least not until he has given the word. When an *ariki* leaves or returns from an overseas voyage, he is carried down the beach and set in the canoe. And he is never permitted to go without a substantial escort to assure that his needs will be taken care of.[9] If he is merely going fishing for the day he may walk down the beach, but he is expected to sit in the canoe while the other members of the crew push it through the surf and risk injuring their feet on the sharp coral reef. Any visitor of note is expected to undergo a greeting ceremony in which he crawls up to the two chiefs and attempts to press his nose to their knees as a sign of deference. The chiefs grab the visitor's head and pull it up to their own so that they press noses to each other, thus for the moment elevating the guest to their own lofty position. An Anutan seeing the chief for the first time after a protracted absence goes through the same procedure, although not in the same formal ceremonial context. Few sights have impressed me more than seeing a young, educated Tikopian, who spoke fluent English and worked in the Honiara Museum, drop to his knees and press his nose to the shins of the two Anutan chiefs when they walked into the museum during their visit to the Solomon Islands capital in February 1973.

In all these ways the Ariki Tepuko is shown the honor, respect, and deference due him as chief. He is clearly inferior in rank, however, to the Ariki i Mua, and if the two come into a dominance-subservience situation it is the lesser chief who is expected to defer. When the two chiefs are being honored together, Tui Anuta is honored first and given the larger portions and the most desirable foods. (There is always some differential between the two servings, however slight, to signify the difference in rank.) And on ceremonial occasions the Ariki i Mua is always seated on the right, the dominant side; the Ariki i Muri is seated on the left.

These are the cultural rules respecting behavior vis-à-vis an *ariki,* and rarely if ever will an Anutan abrogate them. There are other rules, however, sanctioning generosity and hospitality as well as the church's injunctions to love thy neighbor and forbidding vanity. These injunctions apply to the chiefs, who are expected to embody everything positive about Anutan culture even more strongly than anyone else. Because of this second set of prescriptions the chiefs often treat others with the same respect and deference to which they themselves are entitled on account of their chiefly status.[10]

The Ariki i Mua stands at the apex of Anuta's political structure. He is called Tui Anuta ("Lord of Anuta") and he is just that—the high chief of the entire island. He generally consults with his *maru* and the second chief before issuing instructions to the island, but he need not do so. Whenever he speaks his word is law—although this should not be taken to imply that the law is never broken.

On any matter of policy affecting the entire island Tui Anuta has the ultimate say except in matters relating to the church. And even there his influence is second only to that of the catechist, his younger brother.[11] In the wake of a severe cyclone which struck the island in February 1972 there was a considerable food shortage, and the chief determined the policies for coping with this problem. It was he who decided that during the recovery period Anuta's population would prepare and consume food as a single unit, and it was he who imposed a temporary *tabu* on the use of green coconuts to assure there would be enough mature coconuts for cooking during the period of scarcity. Morever, it was the chief who decided on the types of food which would be prepared in order to preserve coconuts for future use. He has called for his subjects to join together in building a new church where services would be conducted in Mota (until recently the official language of the Melanesian Mission) rather than the English used by the present catechist in the old church at St. John; he has called for them to join in repairing an aqueduct which had been destroyed during the storm.

In the matter of maintaining public order it is again the first chief who has the ultimate legislative, executive, and judicial authority. On 9

August 1972 a group of children was caught stealing watermelons from someone's gardens. That evening after church, without consulting anyone in advance, the chief called the island together and announced that from that time until further notice no child (including persons of fifteen and even sixteen years of age) was to venture outside his or her house unless accompanied by an adult. I expected this dictum to be halfheartedly followed for a few days and then for the children gradually to slip back into their old behavior. It seemed that over a protracted period the proclamation would be unenforceable, but to my amazement it remained in force and was quite strictly followed right through the time I left the island in January of the following year. When conflicts break out among his subjects it is the chief's job to resolve them. He may assign specific people to work at specific tasks like gardening, fishing, or making oven at a specific time. Such a command takes precedence over all other plans.

The Ariki i Muri, in general, has the same powers and responsibilities as the Ariki i Mua. Although these vary only in the degree to which they are possessed, there are some respects in which this quantitative variation is sufficient to produce a real qualitative difference.

The whole island owes allegiance to the second chief. He is respected as an *ariki,* and he has the authority to issue commands on his own initiative if the Ariki i Mua is not present at the time. However, he is primarily responsible for his own *kainanga.* Anyone wishing to leave the island must first obtain permission from his chief, and except for members of the Kainanga i Tepuko this means permission from the Ariki i Mua. The Ariki Tepuko may instruct members of his *kainanga* to make oven or engage in special work projects. While he may issue similar instructions to members of other *kainanga* and be obeyed, it is not by the same intrinsic right. When members of the Kainanga i Rotomua or the Kainanga i Pangatau are asked to which chief they listen, they either show confusion or say that they listen to both. I was even told by a few informants that if the two chiefs issued contradictory instructions they would listen to "the one who is right."[12] Yet the level of the second chief's political authority is such that at various times in the island's history when no Tui Anuta was in office it is said that one of the leading men from the Kainanga i Mua, and not the Ariki Tepuko, had primary responsibility for watching and caring for the island.

The Kainanga i Pangatau and the Kainanga i Rotomua do not have chiefs, but they do have heads. The Kainanga i Pangatau has three lines: one descended from Nau Ariki, the elder of Tearakura's two sisters; one from Nau Pangatau, the younger sister; and one from Pu Matangi, a man who immigrated from Tikopia several generations later. Each of these three "houses" has its own head. The house descended from Nau Ariki is led by Pu Nukutamaaroa, that descended from Nau Pangatau by Pu Penuakimoana, and that from Pu Matangi by Pu Tuapi. As is to be expected, the line of highest rank is that descended from Nau Ariki, but for some reason which no one seemed able to explain the immigrant line was second in rank and Nau Pangatau's was left on the bottom.

The three leaders are ranked according to the lines from which they have come. Each is responsible primarily for his own house, although they are referred to collectively as the three heads *(nga pokouru e toru)* of the Kainanga i Pangatau. But they are not in any sense chiefs. They have no *ariki* title, are not deferred to in the manner of chiefs, are not given *pakaariki* portions during disbursement of food, and do not sit with the chiefs on ceremonial occasions. While they are responsible for ensuring proper behavior on the part of their subordinates, they do not make policy decisions as do chiefs, and they derive their position from the *pono* (general assembly), which ultimately means appointment by the Ariki i Mua rather than by genealogical seniority. In fact, of the three only Pu Nukutamaaroa is the genealogically senior male of his house. Nor is it even necessary that there be three heads for the *kainanga;* in previous times there had often been but a single head. It is because he thought that Pu Nukutamaaroa, being generally unaggressive by nature, could use some help in keeping an eye on his *kainanga* that the *ariki* appointed the other two—men who are much less reticent about asserting themselves— to assist him at running things smoothly. Moreover, unlike a chief, a head of one of the lesser *kainanga* may step down when he reaches an age at which the responsibilities of his position prove an undue burden.

These comments on the heads of the Kainanga i Pangatau apply in principle to the Kainanga i Rotomua as well. During most of the time I spent on Anuta, however, only one adult male from that *kainanga* was present on the island, which made the problem of determining a leader rather a simple task. In most cases, due to its small size the Kainanga i Rotomua participated along with the Kainanga i Pangatau in collective activities.

THE *Maru*

On Tikopia the word *maru* is used to denote close agnatic male kinsmen of each of the four chiefs, and it is they who are primarily responsible for seeing that the policies of the *ariki* are implemented. On Anuta, on the other hand, all males of responsible age in the two chiefly *kainanga* are referred to as *maru* or *tangata tu* in contrast to the men of the lesser *kainanga,* who are known as *pakaaropa.* The Anutan *maru* are expected to perform in the same capacity as their Tikopian colleagues, advising the chiefs, executing their decisions, and maintaining order on the island. But since one is a *maru* by virtue of his *kainanga* affiliation it has the appearance of a social stratum rather than an office, and Firth's translation of the term as "executive officer" seems somewhat inappropriate to the Anutan situation. Members of this stratum have responsibilities which they fulfill to greater or lesser degrees, but one who fails to shoulder his responsibilities does not lose his *maru* status by virtue of that fact.[13]

Approximately once a week—generally on Sunday evenings—the chiefs and their *maru* gather together for a meeting known as *te araara o nga maru mo nga ariki* ("the discussion of the *maru* and the chiefs"). Current problems and forthcoming major events as well as the general state of the island are thoroughly discussed, and everyone is given a full opportunity to make his voice heard. No votes are ever taken, however. After all sides of an issue have been heard, the final decision is up to the first chief, and to a lesser extent the second.

The morning after such a meeting a *pono* or general assembly of the entire island is called at which the decisions of the previous night are relayed to the people by the *tangata tu* or, on occasion, by the chiefs themselves. It is then up to the *maru* and the heads of the Kainanga i Pangatau and the Kainanga i Rotomua to ensure that the dicta of the *pono* are carried out.

The words *maru* and *tangata tu* refer to the same group of men, and there is no clear dividing line separating the contexts in which it is proper to use one term or the other. I have the feeling, however, that *maru* is the generic term for persons holding the rank and for the rank itself. *Tangata tu* literally means "standing man." Firth has suggested (personal communication) that *tangata tu* denotes a "standing man" in the sense of being a leading man, and he has pointed to a possible etymological relationship between *tu* of *tangata tu* and Tui, the title for a chief. I find this view quite plausible, and it is supported in my experience by the description of one of Anuta's leading carpenters as *"te tipunga tu* of this island." An alternative interpretation is that while *maru* denotes a social group, *tangata tu* connotes the role of "standing in" for an *ariki,* speaking for him in the *pono,* maintaining order, and seeing to it that his orders are carried out.

Pu Tokerau once explained to me that as the chief's brother his proper designation was not *maru* but *tama nga ariki* ("child of the chiefs"). This conforms with Tikopian usage, and it is true that on occasion he stood somewhat aloof from the political process, allowing Pu Paone, Pu Maravai, and some of the others to take the leading roles. He had the right to step in, however, at any time he wished, and not infrequently he exercised this right. In practice he and the chief's other brothers as well as the sons of the second chief were referred to as *maru* and they acted the part, which leads me to suggest that *tama nga ariki* is not a category to be distinguished from the *maru* but is in fact a subspecies.

In the *araara o nga maru mo nga ariki* and the *pono* are discussed matters at all levels of seriousness. People have been instructed to make certain to relieve themselves below the high-water mark on the beach so that the noxious matter will be carried away by the tide. I have heard instructions not to use green coconuts and to make sure that any papayas picked were properly ripe in order to conserve resources in a time of scarcity. Instructions have been given to dump garbage in the sea rather than leaving it to rot on the paths or in the villages. It is at the *pono* that people were reminded not to let their children go unsupervised, and after a time it was announced at a *pono* that several youngsters were to be excepted from this regulation because they had dutifully obeyed the assembly's instructions up to that time.

The decisions on who would lead the Kainanga i Pangatau and the Kainanga i Rotomua, like all the others noted above, are the ultimate responsibility of the two chiefs, and especially the Ariki i Mua, but according to the native formulation they are appointed by the *pono*. Normally the leader of a *patongia* is the eldest son of the last head. When exceptions are made, the decision to break with usual tradition, it is said, must be ratified by the *pono*. In short a policy decision may be instigated by anyone, but the chief has the ultimate say. He speaks, however, through the mechanism of the *pono*, and it is not until the *pono* has spoken that the decisions become official.[14]

A *pono* is called by the Ariki i Mua or possibly by both chiefs, generally—although not necessarily—in consultation with the *maru*. A chief may speak for himself at the assembly to enhance the dramatic effect of what is said, but this is rare. A *pono* might be called at any time, but most often it takes place on Monday mornings immediately after church, since the usual time for the "council" meetings is Sunday night and this is the earliest time thereafter at which it is convenient to call the whole island together. Before construction of the new church, the island's population would gather in the coconut-leaf shade house just outside the old church house at St. John, and the leading *maru*, Pu Maravai and Pu Paone, would relate the previous night's decisions. Sometimes certain decisions would be related by one and the rest by the other; at other times they would both speak on the same topic to reinforce each other's words. Other *maru* would then add their opinions and everyone was free to raise questions, but only after the two leaders had finished.

After completion of the new church at St. James, except for especially important occasions the island was divided in two, and one of the two leading *maru* addressed the group at St. John while the other instructed the group at St. James. Aside from this, however, the procedure remained unchanged.

It should be noted that while Pu Maravai is of the senior line next to the chief in the Kainanga i Mua, Pu Paone is genealogically only the sixth-ranking man in the next line. His position in the *pono* is due to his recognized status as "the wisest man on the island" at the present time, the exemplary life he is known to lead, and the esteem in which his words are universally held. His ability to understand and solve problems and to put the supreme virtues of generosity and hospitality into practice in his own life effectively compensate for any genealogical deficiency and make him the most respected of the *maru,* on a par with his unquestionably senior colleague as cohead of the all-important *pono.*

The *maru* have political responsibilities and authority but they are not chiefs and are not honored as such, although one of the *tama nga ariki* may stand in for the chief and take his place of honor at important celebrations if the *ariki* is unable to attend. Aside from this the *maru* derive their ritual honor—as opposed to political deference—more from their age, sex, and kinship status than from their position in the political system.

The *Pakaako*

Ako is the Anutan word "to learn" and *paka* is the causative prefix; thus *pakaako* is the verb "to teach" and the generic term for "teacher." It also has a more specific reference to the catechist and his assistants, since their job is seen as being to teach the island to follow the ways of the church.

The church is a central institution on Anuta, second to none. It is the Anutans' protection from natural disaster and insurance for their continued well-being. Positions of rank and power as well as most normative rules for correct behavior are justified by reference to church doctrine as it is understood by the natives, and it is the church which regulates the Anutans' work schedule and ceremonial calendar more than any other single factor. Thus the catechist is one of the island's most important men in his role as head of the church. He is honored accordingly.

In terms of formal behavior the catechist is not shown the deference of a chief. A man will not step aside to let the catechist pass by unless he is already obligated to do so on grounds other than his position in the church. The same may be said for standing in his presence, turning one's back on him, and other signs of deference normally exhibited toward one of higher rank. In his dealings with the chief the catechist is ritually subordinate. At general food distributions, however, in addition to the *pa-*

kaariki special baskets are apportioned to the catechist, his assistants, and the local schoolteacher. This type of prestation is referred to as *te pakamisionari*. It differs from the *pakaariki* in that it is smaller, and if a *pakaako* is absent his gift is simply omitted. If a chief is away, the *pakaariki* is retained and presented to someone acting in his stead.

Pu Tokerau has three assistant catechists: Pu Maevatau, a man in his forties who has served in this position since the early 1960s; Judah Mataamako, a young man of about eighteen who was appointed in August 1971; and Harry Matakiapo, the first chief's twelve-year-old son who was appointed at the same time as Judah. Since Harry's *patongia* already receives both a *pakaariki* and a *pakamisionari* prestation through the Ariki i Mua and Pu Tokerau, however, they decided to forgo their rights to an additional prestation in his behalf. On the other hand Pu Nukumairunga, the schoolteacher, is not intrinsically entitled to a *pakamisionari* prestation despite his designation as a *pakaako* because his teaching role is not directly related to the church. Since he is an immigrant from Tikopia and a cripple (his legs are paralyzed and atrophied from a bout with polio during the 1950s) and is recognized as making a valuable contribution to the island (in addition to teaching the young children he operates the radio, dispenses what medicines are available, and on occasion renders his services as an interpreter for visiting dignitaries), Pu Tokerau and the chief decided it would be appropriate for the community to issue him a gesture of its sympathy and appreciation by including him in the *pakamisionari* disbursements.

The catechist instructs the people, as do the chiefs and the *maru,* and although his proper sphere is church-related matters there is no clear dividing line between sacred and secular affairs since virtually everything has its sacred side. He instructs the populace in correct moral behavior and organizes ceremonies and feasts related to the church. He may organize fishing expeditions or tell people to prepare an oven for an upcoming celebration, and he along with the companions of the Melanesian Brotherhood is responsible for ensuring the proper upkeep of the church and its equipment. In terms of personal efficacy or power *(manuu)* he is put in the same general class as the two chiefs, and when he speaks the awe with which he is listened to is comparable to that afforded an *ariki.*

COMPANIONS OF THE BROTHERHOOD

The Melanesian Brotherhood is an order of friars founded by a young man from Guadalcanal during the reign of John Steward as fifth bishop of Melanesia. Members of the brotherhood are expected to take vows of poverty and chastity for short periods, which may later be extended if the member so wishes. There is no compulsion to maintain membership beyond the minimum two years, and there is no stigma attached to leaving after this period. Their goal is to assist the official clergy of the Anglican church in bringing new Solomon Islanders to the faith and strengthening the faith of those already converted (Fox n.d.). According to their handbook (Melanesian Mission n.d.:1), the companions are:

1. . . . baptized members of the Church, men, women, and young people who are joined to the Brothers in their work for the kingdom of God.
2. They help the Brothers
    by praying for them and their work
    by giving money and useful things to the Brotherhood
    by taking care of Brothers when they come to visit them or travel through their districts.
3. As the Brothers work for the kingdom of God in places to which they are sent out, so the Companions work for the kingdom of God in the places where they live.

    They help the people who live around them,
    to know and worship God,
    to be strong in the faith,
    to keep the commandments of God and to serve him truly in their daily lives,
    to work for the good of all, serving one another in love and true fellowship,
    to be faithful members of God's holy Church.
They do all this by their good example and in other ways.

On Anuta there are no Melanesian Brothers, but there is an organization calling itself *te Companion,* members of which serve as lay assistants to the catechist and help carry out the day-to-day details necessary for keeping the church in good repair and its activities in smooth operation. They perform various social services, help the infirm and others who cannot care for themselves, and participate in the making of decisions regarding church policy. Services in the new church at St. James are run by the companions, the four *pakaako* all concentrating their efforts in the old church at St. John.

The companions are highly respected and appreciated for the services they perform. Moreover, they are believed to hold a great deal of power *(manuu)* because of their association with the church. As a result they are listened to with respect when they speak, but they are rarely afforded the outward signs of ritual subordination on the basis of their companion membership.

As with the position of *pakaako,* the companion is not a traditional title and there are no genealogical requirements for membership. One must be willing to put in some extra time for prayer (about fifteen minutes a day after the regular services have disbanded), several hours a week for meetings to discuss church policy, and the time, effort, and responsibility for performing the religious and social services for which the companions were organized. Yet the chiefs and their assistants continue to feel a responsibility for the smooth running of the religious system. It is for this reason that the first chief's younger brother is the head catechist and the *ariki*'s son is one of the assistants, and it is for the same reason that both chiefs and the leading *maru* have assumed responsibility as members of the companions.

RANK AND SEX

Men outrank women both in honor and in political power. In fact women have no formal power in the political sphere; any influence they hope to exert must be wielded informally on a domestic level through their persuasive powers or aggressive personalities.

There are no women *maru,* and aside from Nau Ariki, of whose role nothing is known, no female chiefs. Women have no voice in council meetings or the *pono* except perhaps indirectly through their husbands. At a meeting which was called one night to discuss whether the island should accept relief supplies from the government at the possible expense of comprising its sovereignty, all the men—*pakaaropa* as well as *maru*—were encouraged to come and express their opinions. Few women attended, however, and those who did show up were given no opportunity to speak.

In terms of personal relations there is a great deal of individual variation, but when a man has his mind made up the woman must give way. There were times when Ta Notau ("the Notaus") would come to visit in my study while I was attempting to concentrate on some work. After several moments' pleasant chat Nau Notau, a strong-willed, intelligent woman, would realize that I wanted to get back to my work and would suggest to her husband in no uncertain terms that they should leave. Invariably he would acquiesce.

On the other hand, I can recall a night I was visiting Ta Paone rather late. I was talking with Pu Paone over dinner while his wife had started to doze off. When we had finished our meal he called to his wife to rouse her, and after several attempts he managed to obtain a grunt of acknowledgment. With his wife now half awake he told her we had finished eating and that she should put the food away. She made no move in that direction, indicating that she was too tired and her husband should put the food away himself. He again roused her and repeated his instructions, but with the same effect. After two or three more tries, each time putting his command in somewhat stronger terms, she finally capitulated and grudgingly carried out his bidding. She then went back to sleep while Pu Paone and I continued our conversation. Perhaps twenty minutes later he decided he wanted to get something down from the rafters to show to me, and once again he roused his dozing spouse. She was no more anxious to get up now than she had been twenty minutes before, but after a few stern rebukes from her husband Nau Paone gave in once more and got down the objects in question. It is significant to add that this relationship of dominance and submission was in no way affected by the fact that Nau Paone is the sister of the island's high chief.

In terms of honor and respect women also rank below men. A man may point his feet at a woman while sitting on the floor whereas the reverse would be a severe insult. A man may turn his back on a woman or stand in her presence while she is seated. A woman may lie down pointing her head at a man's legs whereas for a man to do this would be extremely demeaning. If a man and woman meet on a trail, the woman is expected to step aside and let the man pass. For a woman to touch a man's head except on his explicit instructions is disrespectful in the extreme, whereas a man may touch a woman's head without any connotation of disrespectful behavior—unless, as in most of these cases, restraint is required by the kinship system. Inside a house men may sit on the seaward side—the place of honor—whereas women must be confined to the inland portion. Even in church, where the congregation is segregated according to sex, the women sit on the left (the inferior) side while the men sit on the right.

RANK AND KINSHIP

In the Anutan language a relationship between two or more people may be indicated by the word *tau* followed by the term for the senior partner to the relationship. Thus a mother's brother and his sister's child are referred to as *te tau tuatina* and a father and child are *tau tamana*.[15] In this section I propose to list the various relationships that exist in the Anutan kinship system and describe briefly the quality of the relationship from the point of view of dominance, subordination, familiarity, and restraint.

Tau tupuna ("grandparent-grandchild")

The *tau tupuna* relationship[16] is one of close friendship and solidarity. They may joke and tease each other, use each other's proper names freely, and even talk about sex. If there is any difference in rank, it is in favor of the *tupuna* ("grandparent"). Thus we find the term *nuna,* which may be used in speaking to or about the *tupuna,* as an alternative to using his proper name whereas for the *mokopuna* ("grandchild") there is no alternative form.

Tau tamana ("father-child")

No one is more highly respected than the father and his brothers. One may not joke roughly with his *tamana* ("father"), utter his name, or discuss matters related to sex. For a man to stand in the presence of his *tama* ("child") while the latter is seated, point his feet toward him, or turn his back on him may not be thought of as very considerate if the *tama* is an adult. But he is within his rights to do so, whereas for the reverse to occur would be a severe breach of propriety. Although one would never consider striking his *tamana,* the reverse is a much less serious offense. In fact, striking one's child lightly to discipline him is perfectly in order until the youngster reaches the age of responsibility.

Tau pae ("mother-child")

In most respects one's behavior toward his *pae* ("mother") closely resembles that toward the *tamana.* The *tama* may not utter her name, and while he is still small she may inflict physical discipline and he is obligated to do her bidding. If the *tama* is male the relationship becomes more complicated when he gets older because of the sex differential. And if the two meet on a path it is often the *pae* who is required to step aside. Moreover, the restraint observable in the *tau tamana* relationship is considerably modified for the *tau pae* by a tendency toward indulgence and to a certain extent even camaraderie. Informants agreed that a child is often taught about sex by his mother; and when a young man decides he would like to marry, the *pae* is frequently selected to go as his emissary and propose to the girl.

Tau makitanga ("father's sister-brother's child")

The *makitanga* ("father's sister") is highly respected. In fact, she is identified with the *tamana* in the minds of many informants. Restrictions placed on interaction between *tama* and *tamana* apply also to the *tau makitanga* relationship, although in situations of ritual honor (in meeting on a path where one party must step aside, for instance) the *makitanga* is generally the one who is expected to defer if the *tama* ("brother's child") is an adult male. As in the *tau tamana* relationship the prescribed restraint is somewhat mitigated by strong ties of affection which continually manifest themselves and are obvious to even a casual observer. While the relationship involves much restraint and mutual respect, the *makitanga* does not command the kind of awe or out-and-out fear which the father's sister is reported to evoke in Tonga or Samoa.

Tau tuatina ("mother's brother-sister's child")

Along with the *tau panau* ("sibling of same sex") relationship, the *tau tuatina* is the freest, most solidary relationship on Anuta. The *tuatina* ("mother's brother") and *iraamutu* ("sister's child") may joke roughly and tease each other. Horseplay is permitted, and even striking each other is not forbidden. They share each other's property, and there are several types of ceremony a *tuatina* is expected to put on for his *iraamutu*. Any difference in rank, however, works in favor of the *tuatina,* who is expected to discipline the *iraamutu* if necessary and teach him proper behavior. While much license is permitted in the relationship, it is unlike Tonga in that the *irramutu* is definitely not "above the law."

Tau panau ("brother-brother" or "sister-sister")

Two or more *taina* ("siblings of the same sex") are referred to as *tau panau.* This relationship, along with the *tau tuatina,* is the most solidary on the island. *Taina* may joke and tease each other or talk about sex. They may play practical jokes or even strike each other. One exception to this rule is the firstborn *(te urumatua),* who must be respected and obeyed, but even here there is a good deal of freedom. When one party to the relationship must defer to the other, as in passing on a narrow path, a younger brother usually defers to an elder and always to the *urumatua.* If the *taina* are only classificatory brothers (or sisters), genealogical seniority takes precedence in formal situations, but this is not strictly followed in most normal dealings.

Cross cousins of the same sex are in a somewhat special category. They are known as *tau panau pakakovikovi* (*"tau panau* in a bad—that is, restrained—relationship"),[17] and the deference one owes to his *makitanga* is carried over to her child. Thus a man may not discuss sex, joke roughly, verbally abuse, engage in horseplay, or strike his *makitanga*'s son. The freedom one is permitted to exhibit toward his *tuatina,* on the other hand, is also carried over so that the relationship is not reciprocal. Thus a man may hit or exhibit other forms of disrespectful behavior toward the son of his mother's brother should he so wish, and the recipient has no alternative but to accept his fate stoically. Such at least is the theory. I have never witnessed this kind of behavior, and in actual practice there is rarely any noticeable difference between the quality of interaction among cross and parallel cousins.[18]

Tau kave ("brother-sister")

The *tau kave* ("siblings of opposite sex") must respect each other, but the extreme restraint exhibited in the *tau tamana* or *tau makitanga* relationship does not apply. The sister does not outrank the brother as she does in Tonga, nor does the brother fear the sister's curse as he does in Samoa. The pattern of brother-sister avoidance existing in much of western Polynesia is absent on Anuta. In fact, true brother and sister may even sleep on the same mat and under the same blanket since the suggestion of sexual relations between them is viewed as being too absurd to consider seriously.[19] A man may not discuss sex with his sister or other close *kave*, although a distant *kave* is an appropriate marriage partner. In general a man is expected to look after the interests of his sisters (classificatory as well as real); but they do not confide in each other about their sexual exploits, and a man accused of violating a woman's honor should be dealt with by the *pono* rather than on a familial level. In general a woman is expected to show ritual deference to and obey her *kave* unless she is considerably older and the *kave* is a small child or she is the *urumatua* and the *kave* in question is "born behind" (born after). The *tau kave* address and refer to each other by their proper names. There is no special term—as there is in the case of many relatives—which may be used as a substitute.

Rumatua ("husband-wife")

The term *rumatua* denotes a married couple. As should be evident from the discussion of the relative positions of men and women, the husband clearly outranks his wife. A man may point his feet toward his wife or stand while she is seated in his presence. A woman may sleep with her head pointing toward her husband's legs; she may not turn her back on him, touch his head, or walk ahead of him on a path. Yet the relationship, it must be said, is characterized by familiarity rather than restraint. A husband and wife may joke with or about each other. They may tease each other verbally, and in areas of female expertise such as infant care or running a household a man often defers to his wife's judgment. Moreover, while final decisions affecting the couple are up to the man, a good husband talks over important matters with his wife before arriving at a conclusion.

Tau ma ("brothers-in-law")

The *tau ma* relationship is marked by respect and restraint. Mild joking is permissible, but without sexual allusions, and practical joking is to be avoided. They may not strike each other, even in fun. They may not touch each other on the head or point their feet at each other, and one may not stand while the other is seated in his presence. They may not turn their backs on each other when seated at close quarters or call each other by their proper names. When using the personal or possessive pronoun to address each other, they must use the dual *(korua)* form as a special index of respect used only for affinal relatives. When one requests assistance, his *ma* is supposed to be prompt and liberal in his response.

Taina tangata-taina papine ("brother-in-law-sister-in-law")

In the sense of being free and solidary, the relationship between a man and his *taina papine* ("sister-in-law") is modeled on the *tau panau* relationship. They are free to joke and tease each other, and they may even discuss matters of sex. They are preferred over all other potential marriage partners. They refer to and address each other by proper names, and while some informants say it is proper for them to use the dual form of the personal and possessive pronouns it is certainly not mandatory. A few informants even considered such usage improper as they felt it placed an unnatural barrier between the two parties. A man outranks his *taina papine* strictly on the basis of the sex differential between them.

Tau pungona ("parent-in-law-child-in-law")

The *tau pungona* relationship is charged with respect and restraint on very much the same order as the *tau tamana*. It is a reciprocal relationship with neither party inherently outranking the other[20] and proper etiquette demanding that each side defer to the other whenever possible. In general it may be said that restrictions on behavior resemble those applying to the *tau ma* except that in the case of the *tau pungona* they must be adhered to even more rigidly.

To conclude this discussion one might note, perhaps with some skepticism as to its propriety, that I have discussed political authority, ritual honor, and freedom and restraint almost as if we were dealing with a single phenomenon. In fact they are distinct entities, but they are closely related insofar as they are all part of the Anutan ranking system. Political and honorific are both modes of ranking, and while they are not entirely congruent there is a good fit between them in most cases. The matter of freedom and restraint is somewhat different, but even here there is an important correlation. Kinsmen of very different rank are bound by the imposition of severe restraints. As they become closer in rank the restraints break down and freedom prevails. An exception to this pattern is seen in the case of certain affines *(tau ma* and *tau pungona)* where the structural potential for conflict is especially great and an imposition of restraint keeps it from coming to the surface.

PRINCIPLES OF RANK

There is a sense in which it is a mistake to speak of *the* Anutan ranking system as if it were a single unitary phenomenon. "Rank" can refer to any ordered hierarchical relationship, and such relationships, often having somewhat different bases and manifestations, run through many aspects of Anutan culture.

Throughout this essay I have made reference to two different ways in which hierarchical relationships manifest themselves on Anuta: ritual honor and political authority. From the preceding discussion it should be clear that these two systems are closely intertwined and follow the same general outlines but are in no sense congruent. Moreover, there are many other different contexts in which ranked relationships occur, and the basis for the ordering is not always the same in each case.

The most important determinant of one's social rank in both the political and the honorific spheres is genealogical seniority. This means that an older son outranks his younger brother, his children outrank those of his younger brothers, and so forth—the individual of the highest rank is the eldest son of the eldest son. Tui Anuta is the genealogically senior male on the island, and Tui Kainanga is the genealogically senior male in the Kainanga i Tepuko. It is on the basis of genealogical seniority that siblings of the same sex are ranked with respect to one another, and it is on this basis that the leaders of the lower *kainanga* as well as the individual *patongia* ("patrilateral extended family"; see Feinberg 1973: 9–11) usually are chosen.

Seniority is not, however, a wholly unambiguous criterion. It works well when applied to members of a single line or in comparing one line with another, but the Anutans do not calibrate it in terms of quantifiable units—and when one is comparing a junior member of a senior line with a senior member of a junior line, it turns out to be of little value. In fact, there are other ways of comparing people which are more relevant for some Anutan purposes than genealogical seniority, and therefore this is a matter with which they rarely concern themselves. This is not to say, however, that the issue is without its implications. I might even suggest that the ambiguity in the relationship between the leading *maru* of the Kainanga i Mua and the chief of the Kainanga i Tepuko—in which the latter is unquestionably superior in honorific terms while the former have often assumed preeminent authority in the political sphere—can be traced to precisely this confusion.

Although Anutans are ranked with respect to each other on the basis of genealogical seniority, once a title has been bestowed upon an individual he is elevated by virtue of his title above the level to which he was entitled strictly on the basis of his genealogical position. A man's genealogical status does not change upon his installation in the chieftainship, but his political power and ritual honor are affected drastically. And if for behavioral or other reasons a man is passed over in favor of his younger brother, the junior relative must be obeyed and respected for his title irrespective of his genealogical inferiority.

At most levels there are both ascribed and achieved (that is, genealogical and behavioral) prerequisites for power and prestige. A chief, for example, should be in a particular genealogical slot, but if his behavior is inappropriate he may be passed over. When this happens, he is passed over in favor of not just anybody selected at random but rather in favor of the man in the most appropriate genealogical slot who exhibits acceptable behavioral qualities.

It is in the middle levels of the political system that the greatest potential for the attainment of achieved status comes into play. Perceptivity, wisdom, persuasiveness, and a willingness to assert himself have elevated Pu Paone above the position in the *pono* to which his genealogical status entitled him, while others have declined to assert themselves and thus lost out on the political influence they could justly claim if they were so inclined. There are traditions of men having risen to extraordinary heights in the political system on the basis of physical strength and fighting skill. Generosity, leading an exemplary life, or having expertise in occupations such as gardening, fishing, carpentry, or navigation, on the other hand, are greatly admired and bring prestige to their possessors, though of an informal sort. It is expected that persons of high rank will manifest these qualities, but their possession in and of itself is insufficient grounds for the attainment of formal rank.

A rather different manner of ordering persons with respect to each other is on the basis of the relative kin categories into which they fall. In general an individual submits to those in ascending generations and dominates those in the generations below him. Even a chief must refrain from using the proper name of anyone he calls *tamana* ("father"). A man is on almost an equal plane with his *tuatina* ("mother's brother") and *tupuna* ("grandparent"), and he is on an equal plane with members of his generation and all affines of the same sex, although in the latter case there is mutual deference and honor.

Rank relations between men and women crosscut those established by kinship. In cases where the kinship system would otherwise prescribe an egalitarian relationship, if there is a sex differential between the two parties the man will outrank the woman. In both political and honorific terms a man outranks his *kave* ("sister of female cousin"), his *taina papine* ("sister-in-law"), and his wife. If the woman is dominant on the basis of kinship but the man is dominant on the basis of sex, as in the *tau pae* ("mother-child") or *tau makitanga* ("father's sister-brother's child") relationships, the problem is usually resolved by each deferring to the other. A man may not point his feet out toward his mother, strike her, or stand in her presence while she is seated because she is his *pae;* she is forbidden to do these things to him because he is a man. There are, however, some aspects of such a relationship which are not reciprocal. On the kinship side the mother (or father's sister) may demonstrate superiority over a man by addressing or referring to him by his proper name, whereas this is a liberty which no son (either real or classificatory) may legitimately take, regardless of his rank in other contexts. On the other hand, a man may sit on the seaward side of the house—a privilege from which *all* women are excluded—and when meeting on a narrow path even a man's own mother is expected to step aside.

Within certain limitations, age is a factor in determining rank as well. Among adults chronological age does not override genealogical seniority, kin classification, or sex. Children, however, are entitled to little formal honor in ranking contexts (as opposed to rites of passage where they may be singled out for special honor but not in such a way as to establish a dominance-submission relationship with anyone else), and they exercise no authority except over those who are even younger than themselves. Even a sister has authority over her younger brother until he demonstrates by his behavior that he has reached a responsible age. I have seen men drop many of the restrictions normally placed on interaction with their *ma* ("brother-in-law") in cases where the latter is a young child.

A firstborn son and daughter occupy special positions above and beyond that of simple age superiority and genealogical seniority. Many ceremonies are performed only for the *urumatua tangata* ("firstborn male") and *urumatua papine* ("firstborn female"). As far as I could determine, the latter is an honorific position rather than one which carries any political power; in fact the ritual preeminence of the *urumatua papine* seems limited to ceremonial occasions. The *urumatua tangata,* in addition to his ritually dominant position, is usually the man who will succeed his father to titles bearing political as well as honorific rank.

Another area in which we find hierarchical relationships to be a dominant characteristic is that of religion. In the traditional system this hierarchy was just another aspect of genealogical seniority and possession of titles. The worshipped deities were generally deceased humans, and the position of a god in the Anutan pantheon varied in more or less direct proportion to his genealogical rank while living as a human being. The most powerful gods were worshipped under the leadership of the first chief, who was also the island's high priest, assisted by the second chief and the leading *maru*. Lower-ranking deities could be invoked by their living descendants under the leadership of the group's senior male.

With the coming of the church, religious rank was no longer directly tied up with genealogical seniority. And although traditional leaders have felt an obligation to assume positions of responsibility in the church, it has not been limited to them. At the same time that genealogical and societal rank have been formally separated from status in the religious order, the structure of the ranking system has simply been replicated in the organization of the church. On the societal level the first chief is formally honored: it is he who has the ultimate authority to make decisions, although he does this in the name of the *pono*. The second chief is given chiefly honor, but his political authority is more analogous to that of the leading *maru* than that of the senior *ariki*. Although the *maru* are not given formal honor, they act as advisers to the chiefs and make sure that the decisions of the *pono* are carried out.

In the church, political power is in the hands of the catechist. His assistants (referred to by the same name, *pakaako*) are also honored by means of the *pakamisionari* prestations. In fact, were an Anutan to describe the relationship between Pu Tokerau and his assistants he would probably say *"Pu Tokerau i mua; rake mea i muri"* ("Pu Tokerau is in front; the others are behind")—the same terms used to describe the relationship between the two chiefs. The companions, on the other hand, have little formal honor as a result of their position. But they do advise the catechist at weekly meetings or as the need arises, and it is their duty to see that the policies of the church *(te rotu* or *te pekau)* in whose name the catechist acts are implemented.

It should now be obvious that there are many different principles according to which hierarchical relationships may be established in Anutan culture. Different principles become operative in different contexts, but they also exist as at least partially independent variables which may intersect and to a certain extent counterbalance each other. Regardless of the context, however, there are two key concepts found in all ranked relationships: *manuu* and *aropa*.

Manuu or *mana*—both terms are used on Anuta to similar effect, but the former is the more common—designates a kind of personal power or efficacy. *Manuu* is believed generally to be possessed in proportion to one's social rank. It is inherited from one's father and flows down genealogical lines. The higher the rank of one's father, the more *manuu* he has to pass on to his sons, and it goes to the eldest son before his next younger brother and so on, so that by the time it gets to the youngest there may be little left for him. In other words, its most common immediate source is genealogical seniority, although the other criteria for rank are factors as well. Women have much less *manuu* than men, and infants have little or none regardless of their genealogical position and sex—it gradually increases as they get older and grow into adulthood. A high title, especially that of *ariki,* brings a great deal of *manuu* to the one who bears it. Despite the varied immediate sources, however, its ultimate source is the same: in the ancient religion it derived from the traditional deities (some informants say Satan); in more recent times it has issued from the Christian God, whom I have often heard referred to in church sermons as *te tapito o te manuu katoa* ("the source of all power").

Manuu is manifested in such qualities as wisdom, physical strength, occupational expertise, and skill in dealing with problems. Ideally, genealogically senior men are also competent individuals, in which case the two principles are mutually reinforcing. Sometimes it happens, however, that a man will demonstrate by either his competence or his ineptitude that he has been granted *manuu* in a greater or lesser degree than one would ordinarily expect him to possess on the basis of ascriptive criteria. This is taken as an indication that the individual is especially favored or disfavored by the gods (or God), and this is ultimately what accounts for the degree of openness there is in the Anutan system of rank.

The sanction behind rank derives from the *manuu* of the superior party. It is said that in earlier times if a chief were annoyed at someone he could curse him with sterility or death, and despite the coming of the church most people are still not convinced that this power has been lost. In fact there were several cases of mental derangement, mostly of limited duration, during my stay on the island which were diagnosed as having resulted from failure to show proper respect and obedience to a chief. The oral tradition relates how Pu Rongomai fell ill because he disobeyed his elder brother, and while I was on Anuta there were at least two illnesses—one proving fatal—which were said to have stemmed from the victims' failure to care properly for their parents during old age. Cases such as these illustrate the dangers involved in paying inadequate respect to persons of higher rank, but the legitimate right to exercise political authority and compel deference comes from ancient tradition *(te tukutu-kunga mai mua)* and one's position as protector and provider for the well-being of his subordinates. A dramatic illustration of this principle took place in 1972.

A substantial food shortage resulted from a severe cyclone which struck Anuta in February 1972—just a month before my arrival. During the recovery period the Ariki i Mua proclaimed that the island henceforth would harvest food and make ovens as a single collective unit until the time of scarcity had passed. His reason was that no one knew beforehand just how severe the food shortage might be, or whether for that matter it might not even develop into a full-fledged famine. It was the chief's feeling that if no corrective measures were taken some of the poorer members of his community might starve to death. He therefore determined to distribute the wealth so that, as he put it, if anyone on the island were to die of starvation everyone should die together. He did not want anyone to have plenty to eat while someone else was starving, so he decided that during the period of scarcity all food resources would be pooled and distributed equitably to the entire island.

If this were the whole story it would be sufficient to demonstrate that the chief assumes an attitude of responsibility for the welfare of the island. But it goes beyond this. In fact the food which was harvested, cooked, and distributed to the island did not come from *everyone's* gardens but from those of the Kainanga i Mua. It was members of this *kainanga* who carried out the preparation and distribution of the food as well. The Kainanga i Tepuko assisted the Kainanga i Mua with contributions from their gardens as well as working around the ovens while the lesser *kainanga* were able to keep their food as reserve or use it for ceremonial occasions. This arrangement, it should be noted, is not related to numerical superiority or material wealth. In fact the Kainanga i Pangatau is as large as the Kainanga i Mua and is somewhat richer in number of gardens, while the Kainanga i Tepuko is a distant third. Rather it is consistent with the position of Kainanga i Mua as the leading *kainanga* and protector of the island. Because Pu Tepuko played the role of first lieutenant to Tearakura during his lifetime, and then as chief of the island after his brother's death, his descendants in the Kainanga i Tepuko assist Tearakura's descendants in their task of caring for the island.

The obligation shared by persons of high rank to care for those below them is manifestation of the general phenomenon known as *aropa*. In different contexts this term may be translated as pity, sympathy, love, or affection, although none of these words really gives the full flavor of the Anutan concept. If an Anutan is away from the island and he misses another, he will say *"Kau aropa ki ei"* ("I *aropa* to him"). I was frequently told before the end of my stay that I should not leave the island because *"Kau aropa ki a te koe"* ("I *aropa* to you"). When one suffers some misfortune he again is told *"Kau aropa ki a te koe,"* although with a rather different connotation than in the case above. An orphan is called a *tama pakaaropa* or "pitiable child."

In most contexts *aropa* may be loosely thought of as connoting what we call "love," but there are also considerable differences in its content and expression. In Western society one does not often utter the words "I love you," and when one does it is supposed to reflect a deep emotional commitment. On Anuta it is more tied up with behavior: actions are constantly explained in terms of one's *aropa* for someone else. Unlike Western concepts of love and friendship, which are taken to be immaterial qualities valued as ends in themselves, *aropa* is meaningful only insofar as it is expressed in material terms. One cannot be on Anuta for long without realizing the tremendous importance attached to the giving and sharing of material goods. In fact a presentation of material goods is often termed *aropa,* the same as the sentiments of which the prestation is taken to be a material embodiment. A gift is often handed over with the words *"toku aropa ki a te koe"* ("my *aropa* to you"), and before I realized this connotation I once asked an intermediary to relay my *aropa* to a friend on Tikopia in the same way we may send our regards or our love. I was rather perplexed by the response—"Where is it?"—until it was explained to me that when somebody sends his *aropa* to someone overseas it is in the form of a material object.

The significance of this concept to the ranking system is best summed up in the very terms by which the men of the two types of *kainanga* are called. The word *maru* refers to shade from the sun or shelter from the rain. A husband may be referred to as his wife's *maru,* and I have even heard a funeral dirge for a dead chief in which the *ariki* was described as *toku maru* ("my *maru*"). When this is put together with the role of the men of the leading *kainanga* who are described by the same term, it may be seen as a unitary concept which might justly be translated as "guardian" or "protector."

The men of the lesser *kainanga,* and the *kainanga* themselves, are referred to as *pakaaropa. Paka* is the causative prefix, and the concept of *aropa* we have just discussed at some length. *Pakaaropa,* then, may be roughly translated as "causing sympathy" or "causing affection." The *pakaaropa* are weak. They do not have enough *manuu* to take care of themselves, and in traditional times they did not carry enough sway with the gods to ensure the continued welfare and prosperity of the island on which they lived. Thus they produce feelings of *aropa* in those with greater *manuu.* This *aropa* is expressed by providing protection both in the supernatural sphere by performing *kava* rites to propitiate the gods (or at the present time by making sure that the operations of the church are running smoothly) and in the temporal sphere by ensuring that they have sufficient material goods to continue living a reasonably comfortable existence. In return for their solicitous behavior the *pakaaropa* owe the *maru* and their chiefs allegiance, obedience, ritual deference, and occasional prestations of material goods as symbols of the *aropa* (translated in this case perhaps as "appreciation") they are obligated to return.

This model, I would suggest, may also be applied to other ranked relationships. Men own the canoes and have primary interest in the gardens.[21] This economic relationship is consistent with their superior *manuu* and fashions their role as protectors and providers for the welfare of their wives and sisters. It is in this context that their ritual and political superiority may be understood.

Parents care for and protect their children, and I suspect that it is because of this assistance and protection that informants say the respect due a father is second to none. Yet, significantly, as they get older and the dependence relationship reverses, respect relations also begin to shift in favor of the child.

Older persons are expected to be more experienced and hence more knowledgeable and generally competent than their juniors, who are dependent upon them for tutelage and assistance. A strong man, great warrior, or man of outstanding wisdom is expected to use his prowess to protect the island from foreign invasion and maintain order. And the church, as the "source of all power," assumes ultimate responsibility for the well-being of the entire community.

The Anutan ranking system, then, is a double-edged sword. One defers to persons of higher rank in the first instance because of their greater *manuu,* but with this *manuu* comes an obligation to exhibit *aropa*. This reciprocity is reflected in the humility of high-ranking individuals who often take it upon their own initiative to defer to those below them in ritual contexts, and also in their role as providers and protectors. In return those of low rank show *aropa* for their benefactors by means of periodic ritual prestations and acceptance of their relative status, thus affirming the legitimacy of the ranking system along with the assertions of political authority and ritual honor which it entails.

NOTES

The fieldwork on which this essay is based was carried out between February 1972 and March 1973 under the auspices of a U.S. Public Health Service training grant. I am indebted to Professor Fred Eggan of the University of Chicago for his helpful advice and encouragement before, during, and after my stay in the field, to Professor Marshall Sahlins and fellow students Joseph Maxwell and John Kirkpatrick of the University of Chicago, who read and commented on a draft of this paper, and to Professor R. C. Green of the University of Auckland and Dr. D. E. Yen of the Bernice P. Bishop Museum for their correspondence and assistance during and since the period of my field study. Above all, however, I would like to express my gratitude to Sir Raymond Firth for originally suggesting that I consider Tikopia's nearest neighbor (in linguistic and cultural as well as geographical terms) for a field site during his tenure as visiting professor at the University of Chicago in autumn 1970 and spring 1971, for the interest he has taken in my work and the valuable assistance he has provided since that time, and for his Tikopia studies to which I could constantly look as a source of guidance and inspiration in the conduct of my own field investigation. I also appreciate his having read and commented on an earlier draft of this paper.

1. The Anutan *kainanga* are closely analogous to Tikopian units bearing the same name, which Firth has chosen to translate as "clan." For further discussion of the Anutan units and their Tikopian counterparts see Feinberg (1973:13–17) and Firth (1966:298–329) respectively.

2. Nau Ariki was the only woman ever to hold this title, and while I was able to confirm with several informants that this was the case, no one seemed to have any idea what powers or responsibilities she may have held by virtue of this title. My best speculation is that it was an honorific position without political authority, perhaps analogous to the "female Tui'i Tonga."

3. Pu and Nau, Anutan titles for married men and women, are analogous in use to the English "Mr." and "Mrs." respectively.

4. In addition to married names all Anutans have one or more personal names and, in recent times, baptismal names as well. It is common practice for a native to be given the same name as a deceased relative or ancestor; thus when there is a reasonable likelihood of confusion due to a convergence of married names, I have added the Christian personal name or both in parentheses. Hence the present Ariki i Mua is Pu Koroatu (Jacob Tearaamanu), not to be confused with his namesake who is mentioned here.

5. For more extensive discussion of this point see Feinberg (1974).

6. With some reservations the *patongia* may be identified as a patrilateral extended family; it is the elementary unit of property ownership, production, and consumption. For further discussion see Feinberg (1973:9–11).

7. In fact there was a third *patongia*—that of Nau Tanukope and her young son Joses Vakairakau. As there was no adult male in the unit, however, its existence was irrelevant to the problem of installing a new chief.

8. I can recall one feast in which a hungry populace waited for forty-five minutes with the food spread out in front of them for the Ariki Tepuko to show up so that they could begin their meal.

9. The Ariki Tepuko created quite a stir when he left in June 1972 to visit his sons in Honiara, capital of the Solomon Islands. When he and his wife went out to the ship without first publicizing their plans, his people simply assumed they had gone out to say good-bye to some relatives they knew were leaving. Thus the chief departed without proper ceremony or an entourage to protect him and care for his needs. Many Anutans were very upset for a long time over the affair.

10. For a fuller and more theoretical account of this phenomenon the reader is referred to the final section of this essay.

11. A catechist is the lowest-ranking clergyman in the Anglican church (but the highest-ranking clergyman on Anuta during the period of my stay).

12. In practice no situation should ever develop to this point, since the two chiefs are expected to defer to each other's judgment and speak in unison. In most cases, if the second chief feels very strongly about something the first chief will accede to his colleague's wishes in order to preserve the principle of chiefly solidarity. But if Tui Anuta is adamant, the only proper course for Tui Kainanga is to defer.

13. If it is necessary to translate *maru* into English the best gloss might be "nobles." The *pakaaropa,* in contrast, would be "commoners." The absolute status differential between these strata in normal daily intercourse, however, is not so great as this characterization might be taken to imply, and therefore I prefer to use the native terms.

14. Perhaps an analogy might be helpful here as long as the parallels are not carried too far. The president of the United States may act on the spur of the moment to commit troops for a police action in some part of the world, and when he does the American people are supposed to rally to his support. Nevertheless, according to the Constitution war-making power rests with the Congress, and it is not until Congress has acted that the action gains an official stamp and the United States is legally at war. On Anuta, rather than two decision-making bodies there is but a single ultimate authority (who may have to speak, however, in two separate forums).

15.   The Anutan terms for mother's brother, sister's child, father, and child are
        tuatina, iraamutu, tamana, and *tama* respectively. For a full listing of Anutan
        kin terms and their approximate English meanings see Feinberg (1973:17–20).
        For a more extensive and, I believe, more accurate account see chap. 3 of my
        doctoral dissertation (1974). Firth (1966:233–235) has noted a similar usage of
        the word *tau* among the Tikopia.
16.   For the sake of convenience I shall identify the relationships to be discussed by
        means of genealogical glosses. It should be emphasized, however, that the Anu-
        tan kinship system cannot be properly understood solely in genealogical terms.
        For a fuller account the reader is referred to chap. 3 of my doctoral dissertation.
17.   The Tikopian term *pakapariki* (see Firth 1966:207–209) is presently used with
        much greater frequency than the Anutan *pakakovikovi,* but many informants re-
        member the indigenous term and can recite it easily upon request.
18.   One informant actually suggested to me that the whole distinction between cross
        and parallel cousins is an alien concept imported from Tikopia. The fact that the
        same distinction between theory and practice exists on Anuta's neighbor, how-
        ever, and the presence of a distinct indigenous term (*kovi* is not part of the Tiko-
        pian lexicon) leads me to look with skepticism on this contention.
19.   This finding confirms Firth's report of a similar practice among the Tikopia
        (1966:178–185).
20.   By this I mean that while one may outrank the other on other grounds this is
        entirely separate from the *tau pungona* relationship.
21.   Unlike their relationship with canoes, women do work in the gardens and are
        said to share in their ownership. A man's ties to his gardens, however, are not
        altered by marriage as are a woman's, and it is in this sense that the bonds be-
        tween him and his land are closer than those linking the land to his sisters or
        wife.

REFERENCES CITED

Feinberg, Richard
1973   Anutan social structure. In *Anuta: a Polynesian outlier in the Solomon Islands,*
        ed. D. E. Yen and Jane Gordon. Pacific Anthropological Records, no. 21. Ho-
        nolulu: Bernice P. Bishop Museum.
1974   Social structure of Anuta. Ph.D. dissertation, Department of Anthropology,
        University of Chicago.

Firth, Raymond
1966   *We, the Tikopia: kinship in primitive Polynesia.* Boston: Beacon Press.

Fox, C. E.
n.d.   *The Melanesian Brotherhood.* London: Melanesian Mission.

Melanesian Mission
n.d.   *Handbook of the Companions of the Melanesian Brotherhood.* London:
        Melanesian Mission.

Cliques, Factions, and Leadership among the Toaripi of Papua

DAWN RYAN

The literature on traditional Melanesian political organization has concentrated on the emergence and activities of the "Big Man." Societies
such as the Trobriand Islands and Wogeo, where hereditary leadership
has been reported, have generally been disregarded as "untypical."
There is, however, a considerable body of material which indicates that
the well-documented and widely reported Big Man type of leadership is
by no means the only one in Melanesia.[1] In particular, the south coast of
New Guinea is a geographical area in which leadership is determined to a
considerable degree by inheritance of office. In this essay, I wish to give
another ethnographic instance from this area and to suggest that contemporary local-level political organization shows a development and adaptation of traditional patterns to meet changing circumstances.[2] The emphasis throughout is on the "working arrangements of society" (Firth
1954:10).

The Toaripi number approximately five thousand people, about three-
quarters of them living in villages on the Gulf of Papua and the rest in
towns throughout Papua New Guinea. The villages are quite large for
Melanesia, generally containing 600 to 700 people, and are situated right
on the coast around the mouths of two large rivers.

The staple foods are sago, fish, and coconut supplemented by sweet
potato, manioc, tinned corned beef, tinned fish, rice, and tea. This list
indicates on the one hand that cash is an integral part of the Toaripi
economy and on the other it shows that the terrain is unlikely to be suitable for cash crops. Sago palms are not generally cultivated, but grow
wild in the freshwater swamps which are so extensive in the area that it is

not easy for people to find dry land for village sites. Cash is a necessary part of Toaripi life, but the only local source is copra sales. This, of course, is one of the reasons why so many people move away to the towns.

The first recorded visit by a white man occurred in 1881, when James Chalmers of the London Missionary Society spent a short time in the Toaripi villages. Since then there have been many changes in Toaripi culture, some quite dramatic. The old religion has been completely superseded by Christianity; large-scale economic enterprises such as trading voyages have stopped; thc number of villages has risen from two to eleven; the arrangement of houses in villages has changed; and so on.

In 1919 the Toaripi participated in a cargo cult known in the literature as the Vailala Madness[3] and abruptly repudiated their traditional culture, especially the religion. Since the 1920s young men have been accustomed to go away to work, and since the end of World War II many families have gone to live in towns. The London Missionary Society and later the Australian administration have provided schools in the area for about fifty years, so that most Toaripi are literate in their own language and a few in English. Since World War II, cooperative societies and a local government council have been formed.

In general, the Toaripi are typical of people in coastal parts of Papua New Guinea: having seen many profound changes in their own culture, involved in a complex way with the outside world, they have yet maintained their cultural distinctiveness while adapting to numerous innovations.

TRADITIONAL TOARIPI SOCIETY

At the time of contact the Toaripi lived in two large adjacent villages at the mouth of the Lakekamu River. Each village contained a number of men's houses which were of great importance in the society. The men's houses were the foci of cycles of ceremonies which were validated by reference to series of myths recounting the adventures of heroes and heroines. Each men's house had associated with it a set of these myths, and the members of the men's houses group *(elavoape)* were thought to be kin mainly because of their association with a common set of myths. Each men's house had stored in it sacred bull-roarers and other religious paraphernalia kept secret from women and uninitiated boys. The men of an *elavoape* arranged for their own sons to be initiated into the secrets of these religious objects, but they coordinated the initiation with those of the other men's houses in the village. All boys initiated at the same time belonged to a village-wide, named age-group. Girls also belonged to the age-group but were not initiated into religious secrets. Members of an age-group *(heatao)* cooperated in various economic activities, and the male members were important in the organization of war parties. There was no hierarchical arrangement of age-groups, nor was there any institutionalized leadership within an age-group.

Within the men's house there were at least two offices: *pukari* and *mai karu*. The *pukari*'s position was inherited patrilineally, but it is not clear how many *pukari* there were in one men's house.[4] The *pukari* had two main sets of duties: he organized and presided over the distribution of food at certain feasts, and he mediated disputes and intervened to stop fights. It is not clear just how he was brought into a dispute or whether his jurisdiction was limited to certain kinds of dispute. If a fight broke out in the village a *pukari* took his badges of office, a string bag and a lime gourd, and went to the scene. If the fighting did not stop he smashed the gourd and tore the bag. At the same time the *mai karu* associated with him, who always belonged to a different men's house, sounded the bull-roarer and all fighting had to stop on pain of undefined supernatural punishment. Later, those who had fought provided a pig for a feast at which the *pukari* received new badges of office and which marked the resumption of friendly relations among the disputants.

This outline of peacekeeping within the village leaves many unanswered questions: Who settled arguments that did not develop into fights? What was done when members of different men's house groups quarreled or fought? What was done to effect the reconciliation that must have preceded the feast? What was the exact relationship between a *pukari* and his associated *mai karu?* None of these questions can be answered with certainty: the institutions had disappeared forty years before I was in the field, and the few who could speak of these times with any knowledge were unwilling to do so because of the general devaluation of the "old ways."[5] It is nevertheless clear that the *pukari*'s peacekeeping activities had a strong ritual component and that such authority as he had derived largely from his association with the bull-roarer. Furthermore, it seems likely that a good deal of informal and private negotiation took place before and after the public intervention of the *pukari*.

Magical formulas were used to help ensure success in warfare and in various large-scale enterprises such as hunting, fish drives, and trading voyages. These formulas derived their power from their association with the myths, and knowledge of them was handed down from father to son. Knowledge of the appropriate formulas was necessary before a person could assume leadership of an enterprise, but it was not sufficient to ensure leadership. This depended on factors such as previous success, the composition of the group involved, and the standing of other people with similar knowledge.

Leadership, in other words, was largely situational: a *pukari* might or might not lead a pig hunt;[6] a man who led one pig hunt might or might not lead the next. Positions of authority were spread throughout the society and were tied to specific situations. The inheritance of knowledge which sustained positions of authority marked off a catchment of people who competed to exercise actual leadership, but there was no provision for the emergence of a Big Man of the kind so frequently described in the literature.[7]

CONTEMPORARY LEADERSHIP AND POLITICAL ORGANIZATION

As I have noted, Toaripi discarded the bull-roarers and other religious paraphernalia in 1919 and made no attempt to revive the old religion when the promises of the Vailala Madness were not fulfilled. Among other things, this meant that the *pukari* no longer had any sanction for their position, nor was magical knowledge of importance in deciding leadership of an activity.

Neither informants' statements nor documentary records provide any but the most sketchy account of Toaripi life between 1920 and 1960, so that it is difficult to set out details of the ways in which activities were organized in this period. There are, however, a few general points that can be made.

Government-appointed village constables were responsible for peace-keeping in the village and were required to take lawbreakers to the district headquarters about forty miles away. The constables apparently mediated and settled minor quarrels, so that only major disputes went to the government office. The constables also had the duty of enforcing government regulations about village hygiene, clearing of paths, repair of rest houses, and the like. They were thus agents of an outside law-enforcement body, and those appointed to the position were not necessarily community leaders who commanded respect or exercised authority recognized by their fellows.

Christian missionaries had been continuously resident among the Toaripi since 1883, and by the 1920s several local men had been ordained pastors. Missionaries, pastors, and deacons were men of influence in Toaripi villages, though it is difficult to obtain detailed information on their activities. It seems, however, that their association with the supernatural lent authority to their words and actions; and in some cases at least the village pastor was a much more important man than the village constable. Between them these two men appear to have taken over many of the leadership functions that had lapsed with the repudiation of the old religion, but it is seldom clear exactly how these functions were carried out.

Contemporary Toaripi have a diffuse pattern of leadership, but leaders no longer have supernatural support for their position. To show how this actually works, I shall discuss the situation in Uritai village, where I spent most of my time in the field. I am concentrating on this one village mainly for ease of presentation; what I have to say applies in general terms to all Toaripi communities.

Age-groups are still important in Toaripi society, having survived the destruction of the men's houses and the disappearance of the old religion. People who begin to go to the village school at about the same time are members of one named age-group. Age-mates cooperate in various economic activities and help each other on numerous occasions, both formal and informal; they are, in fact, friends as this relationship is recognized in the society. But age-groups are not in themselves important in the definition of leaders or in the process of decision making.

Kinship is also an important feature of Toaripi society.[8] It is reckoned bilaterally, with no regular cutoff point. Remembrance of kin ties is related to interest in land. Each named plot is owned by one or more descent groups (cf. Firth 1963:23) consisting of the descendants of the original owners or users of the plot. In theory, each plot has hundreds of owners, and each person has rights to hundreds of plots; in fact, most owners and rights are forgotten. A person knows of his rights to about twenty plots, and he exercises them on about half a dozen, usually some of those on which his parents have worked. If land rights are not exercised for a generation or so, they lapse and the genealogical ties on which they were based are forgotten.

A person is an active member of about half a dozen landholding groups (that is, he regularly works on this land) and is probably a peripheral member of as many more (that is, he has trees on this land or works on it occasionally). The other members of these groups are his recognized kin, with whom he cooperates in many activities and on whom he relies for support in disputes and in large undertakings such as marriage payments and mortuary feasts.

Kinsmen cooperate in everyday work, they help each other on special occasions, they contribute to marriage payments and receive portions of such payments made by others: in other words, they are constantly exchanging goods and services of all kinds. Within this framework, decisions have to be taken on many matters and some activities need leaders. But there is no formal leadership in the general field of kinship. Furthermore, a person has no overall status in this field: he may be an influential member of one descent group but of little account in another. Nevertheless, decisions are made, activities are organized, disputes are settled.

A point to remember is that in any one situation a very small number of people are involved, and they are people who interact frequently and rely heavily on each other for goods, services, and companionship. This means that on some occasions a great deal of time and trouble will be taken to reach a decision satisfactory to all. On other occasions, the very closeness of the relationship means that a decision can be taken quickly and without question from others.

The lack of formal leadership in kin relationships and the process of decision making are illustrated in the two following cases.

Case 1

A middle-aged man whose father had died when he was a small boy had spent all his life working with and caring for his stepfather, who was not a kinsman and had no children of his own. The old man was now feeble and clearly not going to live much longer, and kinsmen had stated firmly and publicly that the stepson would not be permitted to inherit land rights from him. When this became clear, the man began to look to the land of his long-dead father. His first cousins, however, vigorously opposed his attempts to use this land, pointing out that he had ignored them for many years so that they scarcely knew him as a kinsman. He had land from his mother, of course, but did not think this enough for himself or his family. Other kinsmen stepped in and began the long, delicate task of negotiating a settlement: each side in the dispute had been remiss, but it would be wrong to leave a kinsman destitute. The man was to spend more time with his long-neglected kinsmen: visit them, work with them, send his daughters to help mind their children, ask for their help when his son's marriage payment was made. Then, as the estranged kinsmen got to know him and his family, they would begin to feel toward him as they should and he could exercise his land rights as he wished. This was to be a long-term agreement, and I left the village before it had got fairly started. But it does show a situation in which a difficult dispute among kin is discussed at great length and the parties are prepared to try to reach accord over a period of many months.

Case 2

Two women mentioned to one of their male kin that they were planning to plant a few coconuts on a plot of land that all used. The man objected, saying that there were more than enough coconuts on that plot. He suggested that they plant on some other land to which they had rights. The women ignored the objection and planted the coconuts. A few weeks later the man saw the seedlings and tore them out of the ground. When the women heard what he had done and complained to other kin, they got no support. The man had made a proper decision about use of that piece of land, and the women should have heeded it.

We can think of Uritai village as a social field composed of dozens of overlapping bilateral descent groups without any overall organization, hierarchical or otherwise. Each person belongs to several of these groups and is often caught in situations where his loyalty is divided. He frequently has to decide which, if any, of a number of competing calls on his time and loyalty he will heed. The decision is taken according to current needs and interests within a framework of norms and expectations defined by kinship and age-group (cf. Firth 1971:31). In a society such as this, does anyone acquire a reputation as leader? If so, how does he do it? How does he persuade people to follow him? What leadership positions are there?[9]

It is easiest to begin with the last point. There are in Uritai three bodies whose formal organization covers the whole village: the village congregation of the London Missionary Society,[10] which has been in existence since the 1930s; the Uritai cooperative society, formed in 1946; and the constituency that elects two councillors to the local government council, set up in 1958.[11] The village congregation is headed by a pastor, an Uritai man who retains his position mainly because the congregation wishes to keep him. Deacons elected by the congregation assist the pastor; and there are also officeholders in the Torchbearer youth organization. The transfer of pastors and the election and demotion of deacons have to be ratified at an annual meeting of delegates from all the congregations in the district, so that these men are not at the mercy of those who bear them temporary ill will.

The cooperative society is run by a board of directors elected annually by the membership, most of the adult males in the village. They cannot be removed from office during the year without the approval of the government cooperative officer in the area. As for the constituency, the two councillors are elected by all the taxpayers in the village and can be removed from office only by a senior member of the administration.

Altogether there are twenty-two positions in these organizations, and the villagers deliberately keep them widely dispersed: the pastor should not be a councillor, there should not be too many deacons on the cooperative's board, and so on.[12]

The pastor and deacons, the cooperative society's board of directors, and the two councillors are all men of general standing and prestige in the village, but they all realize that they have only a limited sphere of influence. The pastor and deacons make decisions about the conduct of church services. If the congregation is dissatisfied, it must wait until the next general church meeting; the councillors and cooperative directors do not as such have any say in the matter. If the congregation does not pay the annual dues requested by the pastor, he cannot ask the councillors to intervene. On the other hand, he should ask the councillors to allocate men to repair his house because that is part of their responsibilities. The cooperative society's directors cannot organize the village labor force, nor can the councillors instruct the society's storekeeper to vary his trading hours.

Finally, all these people must be careful not to give the appearance of using their formal positions to influence decisions that belong to the spheres of kinship or age-grouping. If they do, they will probably lose their point on that occasion—and very likely their position at the next election. This delicate balance of power is not always maintained. But there is a dispute if a person oversteps the bounds of his authority, and the dispute is mediated by someone who points out the different spheres of influence and repeats that a person in one must not encroach on another.

None of these officers has power to enforce decisions he makes. If people do not agree with what he says, they simply ignore him. Thus we are back to our earlier question: How does anyone become a leader? There is no doubt that some men in the village are more influential than others: their opinions count, and they can persuade others to follow a line of action they favor. This influence occurs in a community that is aggressively egalitarian: all adult men are equal and must be taken into account. But, of course, some are more equal than others. It is true that anyone may offer an opinion on any matter, but only certain opinions count. How does this come about? What are the bases of leadership?

A Toaripi belongs to one age-group and several landholding bilateral descent groups. He is probably a member of the village congregation. If he is a male over the age of sixteen, he is a taxpayer and thus eligible to vote in council elections.[13] If he is an adult male, he is probably a shareholding member of the cooperative society. None of these facts indicates his overall standing in the community. Neither his kinship and age-group affiliations nor his membership in the village-wide formal organizations indicate which side he is likely to support in a dispute. Still less do they indicate the influence he is likely to have on any particular occasion. Nevertheless, political authority is derived from the interaction and balancing of interests served by these various affiliations.

In discussing political authority, or leadership, I shall follow Langness (1973:143–144) in saying that the term *political* refers to public affairs and *authority* refers to the legitimate right to influence, to make binding decisions and to direct the affairs of a set of people according to rules they recognize. This, for the purposes of our investigation, constitutes leadership.

Leadership among the Toaripi emerges from the successful manipulation of interests served by membership of cliques and factions. These may, and frequently do, cut across the affiliations I have already discussed; but such affiliations must be taken into account when cliques and factions are examined. By *clique* I mean a collection of people who share a number of interests and interact frequently in the pursuance of these interests over a period of time. Clique members are not recruited according to any one principle, nor does a clique necessarily have a center or leader.[14]

A Toaripi interacts regularly with only a limited number of those he recognizes as kin. Such interaction implies certain rights and obligations, and it may be to a person's advantage to increase the number of those with whom he interacts in this way. There are among the Toaripi regular mechanisms for extending kin terms, along with some of the attendant rights and obligations of the associated interaction, to people who are not in fact genealogically linked. The siblings of an age-mate may be called siblings; the age-mates of siblings may be called siblings; and children of parents' age-mates may be called siblings.

There are thus cliques consisting of people who call each other and for many purposes treat each other as kin; but these cliques serve interests distinct from those that concern landholding bilateral descent groups. Only by observation is it possible to determine whether a given set of "kinsmen" are acting as such or whether they are acting as a clique. Indeed, observation of behavior is an uncertain guide, since the patterns of interaction are very similar in both cases. It is necessary to determine whether a given set of people consists entirely or principally of those who are genealogically linked; whether they act frequently in public affairs; and whether the composition changes as members' interests diverge. Such cliques are numerous in Toaripi society and are an important component of Toaripi political organization. There are, in addition, cliques formed within the various village-wide formal organizations. Each of these organizations encompasses several cliques which promote divergent though not necessarily conflicting interests associated with it.

A man becomes a leader through his clique memberships; by skillful manipulation of others' interests, he is able to build up a following of those who are under an obligation to return past favors and support. This pattern resembles that of Big Man leadership, but I would argue that there are several significant differences.

A leader who emerges in the way I have outlined is dependent upon followers whose own interests do not always coincide with his. Their continued clique membership, and thus continued support for a particular leader, depends not only upon his furthering of their interests but also upon their continued interest in the aims of the clique to which they belong at the moment. Thus a leader cannot be assured of a following simply by the continued exercise of entrepreneurial and manipulative skills; he is equally dependent on the continued interest of the clique members who constitute his following. This is something over which he has little or no control.

In addition, a leader has a limited sphere of influence, as have the officials of formal organizations.[15] If his following is made up entirely of one clique, then his influence in the community is clearly limited. This is equally true if his following consists of members of several cliques. There is no recognized way in which a man can spread his influence throughout the community and become a leader accepted by all. I have argued elsewhere (Ryan 1969) that an attempt to do this is likely to bring together several influential men in an alliance whose aim is to ensure that the attempt is unsuccessful.

Because Toaripi society is marked by pervasive factionalism, there is no recognized way in which a leader can gain preeminence.[16] No one can recruit followers from all sections of the community because people are divided by factions as well as linked in cliques. Before I expand on this idea, I wish to illustrate my argument with two case studies which highlight many of the points I am trying to make.

Case 3

Kara, who was a local government councillor at the time, organized a trade store, ostensibly as a kin-based operation. He and his children constituted the case. Kara had over the years cared for the orphaned children of his brothers and sister, and the nephews were under a heavy obligation to him. They provided some of the capital needed and those who were still unmarried worked in the store. These young men were not only under an obligation to Kara for his past care; they also expected assistance from him in making up their marriage payments in the future. These factors made them good storekeepers: they did not steal and they gave credit only with Kara's approval. Another of Kara's brothers had been on bad terms with him for many years and refused to contribute to the venture. Other nephews contributed capital and skills such as knowledge of bookkeeping; these men had not necessarily been cared for by Kara and thus were not under any particular obligation to him. Some of them became shareholders so that they could get goods on credit. Kara did not invite all his genealogical kin to contribute; those excluded were generally prominent in mission activities. Kara was cool toward the mission, though he did not openly oppose it.

Others who were invited to participate were Kara's kin only in the sense that they had in the past been affiliated with the same men's house group. The younger generation in this family contained some wage earners who sent money to their parents, who would thus be regular store customers. One daughter had married a schoolteacher who was working on the nearby government station. This man was invited to become a shareholder. He was likely to be a regular customer and might well attract some of his fellow teachers to the store; he, on the other hand, could get credit.

There are several points of interest here. Kara activated a selection of kin ties in collecting capital for the store. But only those kin who were likely to be useful were recruited, and those who became shareholders were furthering interests that had no necessary connection with kinship. Kara was clearly the leader of a kin-based clique whose interests centered on the trade store. It is worth noting that his office of councillor did not enter into this activity, nor did his success in organizing the store enhance his authority as councillor. Later Kara attempted to drive the village cooperative store out of business by using his clique as a power base. He failed—partly because some members of his clique were also members of cliques associated with the cooperative and partly because his success would have given him virtual monopoly of trading in the village. Such preeminence is not to be tolerated among Toaripi.

Case 4

A meeting of the cooperative society, at which eighty people were present, decided by a vote of 77 to 3 to provide more share capital for the Toaripi Association of Native Societies.[17] The three who disagreed were influential men, though only one held office in the cooperative. As each spoke in turn, he told the meeting about his land and kinsmen before going on to detail his past work for the cooperative society. Finally, each outlined plans for the future of the society which would be thwarted if the money were handed over to the association. In reply a couple of men said that the contribution would be of benefit to the community; the cooperative was, after all, the backbone of the village, and there should be no objection to helping it grow strong. The dissenters spoke again, repeating their points. Other men of influence began to speak in their support, and after about three hours of discussion the meeting voted 80 to 0 not to contribute the share capital to the association.

One of my friends who did not agree with the decision said later that there was no point in holding out against the three: if they did not want to contribute, neither they nor their kinsmen would do so, and the cooperative society would be placed in the embarrassing position of having promised to do something and then being unable to fulfill the promise.

In fact, the preambles to the dissidents' speeches had been reminders to the meeting of the size of their kin following; they had also reminded kin in the meeting of the three men's influence in their various kin groups. The men had thus recruited allies and displayed the strength of their followings to the meeting before going on to set out their objections to the original decision.

I have said that cliques are not necessarily in opposition to each other, but they are the components of factions. Factions are, by definition, concerned with conflict and opposition, but a faction is not merely one side in an argument. It persists over a considerable period of time, promotes a fairly consistent and clearly defined set of goals, and is composed of a number of cliques whose interests coincide on these issues or whose opponents on other issues are in the opposite faction.

There are several factions in Uritai village, again with overlapping memberships. The fact that a person belongs to several factions does not necessarily divide his loyalties, because the factions are generally opposed on distinct issues. Thus a person may belong to one faction which promotes the influence of the cooperative society against that of privately owned trade stores, to another faction which opposes the secular influence of the London Missionary Society, and to several kin-based factions which oppose others over interests in land.

A faction always has a leader, either an individual or several allies; the leader is always attempting to recruit new members, either individuals or cliques, the aim being to gain a decisive victory over the opposing faction. In time there is thus considerable change in membership, but the set of interests served remains much the same. On the other hand, cliques form and break up as members' interests change; they last for a shorter time than do factions, and their aims and interests vary.

It is in this general context, then, that leaders emerge. They attain authority over their following by promoting followers' interests. Followers are loyal so long as their diverse interests are served by the leader. And followers belong simultaneously to several cliques, so that there is always the possibility of divided loyalties. When such a conflict of loyalties occurs, a person resolves it by attempting to balance the various interests involved so that he attains the greatest advantage possible.[18] In my discussion of Case 3 above, I indicated that such calculations by followers can thwart a leader's attempt to gain victory. Factions in Uritai village last for considerable periods of time, and faction leaders are among those who are influential in the community at large. Even though they serve partisan interests, they have to be taken into account if any general decision is to be implemented.[19]

Elected officers of the formal organizations are also influential in the community at large. Their election may reflect their importance in the arena associated with the organization, though some officers are obscure men. Their election does reflect an attempt to ensure that several cliques within the organization are represented, and officeholders are seldom re-elected many times.[20] This reflection of clique interests explains the reluctance to have too much overlap in membership of the various elected offices: a clique may obtain influence in several organizations and its leaders may thus be in a position to assert overriding authority throughout the community.

Thus political organization in Uritai village can be seen as consisting of cliques and factions in which interests of all kinds are expressed and furthered. Since leaders and followers alike are constantly striving to balance interests in order to obtain the greatest advantage, alliances are constantly made and broken and an individual has little chance of attaining preeminence. At any one time there is a set of men who are generally influential in the community, but because of the way in which they have attained influence they do not form a clique, nor in ordinary circumstances do they form a temporary alliance to attain a common goal. Not all these men are influential on all occasions, so leadership is fragmented and situational.

This represents a continuation of principles discernible in traditional Toaripi society: situational leadership, with a leader on any given occasion reflecting sectional interests in the community. There is no longer a hereditary basis for leadership outside kin groups or kin-based cliques. Nor is there a supernatural basis for leadership save, perhaps, in the London Missionary Society congregation.[21] Nevertheless, I would argue that the present arrangement represents continuity and adaptation of organizational principles to meet changing circumstances and that cliques and factions should be seen as an integral part of Toaripi social life in the past as well as in the present.[22]

NOTES

1. Seligman (1910), Malinowski (1922, 1935), Wedgwood (1958-1959), Hogbin (1940-1941, 1969-1970), Williams (1940), Groves (1963), Salisbury (1970), Hau'ofa (1971), and Young (1971) have all reported forms of leadership that do not fit the Big Man pattern.
2. The fieldwork on which this essay is based was carried out between 1960 and 1962. The ethnographic present refers to this period.
3. See Williams (1923) for an account of this movement.
4. The material on men's houses and their offices was collected forty years after they had disappeared, so that many details are confused or uncertain.
5. This is the portion of the doctrine associated with the Vailala Madness that has persisted. See Ryan (1969).

6.   If he did so, it was because of his knowledge of the appropriate magical
     formulas, not because of his office as *pukari.*
7.   As used by Mayer (1966:102, 115), a person's catchment consists of those people
     to whom he or she is linked as the result of their mutual involvement in a "series
     of purposive action-sets in specific contexts."
8.   The relationship between landholding and bilateral descent groups is one that
     also obtained traditionally.
9.   My thinking about these problems has been considerably influenced by
     Langness' stimulating paper (1973).
10. Now part of the United Church of Papua New Guinea and the Solomon Islands.
11. The organization of local government councils and their component electorates
     has changed somewhat since 1960–1962.
12. I have omitted mention of the two women's organizations in the village because,
     insofar as their officers took part in public political activity, they played a sub-
     sidiary role; moreover, none of the women was concerned in leadership contests.
     The officeholders in the Torchbearer organization have been omitted because
     their activities were generally subsumed under those of the pastor and deacons.
13. Women are not required to pay tax; only those who do so are eligible to vote.
14. This definition of clique follows closely that of Boissevain (1974:174).
15. Officials may or may not be leaders in this sense.
16. I use the term *pervasive factionalism* to indicate that factions often persist over a
     long period and are an integral part of political organization (cf. Nicholas
     1965:22).
17. The association, whose name has since been changed, consists of all the village
     cooperative societies in this area.
18. This approach clearly owes much to the work of Fredrik Barth, especially his
     1966 paper.
19. Case 4 indicates the way in which such people can negate the effectiveness of a
     decision they disagree with.
20. This is not true of the mission congregation: the pastor had been in the village for
     more than ten years, and the deacons were seldom replaced. In the two years I
     was in the village, only two of the twelve lost their positions.
21. The evidence for such a basis is sketchy, and in any case it does not give the
     congregation officeholders preeminence over those who are officers in the
     "secular" organizations.
22. Compare Nicholas (1965:22).

REFERENCES CITED

Barth, F.
1966   *Models of social organisation.* Royal Anthropological Institute Occasional
        Paper no. 23. London.

Boissevain, J.
1974   *Friends of friends.* London: Blackwell.

Firth, R.
1954   Social organization and social change. *Journal of the Royal Anthropological
        Institute* 84:1–20.
1963   Bilateral descent groups. In *Studies in kinship and marriage,* ed. I. Schapera.
        Royal Anthropological Institute Occasional Paper no. 16. London.
1971   *Elements of social organization.* 4th ed. London: Watts.

Groves, M.
1963   Western Motu descent groups. *Ethnology* 1:15–30.

Hau'ofa, E.
1971   Mekeo chieftainship. *Journal of the Polynesian Society* 80:152–170.

Hogbin, I.
1940–
1941   The father chooses his heir. *Oceania* 11:1–39.
1969–
1970   Food festivals and politics in Wogeo. *Oceania* 40:304–328.

Langness, L.
1973   Traditional political organization. In *Anthropology in Papua New Guinea,* ed.
            I. Hogbin. Melbourne: Melbourne University Press.

Malinowski, B.
1922   *Argonauts of the Western Pacific.* London: Routledge.
1935   *Coral gardens and their magic.* London: Allen and Unwin.

Mayer, A. C.
1966   The importance of quasi-groups in the study of complex societies. In *The social
            anthropology of complex societies,* ed. M. Banton. London: Tavistock.

Nicholas, R. W.
1965   Factions: a comparative analysis. In *Political systems and the distribution of
            power,* ed. M. Banton. London: Tavistock.

Ryan, D.
1969   Christianity, cargo cults and politics among the Toaripi of Papua. *Oceania*
            40:99–118.

Salisbury, R. F.
1970   *Vunamami.* Berkeley: University of California Press.

Seligman, C. G.
1910   *The Melanesians of British New Guinea.* Cambridge: Cambridge University
            Press.

Wedgwood, C. H.
1958–
1959   Manam kinship. *Oceania* 29:239–256.

Williams, F. E.
1923   The Vailala Madness and the destruction of native ceremonies in the Gulf
            Division. *Papua Anthropology Report,* no. 4. Territory of Papua.
1940   *Drama of Orokolo.* Oxford: Oxford University Press.

Young, M. W.
1971   *Fighting with food.* Cambridge: Cambridge University Press.

From Cargo to Politics:
The Transformation of the Yali Cult

JAMES G. PEOPLES

Since cargo cults are usually considered to be religious movements, one might expect that a study of the cults which pays homage to Professor Firth would draw most heavily upon his substantial contributions to the anthropological study of religion, including his recent writings on symbolism (Firth 1973). In this essay, however, I propose to examine a cargo cult in the light of ideas Professor Firth first devised as an aid to understanding secular (that is, nonreligious) social behavior.

AN ORGANIZATIONAL APPROACH TO CULTS

Specifically, this essay begins with the concept of social organization, first popularized in anthropology by Professor Firth (1954, 1963) and recently refined as an analytical tool by economic anthropologists such as Barth (1966) and Belshaw (1967). An organizational or processual approach to behavior entails an inquiry into the goals of the actors, an examination of the means available to them to satisfy these goals, and an analysis of the factors which influence their choices among these means (Firth 1954:4, 9–10). An ideological approach, by way of contrast, focuses on the culturally determined beliefs and normative orientations of the actors as primary forces in social action: hence the occurrence of a cult is regarded as a consequence of beliefs in the supernatural origin of cargo and in the efficacy of ritual acts in obtaining it (Jarvie 1967; Lawrence 1964). This essay intends to demonstrate the utility of the concepts of social organization, process, and strategy in explaining why a particular cargo leader, Yali of the Madang District in New Guinea, became a cargo prophet. Moreover, I intend to specify the conditions which enabled the cult to evolve into a political movement.

Empirical data on the Yali cult were collected by Peter Lawrence (1964, 1971) and presented in his excellent monograph *Road Belong Cargo.* More recent data, published by Morauta (1972), indicate that the cult has been transformed into a political, even nationalistic, movement with widespread appeal to the people of lower socioeconomic categories. By demonstrating that the Yali cult grew out of the interaction between Yali, minor prophets, the people of the Madang District, and the administration, I shall specify the conditions and relationships which enabled this transformation to occur.

Before reexamining the evidence within the framework of strategy and organization, it will be helpful to review Lawrence's own explanation of the Yali cult. Lawrence seems to believe that cargo cults occur because of the combination of preexisting Melanesian religious beliefs and the new situation of relative material/political deprivation brought about by the structure of colonialism. He notes that aboriginal Melanesians believed that their material culture was invented by deities and delivered to humans by their ancestors (Lawrence 1964:7, 16–17, 29–33; 1970a:268, 283; 1971). When missionaries proselytized the Madang area, the Garia and Ngaing people and their neighbors came to believe that God and Jesus were the source of European material culture and that whites had to perform ritual acts to obtain their cargo (Lawrence 1964:74–78; 1970b: 303; 1971:306). This belief was made possible by the twin facts that whites seemed to perform no labor to obtain their cargo and that aboriginally there was no linguistic distinction made between secular labor and its accompanying ritual (Lawrence 1964:228, 248–249). Given that Melanesians feel relatively deprived and cannot conceive of any secular means to match the wealth and power of Europeans, it is indeed rational for them to turn to ritual acts to improve their situation.[1] This explanation seems to account completely and plausibly for the origin of the cargo *ideology,* if ideology is defined (for present purposes) as a set of ideas explaining the origin of cargo together with a prescribed means of obtaining it.

Applying this explanation to Yali's conversion to a cargo cult, Lawrence maintains that Yali shared his own culture's assumption that Western technology was made by deities and that ritual activity was a viable way to obtain it (1964:126–128, 252–253). Lawrence seems to view Yali as a genuine prophet who fully believed in the efficacy of cult rituals in acquiring cargo from the deities. The evidence on this matter is contradictory, however. There is some evidence that Yali had "forgotten" much of his cultural heritage (ibid.:173). Moreover, he had a history of involvement and friendship with Europeans and had even been to Port Moresby, Brisbane, and Cairns and observed the manufacture of Western goods (ibid.:123). Further, he had held a position with the administration in which one of his primary duties, which he carried out with apparently honest zeal, was to repudicate all forms of cargo ritual as ineffective and to attempt to organize purely secular programs for development.

Lawrence (1964:127-129, 252-253) attempts to show that Yali's experiences with European culture and technology were only superficial and that "in the last analysis, Yali's social and intellectual outlook was still that of a southern Madang District native." But "in the last analysis" we can never get inside Yali's head. We shall never know what he believed about the ultimate source of cargo. Since this is true, it is preferable to explain Yali's eventual acceptance of the role of cargo leader in terms of an organizational framework and view his statements about his beliefs (related long after the fact to Lawrence) as part of the strategy Yali adopted to attain his goals.

Granted, then, that Lawrence's general ideological explanation of cargo cults does indeed account for the origin of the Yali cult's ideology and doctrine, he does not address himself explicitly to the manner in which this ideology became a force for action in the context and structure of the colonial situation. Phrased differently, we may accept that the cargo ideology exists as a set of ideas due to the nature of indigenous beliefs about the source of wealth. But it was only one of several available ideologies which prescribed how Melanesians could obtain wealth: according to Lawrence (1964), there was Yali's own earlier secular program of cooperation with the administration; there was the view that adherence to Christianity and abandonment of old beliefs and rituals would bring success; there was the administration's emphasis on gradualism. And no doubt there was also the planters', miners', and labor recruiters' position that wealth could best be obtained through the sale of export crops and wage labor. Why then was the cargo ideology finally adopted by Yali, when it contradicted his earlier program and when he knew it would jeopardize his position with the administration? I suggest that Yali's eventual acceptance of the role of prophet is best interpreted as a pragmatic political act—an act intended to consolidate and legitimate his status and power with the Madang people.[2]

This essay attempts to demonstrate that this act was made necessary by the nature of the interaction between Yali, minor prophets, the general Madang populace, and the administration, an interaction which had been occurring for over two years prior to Yali's becoming a cargo leader. By emphasizing Yali's political goals, we can better understand why the cult was transformed into a political movement, for as a politician Yali would continually attempt to alter the movement's goals and doctrines if its former ideology proved insufficient to legitimate the power of its leader and maintain its following.

Political interpretations of cargo cults abound in the literature. The cults have been viewed as "forerunners of Melanesian nationalism" (Guiart 1951), as protests against colonialism (Lanternari 1963), as an attempt to force Europeans to recognize the validity of indigenous concepts of status (Cochrane 1970), and as a kind of phase through which Melanesians pass in their evolution toward political parties (Worsley 1968:255). Even when they are considered to be religious responses to deprivation and stress, the cults are often seen as containing the seeds of a political movement: the cultic elements drop out, the prophet becomes a political leader, and instrumentally rational activities and organizations replace ritual as a means for attaining wealth and power. Worsley (1968:170–194) comes to exactly this conclusion for the Marching Rule and Paliau movements, and Hobsbawm (1965:58–62) believes the same evolutionary scheme applies to certain millenarian movements in Europe. I agree with this interpretation of the cults as dynamic phenomena. I do not view the transformation of the Yali cult as an evolution from a "cultic" to a "rational" response to the colonial structure, however, for this implies that the two responses are mutually exclusive. Rather I shall investigate the possibility that from the outset of the movement, the "cultic" ideology was used "rationally" (almost as if it were a resource) by Yali and minor prophets in order to attain their own political goals.

THE TRANSFORMATION OF THE YALI CULT

Cargo cults have occurred sporadically in the Madang District since 1871. Lawrence (1964) distinguishes five periods of cargo belief, not all of which became organized movements. The first (ca. 1871–ca. 1900) seems to have been limited to the coast and consisted merely of statements about the identity of early white visitors. White men were seen as spirits of the dead or as pagan deities who had invented a new material culture and were now going to give it to the people.

The second period of belief (ca. 1900–ca. 1914) also explained the contact situation in traditional terms, but by this time the people had come to believe that whites were merely men to whom some native deity had given a superior material culture. As with the first belief, there was no ritual performed to hasten the giving over of cargo from the deities to the people. This myth also had a limited distribution: it did not occur beyond the Sik-Bongu coastal strip. In the third period (ca. 1914–ca. 1933), the people embraced Christian teachings as the true road to the cargo. It was believed that missionaries would reveal ritual secrets if the natives would accept Christianity and observe its taboos. This belief was uniform over most of the district from Garia to Madang and the Rai Coast, and Lawrence (1964:63–85) believes that the percentage of the population supporting it was "probably very high."

The fourth period of cargo belief (1933–1945) seems to have been a reaction to the failure of the third. Lawrence includes three major cults in this period, each of which occurred in a different region, while the remainder of the southern Madang District continued to hold the beliefs characteristic of the third period. The first of these three cults, the Letub doctrine and ritual (ca. 1937–1942), was syncretic and involved the revival of sacrifices to the spirits of the dead and the traditional Letub dance. From 1940 to 1942 the cult gained a large following around Madang town, but it never achieved a centralized organization under a single leader. From Lawrence's evidence (1964:96), there seem to have been many local variants. A second cult flourished from 1942 to 1944 in the Lutheran-dominated hinterland of Yabob village; unlike Letub, this cult had a single leader, Tagarab of Milguk village, and a rudimentary hierarchical organization. Tagarab's cult was also syncretic in its doctrine but competed with Letub over differences in detail. A third cargo activity, the Bagasin Rebellion of 1944, was both a cult and a military uprising, the latter made possible by war materials left behind by the retreating Japanese. Kaum, a former follower of Tagarab, established a military camp in the Bagasin area and planned to attack Madang. But the movement also had ritual elements: prayers to the cargo deity and ancestors, food offerings, destruction of gardens and pigs, hymns, and confessions accompanied the military preparations (ibid.: 87–115).

The situation that emerged at the end of 1944 was one of widespread anti-European sentiment and dissatisfaction with economic, social, and political conditions. The ideology of one cult or another had touched most of the villages in the district in the recent past. But as Lawrence (1964:115) writes: "So far, despite the dissemination of doctrine, actual cargo activity had been carried out on a limited regional basis under the direction of purely local leaders, who had their own idiosyncrasies of doctrine and were at times divided by petty rivalries."

Thus far the cults lacked organizational unity. They had remained local phenomena, and among traditionally distinct sociopolitical groups, cargo doctrines and myths had been as much a source of conflict as one of harmony. Even by 1944, however, the presence of the cults revealed the existence of a second kind of unity in the district, a unity of aspirations. Despite the variations in local manifestations, the widespread appeal of the cults would seem to indicate that the desire for cargo and improved status vis-à-vis Europeans crosscut traditional ethnic and sociopolitical divisions. It is by virtue of this unity of aspirations that Yali sought to legitimize his position and popularize his program, and while doing so he promoted organizational unity across traditional boundaries. The processes by which he achieved this are worth looking into.

In 1943, when the Japanese still occupied Madang District, Yali and other natives had heard a propaganda address from a European officer. Yali's account of the speech is given by Lawrence (1964:124): "In the past, you natives have been kept backward. But now, if you help us win the war and get rid of the Japanese from New Guinea, we Europeans will help you. We will help you get houses with galvanized iron roofs, plank walls and floors, electric light, and motor vehicles, boats, good clothes, and good food. Life will be very different for you after the war."

This address, intended to gain native recruits and mobilize anti-Japanese sentiment, gave Yali high hopes that the Australians would give large quantities of cargo to the Madang people if they cooperated with the secular programs of the administration. Yali had already been active as native *tultul* (assistant village headman), policeman, and soldier. He had visited Queensland (Brisbane and Cairns) for six months' training in jungle warfare, where he learned that Europeans, too, had to work and organize to obtain their material culture (ibid.:123–124). In January 1945 the administration was searching for capable and popular local leaders who could persuade the Madang people to ignore cargo cult prophets and cooperate with secular programs. Yali was their man.

In early 1945 Yali conversed with an administration officer in his own Ngaing area of the Rai Coast. Yali was concerned over the bad reactions of his people to the good intentions of the Australians, and the officer reassured him that conditions would soon start to improve. Unfortunately, but most significantly for later events, the conversation was overheard by a villager who spread an exaggerated account of how the people were soon to get massive amounts of cargo. Yali was invited by the administration to give a speech to what he imagined would be a small crowd of local people, but to his surprise people from all over the Rai Coast appeared to hear the person they apparently regarded as a new cargo prophet. Yali told them, in brief, to support the Australian programs and help drive out the remaining Japanese and they would be rewarded.

The speech was so successful, and the people so abashed at their previous conduct, that Yali was invited to repeat the performance in the town of Madang. But after he left Madang in July 1945, his words there also began to be corrupted: his claim that he had seen European methods of food production while in Australia was distorted to imply that he had seen methods of cargo production and the cargo deity himself. It was said popularly that he had been killed during the war, had gone to heaven, and would now get cargo. The leaders of both the Letub and the Tagarab cults now claimed association with Yali and performed their rituals in his honor. In August 1945 one village even referred to Yali as the "Black King" (ibid.:133–137).

These events have been reported in detail because they reveal that, from the outset, Yali's words and actions were widely misunderstood by the Madang people. Until he later adopted the cargo doctrine, Yali's view of himself never coincided with the people's conception of his role as cargo leader nor with the administration's view of him as secular propagandist (ibid.:138–139). His relationships with both the people and the administration were characterized by what must be called mutual ignorance. Yali's words were, in effect, swept up into a new cargo movement which took the very form both Yali and the administration thought they were trying to prevent. Already Yali's position with the administration was in the process of being legitimated to the Madang populace, but this legitimation was not taking the pattern which Yali and the administration anticipated or desired.

Yali had already received official sanction from the administration. Since cooperation with Australian programs was improving as a result of Yali's speeches along the Rai Coast, in January 1946 the district officer reaffirmed his support of Yali's secular program and again urged him to refrain from involvement with cargo cults. Yali readily accepted these terms. Even the Catholic and Lutheran missions, doubtful at first, soon attempted to win Yali's approval, for they realized that he could help spread Christianity (ibid.:137–138). When we add to these observations the fact that Letub and Tagarab cultists were also claiming association with Yali, the situation which emerges is one of interacting interest groups with different goals and means, all of whom were trying to use Yali's influence and popularity to further these disparate interests. Moreover, the bases of Yali's legitimation to the administration and to the people were incompatible: to the people he was the leader of a new cargo movement; to the administration he was the personification of the rational, cooperative native working to better the lot of his own people.

At the end of 1945 Yali began the Rai Coast Rehabilitation Scheme, a secular program designed to promote cooperation with the administration. People were to stop living in hamlets and group into villages which were to be kept clean and free of marauding pigs; children were to attend mission schools; villagers were to build roads, maintain personal hygiene, have more children, and provide plantation labor and hospitality for Europeans (ibid.:142–144). The district officer was impressed with the success of the scheme, but like Yali's previous activities it soon attracted the interest of cargo enthusiasts from the Rai Coast and at Madang. Yali's house was surrounded by former mission helpers turned cargo cultists who wished to enter his service and incorporate the rehabilitation scheme into the cargo movement. One of these men, Kasan, eventually became Yali's chief secretary; he and other "mission helpers" attempted to persuade Yali to adopt the quasi-Christian cargo doctrine, be baptized, and repudiate pagan rituals.

Yali remained unconvinced by these efforts but "omitted to make it quite clear to the people in general, and Kasan and his associates in particular, that the rehabilitation scheme and the cargo movement had nothing in common" (ibid.:146). Even more important, Yali did nothing to prevent Kasan and his followers from using Yali's name and distorting the scheme to aid in the dissemination of cargo propaganda along the Rai Coast (ibid.:145–147). As a result, the rehabilitation scheme was now also associated with the cargo ideology and the popular conception of Yali as a man in contact with the cargo deity was strengthened.

By this time Yali was beginning to realize that his status with the people depended upon popular belief in his superhuman qualities (ibid.: 147). It might appear that the remainder of his career could have gone in either of two directions. He could support the cultists and adopt the role of cargo leader, thus sacrificing his relationship with the administration; or he could dissociate himself from the cargo movement, thus trading most of his popular support for a formal administrative post. In fact, however, the second alternative would not have worked, for Yali's position with the administration was based on his popularity and status with the people. Ironically, if Yali had unambiguously repudiated the cargo enthusiasts, the people might have ceased to cooperate with the rehabilitation scheme and this, too, would have eroded his relationship with the administration. Since at this time Yali was unwilling to give up his position with the Australians by becoming a cargo leader, he adopted a strategy of remaining noncommittal. Lawrence (1964:148, fn. 1) says that Yali admitted to him that this was his intention. Yali made a public statement which he knew would be interpreted by the people as tacit support of the cargo movement but would be seen as anticult by the administration (ibid.:148). In this way, Yali hoped to persuade both sides that he was doing what they wanted and so keep the support of both the cultists and the administration. This strategy was a success: the district officer believed the rehabilitation scheme to be working as planned, and a patrol officer wrote that Yali seemed to be discrediting the cargo movement (ibid.:150, fn. 1).

Despite these pronouncements, by the end of 1946 the practical achievements of the rehabilitation scheme were overshadowed by the cargo cultists' manipulation of Yali's position and ideas and the misinterpretation of his secular scheme (ibid.:150). Still, the apparent success of the scheme led the district officer to invite Yali to tour the Bogia area (outside Madang District) to promote cooperation and appoint loyal village boss boys. During this journey, a dignitary of the Catholic mission at Alexishafen offered to support Yali's work if he also used the tour to denounce polygyny; if Yali refused, the priest said the mission would openly oppose his future activities. Yali agreed to this proposal, but the arrangement backfired when the enforcement of monogamy led to suicides. Yali was "severely reprimanded" by the district officer and again warned to remain neutral in religious matters (ibid.:150–152). Yali blamed this rebuke on the Catholic mission and native Christians and decided at last to take a strong position: he would let it be known that, although he himself was pagan, he would remain totally neutral in his religious policy and devote all his energies to secular affairs (ibid.:153).

At this point, Yali seems to have wanted to consolidate his position in an attempt to gain more control over those who were distorting his program and harming his reputation with the administration. He installed boss boys in the villages around Madang and on the Rai Coast and indicated that they took precedence over the administration-appointed *luluai* and *tultul*. Since these men owed allegiance only to Yali, they did give him some personal control, although insidious activities still went on in many areas (ibid.:156). Yali's attempt is important to the thesis argued here because this seems to have been the first time a multivillage structure under the personal control of a Madang native was institutionalized. It was partly Yali's attempt to defend his program from the inroads of cultism that led to this structure. Thus, contrary to Worsley's (1968:228) suggestion, it was not through the cults themselves but in reaction to them that the first panregional organization came into existence.

It is during Yali's absence from August to December 1947 that the actual motives of his "followers" come into sharp focus. In August the administration sent Yali to Port Moresby for special training and indoctrination into the Australian program. Without Yali's personal control over their activities, minor cargo leaders speculated that he was collecting cargo for the people from Port Moresby and would return as district officer. There was an upsurge of cargo activity in the Bagasin area beginning in August, in Garialand from November to December, at Dumpu in the Ramu Valley from August to November. In Madang town the Letub cult was revived and a former leader named Kaum began a new cult which lasted about two months. When Kaum was transferred to Saidor on the Rai Coast, the cult was revived there as well as among the Nankina-Mok people (Lawrence 1964:158–165). Most of the southern Madang District was plunged into cargo activity during Yali's four-month absence, and local prophets further mythologized his experiences and claimed association with him.

Yet what happened when he returned to the district was determined not by these events but by the information Yali received during his stay in Australia. This period seems to mark the turning point in Yali's movement. He had undertaken the journey with high expectations both for his people and for himself. Since the Madang people were beginning to cooperate with the development plans of the Australians, Yali expected to be told that the administration would soon begin delivering the "building materials, tools, an electric light plant, machinery for tinning meat, and trucks to solve transport problems" (ibid.:157–158).[3] For himself, he hoped to return as patrol officer. Both aspirations were frustrated. He was told that a free handout of bulk cargo was out of the question. Moreover, the administration's policy would be to spend large sums on long-range economic, educational, political, and health development. Yali recognized the implications of this fact for his position in the district:

> As Yali well realized, the bottom had dropped out of his rehabilitation scheme. Everything he had said to win friends for the Europeans—on the Rai Coast, at Madang, on Karkar, and at Bogia—had been based on the assumption that soon the administration would demonstrate its goodwill by guaranteeing a rapid improvement in native living standards. His followers at home were daily expecting an announcement of this kind and now, with nothing but his shame, he had to return and face them. How was he to explain that there was to be no immediate and tangible reward but only general promises of new schools, hospitals, and opportunities to engage in business enterprise in the future? These were things which they neither clearly understood nor appreciated. It was hardly to be wondered that he had little stomach for the remainder of his official programme. [Ibid.:170]

Nor was Yali's personal ambition to achieve a status equal to whites in the administration to be satisfied: instead of being made a patrol officer, a special post was created for him—the administration's foreman or overseer. Although this appointment gave Yali a higher status than any other indigene, it was clear that in European eyes he remained just another *kanaka* (ibid.:169–171).

The events in Madang District and at Port Moresby during these four months are important for two reasons. First, they reveal the true basis of Yali's legitimation in the district: due to the activities of minor prophets attempting to widen and consolidate their own control, Yali was popularly considered to be the leader of a cargo movement far greater in scope than any of the preceding cults. Minor prophets in the Bagasin area, for example, seem to have thoroughly mythologized Yali's past experiences, his visit to Port Moresby, and his person (ibid.:159–161). Yali's popular support was clearly due more to the people's false conception of him as cargo leader than to his position as secular spokesman for the administration. Second, in Port Moresby Yali acquired new information about his own position in the eyes of the administration and about the Australian program for development. He came to believe (rightly or wrongly) that the Australians still thought of him as inferior to Europeans (ibid.:171).

Yali thought he had been betrayed by the administration: despite his successful efforts at increasing cooperation with Australian programs, the people would still have to wait years to acquire cargo. This new information led Yali to revise his earlier determination not to sacrifice his position with the administration. He now realized that his former conception of this position was erroneous and it was now obvious that the rehabilitation scheme would not be effective in acquiring cargo. Yali knew, from his earlier relations with minor prophets and the people as well as from letters he received from home while in Port Moresby, that his status in Madang District was based on the popular belief that he could acquire cargo. Therefore, in Lawrence's words (1964:176): "Yali obviously needed a new policy to neutralize the people's disappointment when he returned empty-handed, and save himself from the disgrace and obscurity which were the fate of all cargo leaders who failed to live up to their promises." If Yali was to keep his populace status and maintain his legitimacy in the eyes of the people, he needed a new strategy.

At first Yali attempted to establish his legitimacy on a completely different basis. He decided to revive paganism, thus dissociating himself entirely from the quasi-Christian cargo doctrine. The people were to abandon all hope of ever gaining cargo and a European life-style and seek only to obtain the benefits of their traditional religion: more pigs and larger crops. In December 1947 the district officer, alarmed by the wave of cargo activity during Yali's absence, invited Yali to give a public address in January 1948 to denounce the cargo activity once and for all. This Yali did, denying that he was a spirit of the dead and stating that he would never have anything to do with cargo ritual. Yet even Yali did not realize the tremendous support rallied for the cargo movement by minor prophets during his absence. Given the events which had occurred in the district from August to December 1947, the pagan revival was doomed to failure, although it did meet with success from February to March 1948 in a small strip along the Rai Coast. It became apparent to Yali that the pagan revival was an inadequate legitimation to the general population, since it did not embody "values in which the followers have an 'interest' " (Worsley 1968:xii).

Upon his return from Port Moresby in December 1947, Yali was again courted by several minor prophets and even witnessed some cargo rituals and dances. Yali still refused these invitations, even though he knew that he could easily coordinate the Letub and Tagarab cultists under his personal direction. In April 1948 he was approached by a new prophet, Gurek from Hapurpi village, who suggested that Yali's own Ngaing deities were the source of cargo. Lawrence (1964:192–193) makes much of this factor as the "cause" of Yali's decision at long last to support the cargo movement, since it overcame his fear of being accused of stealing other peoples' ritual secrets. Yet the facts presented here suggested that Yali's decision was the result of his calculation that in order to maintain his status he must assume the role which would give him the widest and firmest basis of support.[4]

As a result of his interaction with the Madang people and the minor prophets, Yali had learned that his popularity rested on the people's belief that he knew the "road to the cargo." This popular belief, as we have seen, resulted largely from the self-interested activities of minor prophets as they tried to associate Yali with their own doctrines. As a result of his interaction with administration officials while in Port Moresby, Yali had learned that his rehabilitation scheme would not induce the administration to hand over the cargo. Given these two pieces of information, the best way and perhaps the only way Yali could maintain his popular status was to continue to allow the people to think he could deliver cargo by becoming what most people assumed him to be: a cargo prophet. This would certainly ensure his legitimation with the people. And if he could keep his future activities secret from the administration, which had so far shown itself to be ignorant of the real reason for Yali's popularity, he might also keep his official sanction.

During 1948 the new ritual and belief, which held that native deities were the source of cargo (and hence may have been compatible with the pagan revival), spread to nearly all the Rai Coast and thence to Bogati, Madang, and the Ramu and Bagasin areas. During this spread, the movement incorporated preexisting "small-scale" cults (Morauta 1972: 434). Kaum, for example, borrowed heavily from Gurek's doctrine and claimed to work together with Yali and Gurek to bring the cargo deities back to New Guinea (Lawrence 1964:196).

Aside from Yali's popularity, one reason for the widespread appeal of the movement was that its doctrine was more vague or flexible than those previous to it. Thus in most villages the exact nature of Gurek's myth was unknown. And, perhaps as important, there was no attempt to designate any one group's particular set of gods as the cargo source—deities of taro, yams, war, the Kabu ceremony, and any others regarded as the exclusive property of a local group could all be seen as the source of cargo (ibid.:197, 255). Further, the explicit versions of the cargo doctrine differed widely in different areas.

The new cargo doctrine, then, was not uniform either in its specific ideology or in its ritual. This meant that Yali was able to legitimate his status in slightly different terms in different areas. Unfortunately, there is no way of knowing whether the flexibility of this doctrine was a conscious strategy of Yali and Gurek intended to widen their appeal or a by-product of the activities of minor leaders as they sought to manipulate the new dogma.

The formal structure of the cult (summarized in Lawrence 1964:205, diagram 1) is important for later events. In almost every village Yali had previously appointed, or now appointed, a boss boy who claimed authority from him. However, it was only along the coast between Matokar and Saidor that the organization was elaborated over what it had been prior to 1948, and only the strip between Saidor and Mindire was under Yali's direct control. In these areas, Yali's organization was pyramidal and included his secretaries, policemen, lieutenants, and village boss boys.

Yali himself, still supported by the administration as foreman-overseer, became an independent autocrat and lived in luxury in one of three houses in three different villages where he was served by his younger male relatives. Along the Rai Coast, Yali had nine men in his police force and six main lieutenants plus boss boys; in addition to this formal organization he relied on a personal network of traditional kinship, trade, and affinal relationships. Around the area of Madang, Yali had main lieutenants in five villages and boss boys in most of the others, but these men seem to have been semiautonomous in their decisions (ibid.:203–208). Though details are lacking on the actual workings of this structure, enough data are available to demonstrate that it covered a wider span and provided a wider structural basis of communication and common action than any previous organization under native control.

In addition to his role as leader of the cargo movement, Yali still held the formal administration office of foreman-overseer. This enabled him to claim to the people that the administration had put him in charge of the Rai Coast. He used this official backing to impress upon the people that those who supported the Christian missions instead of his own doctrine were subject to punishment by the administration—that is, himself. To maintain his official sanction from the Australians and to keep from being jailed, Yali had to keep his cargo activities secret from the administration. Toward this end he broke the communication links between Australian officers and the Madang people by assuming the duties of the subdistrict court for native affairs and holding his own meetings. Henceforth, he told the officers, they were not to concern themselves with "petty disputes." These would now be settled by village headmen, boss boys, and himself. At the meetings, Yali officially was instructing headmen and boss boys on the reconstruction plan, but in fact he was promoting the cargo doctrine and ritual. By these means he established the "political cover behind which the ritual could be safely performed" (ibid.:211). Thus for years it was difficult for the administration to determine whether or not Yali was responsible for the movement.

Pressure from the missions and planters, the brutality of Yali's policemen, and the appointment of a new patrol officer all combined to lead the administration to remove many of the official sanctions that by May 1949 had so far saved Yali from prosecution. Gurek left for his own village and the people began to lose the cargo enthusiasm. By early 1950 Yali too became disappointed and allowed the cult to lapse. Pressure from the missions led to investigations by the administration and police. As a result, Yali was sentenced to jail in July 1950.

During the five years of Yali's imprisonment, his political organization ceased to function: the police force was disbanded and the boss boys, though allowed to remain, were now placed third in command in their villages below the *luluai* and the *tultul*. According to Lawrence (1964: 221), this "marked the end of cargo activity as a widespread coordinated movement in the southern Madang District," although between 1950 and 1961 there were isolated outbreaks, led by purely local leaders, which lacked central organization. We know very little about these numerous small cults, although Lawrence (1964:266–268) summarizes their doctrines and distribution. He noted in 1964 that the cults were likely to remain a problem in the subdistrict by contributing to passive resistance to the administration's policies and that the leader of such resistance was likely to be Yali. Later events proved this to be a perceptive statement.

To summarize, the following facts, presented above, are central to my argument that the cult's dynamic potential was realized in a transformation:

1. During the secular phase of the movement (late 1945 to early 1948), the relations between Yali and the Madang people as well as between Yali and the administration were structured by what has been called mutual ignorance. All parties in the interaction assumed that the motives of other parties coincided with their own. This meant that from the outset Yali's movement gained the support of a variety of political and ethnic groups with disparate and conflicting interests, who were thus at least nominally united in a common program. This

situation also implied that the movement could have developed in any of several directions, depending upon which interest group was able to exert the most influence over Yali's decisions. In short, the movement was potentially dynamic.

2. The activities of minor prophets in persuading their followers that Yali supported their cult doctrines resulted in the belief by the bulk of the Madang population that Yali was a greater version of a cargo prophet, a role familiar to the people due to previous small-scale cults. Early in his career Yali misunderstood this fact, but as his knowledge of the true reason for his popularity increased, his strategy evolved into allowing both the administration and the cultists to think they had his support. Later he adopted the role of cargo prophet while keeping the administration ignorant of his cargo activities.

3. Yali tried to legitimate his secular position with the administration in at least three ways: as secular spokesman, propagandist, and implementer of the administration's programs (the rehabilitation scheme); as religious leader (the pagan revival); and as cargo prophet. Although I do not wish to argue that Yali could not have legitimated himself by assuming any other role than that of a cargo prophet, it is significant that this was the only role in which his attempts were effective.

4. Yali created organizations in both the secular and the cult phases of the movement which were panvillage and panregional. This was not, as Worsley hints (1968:228), merely an unconscious effect or by- product of the movement. It was a positive attempt by Yali to consolidate his control and increase his direct influence.

5. During the cult phase Yali's movement absorbed local cults led by minor prophets. Small-scale cults were thus united into a single movement with a single organization and leader.

6. From the outset of his career and throughout the cult phase of his movement, Yali is better considered as a clever political strategist than as a prophet who believed in the efficacy of ritual in obtaining cargo. As a politician we would expect that Yali, like most politicians everywhere, would continue to adapt his role and ideological program to the force of circumstance.

It follows from these points that the cargo ideology, though ineffective in achieving its explicit aim to acquire cargo, provided the motive force for a new organizational unity of Madang villages. In fact, as I shall show, this ideology was more effective than an alternative organization of a "rational" kind introduced by the Australians. The ideology's success in this regard is due to its "competence," in Nadel's terms (1957), in building upon what was common to most of the people of all Madang villages: the desire for European wealth. That Yali was only able to attain legitimacy through cargo ideology, and not through a rational secular program or a return to nativism, indicates that the cargo cult was one way (and the only way which seems to have been successful) in which the existing unity of values and goals can be forged into an organization for political action completely in indigenous hands.

Nothing further is known of Yali's activities until we read in Morauta (1972) that Yali was an open electorate candidate to the House of Assembly in 1964 and 1968. Morauta also indicates that the cult had been transformed into a political movement by 1968. Though still recognizably cultic in its aims and much of its ideology, the cult's secular practices, organization, and clientele reveal its political elements. As Morauta (1972:444) remarks:

> The cult certainly has much of the spirit of nationalism—the rejection of what the Europeans have brought—of Christianity, Administration, in many cases of Western-type courts and medicine, to which traditional organization and methods are preferred. Then there was Yali's candidature in two national elections. The political aspirations of the cult were sharply focused too in 1969 when Yali declared that "Independence" would occur under his auspices on 1 August.

That Yali is still a political pragmatist using the cult ideology to maintain his own status is revealed by his reaction when independence did not occur:

> However on the great day nothing whatever happened and when I saw Yali a few weeks later he said: "What did you expect? How could I bring about independence? Where are our guns? Where are our tanks? Where are our bombers?" [Ibid.:444]

Morauta also argues that the cult reflects the interests of an incipient social class in the Madang area:

> I do not think that so far there are many signs of the growth of social classes within native society, at least in terms of relations between employer and employee. But it does seem that significant differences exist in terms of successful participation in the cash economy, in the control of cash and cash-producing resources. . . . It seems that cargo cults are one of the few instances where we might be justified in talking about class action or class consciousness in New Guinea. . . . [Ibid.:441]

She goes on to say:

> Yali's cult is related to forms of social stratification in the Madang area. These social strata cut across traditional corporate groups, the clans and villages. . . . In several aspects of their lives, Yali's supporters objectively and consciously feel they have more in common with certain members of

other villages than they have with some members of their own. . . . Yali's cult represents the articulation of these interests in political action. . . . [Ibid.:444–445]

Morauta provides quantitative data to support her contention that a rising "class consciousness" in the Madang area is articulated by the cargo ideology.

The effectiveness of Yali's cult in articulating the interests of the lowest stratum of different villages is revealed by a negative case: the Ambenob Local Goverment Council. Lawrence (1964:270–271) perceptively predicted that the cargo movement might compete with the council for the loyalty of the Madang people; as of 1968, this prediction had been fulfilled. The council is obviously a "functionally specific" political organization, yet it is significant that the Madang people have not regarded it as an organization which reflects, organizes, and helps them attain their aspirations on a panvillage level. For the council has been ineffective in combining villages into a single structure:

Council elections tend to follow village lines. People see candidates largely as village candidates and vote for their own man. . . . Equally, once elected, a councillor is seen as a village and not as a ward (i.e., multi-village) official. The councillor's influence in disputes, etc., rarely goes beyond the boundaries of his own village. In the other villages of his ward completely unofficial and unpaid deputies (known as *komiti*) perform his duties and have the status of councillor. [Morauta 1972:445]

The significance of this negative case is apparent. For here is a rational institution, one apparently much better adapted organizationally and ideologically to attaining the goals of the Madang people, yet it has not provided a structure which instills in the people a sense of common purpose and responsiblity. This "modern" political structure has failed to accomplish what the Yali cult achieved even before it was transformed: an effective regional organization under indigenous control which can override traditional boundaries and loyalties and thereby, after transforming itself, provide a wider basis for political action by an incipient lower class.

CONCLUSION

I have tried to show that the concepts of strategy and process, which evolved in anthropology largely out of Professor Firth's concept of social organization, provide a more complete explanation of Yali's eventual adoption of the role of prophet than does an ideological explanation. Once we assume that Yali's actions were intended to consolidate and increase his status with the Madang people while maintaining his position with the administration, the decisions he made about which roles to adopt, which relationships to activate, how much information to give the administration about his activities, and how best to establish his legitimacy all become intelligible as rational decisions. We have seen that conditions over which Yali had little control—the success of minor prophets in convincing the people that Yali was allied with their movements, the refusal of the administration to make Yali a patrol officer, the people's misunderstanding of his rehabilitation scheme and refusal to revive paganism—constrained his behavior and narrowed his options.

Finally, I wish to suggest that it may be a mistake to oppose cargo cults to political movements on the basis of whether their ideology is "millenarian" or "secular." From the outset Yali's movement attracted a range of interest groups who had different conceptions of its goals and means and who supported Yali for a variety of reasons. This conglomerate nature of the movement still persisted in 1968, when it was difficult to characterize it as religious or secular (Morauta 1972:443). Although in 1968 the movement was ineffective in attaining some of its goals (like independence and cargo), it did provide a multivillage organization for political action by an incipient lower class. In this respect, it proved more successful than a functionally specific political organization, the Ambenob Local Government Council. This may be because the council reflected the interests of the economically and politically powerful elements in the subdistrict, whereas the cargo movement (which seems to have become institutionalized) expressed the interests of subordinate groups.

At any rate, in judging whether a movement impedes, promotes, or is neutral for political and economic development, what is most important is not the movement's ideology. For ideologies, as sets of ideas accepted as valid by a large number of people, are adopted by leaders to justify their status and create popular support for their power and actions. (See Mannheim 1936:50 for a similar view of ideology.) In brief, the ideology espoused by a political leader to legitimate his or her actions may have little to do with either the leader's personal beliefs or the concrete effects of those actions on society. Admitting this fact would lead us to view the effects of cargo cults on development with a less prejudiced eye.

NOTES

I wish to express my deep appreciation to Richard T. Curley, William G. Davis, and Henry J. Rutz for their very helpful suggestions on the manuscript, but the interpretations and conclusions are solely my own responsibility.

1.   Jarvie (1967:app. 3) agrees with this characterization of Lawrence's theoretical position and congratulates him for emphasizing that cargo cults must be considered as rational phenomena, since the means used to acquire cargo are logically consistent with indigenous beliefs about the origin of Western goods.

2. Professor Firth himself has offered a similar account of the contingent relationship between cargo belief (ideology) and the existence of a widespread social movement based on that belief. In attempting to explain why no cargo cult has occurred on Tikopia, Firth (1967:161) points out that there were at least two "prototype" cargo cult ideologies which never got beyond the stage of rumor:

    There can be a *"cargo"-cult type of behavior,* without it attaining the organized coherence of a movement or cult development. One important element in such development would seem to be a charismatic leader. He must be more than a catalyst; he must be able to fuse together the various elements available and apply them to the common goal. On the other hand, in so doing he is likely to enter a field of competing status relations. Here an organized chieftainship is likely to inhibit the implementation of his ideas.

    The documented presence of a cargolike ideology in Tikopia which never developed into a movement indicates that belief alone does not explain the existence of the movement. Stanner (1958:25) concurs, noting that "our insight into the cults will grow in the measure in which we abandon the effort to base interpretations on the primacy and efficacy of belief."

3. It seems to be true, as Lawrence suggests, that Yali never fully understood that the administration's plans were for long-term improvement in living standards by the peoples' own rational economic effort. Yali apparently believed that the Australians wanted the natives to do certain things which the rehabilitation scheme had indeed initiated. As soon as these were accomplished, the goods would be delivered.

4. Lawrence (1964:193) mentions this factor as a second element in Yali's decision, noting that he realized Gurek would be a serious rival unless Yali joined forces with him. I hope I have not done an injustice to Lawrence by characterizing his approach as ideological, for there are many other places in his monograph where his interpretation is similar to the one presented by this essay (ibid.:176, 210, 252–253). But it is certainly clear that Lawrence thinks Yali joined the cargo movement because he "believed in" the supernatural origin of cargo.

REFERENCES CITED

Barth, Fredrik
1966   *Models of social organisation.* Royal Anthropological Institute Occasional Paper no. 23. London.

Belshaw, Cyril S.
1967   Theoretical problems in economic anthroplogy. In *Social organization: essays presented to Raymond Firth,* ed. Maurice Freedman. Chicago: Aldine.

Cochrane, Glynn
1970   *Big men and cargo cults.* Oxford: Clarendon Press.

Firth, Raymond
1954   Social organization and social change. *Journal of the Royal Anthropological Institute* 84:1–20.
1963   *Elements of social organization.* Boston: Beacon Press (original 1951).
1967   *Tikopia ritual and belief.* Boston: Beacon Press.
1973   *Symbols: public and private.* London: Allen and Unwin.

Guiart, Jean
1951   Forerunners of Melanesian nationalism. *Oceania* 22:81–90.

Hobsbawm, E. J.
1965   *Primitive rebels.* New York: Norton (original 1959).

Jarvie, I. C.
1967   *The revolution in anthropology.* London: Routledge.

Lanternari, V.
1963   *The religions of the oppressed.* New York: Knopf.

Lawrence, Peter
1964   *Road belong cargo.* Manchester: Manchester University Press.
1970a   Daughter of time. In *Cultures of the Pacific: selected readings,* ed. Thomas G.
          Harding and Ben J. Wallace. New York: Free Press (original 1965).
1970b   The Ngaing of the Rai Coast. In *Cultures of the Pacific: selected readings,* ed.
          Thomas G. Harding and Ben J. Wallace. New York: Free Press (original 1965).
1971   Cargo cult and religious belief among the Garia. In *Melanesia: readings on a
          culture area,* ed. L. L. Langness and John C. Weschler. New York: Chandler
          (original 1955).

Mannheim, Karl
1936   *Ideology and utopia.* London: Routledge.

Morauta, Louise
1972   The politics of cargo cults in the Madang area. *Man* 7:430–447.

Nadel, Siegfried Frederick
1957   *The theory of social structure.* Glencoe, Ill: Free Press.

Prattis, J. I.
1973   Strategising man. *Man* 8:46–58.

Stanner, W. E. H.
1958   On the interpretation of cargo cults. *Oceania* 29:1–25.

Worsley, Peter
1968   *The trumpet shall sound.* New York: Schocken Books (original 1958).

From the Mouths of Babes: Reflections of Social Structure in the Verbal Interaction of Part-Hawaiian Children

STEPHEN T. BOGGS

Now Junyə Boy, get *o-off*. Look you droppin the *coo*kies.
Like dis?
Sit down! Gö all the way back. [pause] Si' ahp! Sit like *di-is!* [pause] An *cross* yo' leg—nobo' + no^n + like see you' peepee.

—Honolulu, 1971

[Saupuke's] elder cousins, children of six to nine, take a considerable hand in his upbringing, and the little girls in particular give him severe commands as to how to conduct himself. . . . As he goes to put back the plug his cousin intervenes, "Give the plug here," then "Run and hang it up" she says, sticking in the plug firmly and giving him the bottle. Then as he quietly complies, "Go to the back," an injunction to retire to the rear of the house away from people of importance, and finally as a parting shot the order comes, "Don't go walking about on the mats"—all of which he obeys without a murmur and sinks down in obscurity.

—*We, the Tikopia*, pp. 149–150.

"It is necessary to give concrete detail about small points of behavior in order to indicate the contours of the Tikopia family," Firth wrote in 1936, because the apparently trivial incidents of everyday life "in reality form the substance of the kinship pattern" (1957:138). When I began studying anthropology in 1947 in Professor Firth's seminar, I formed the conviction that his was the only objective way one could study how children learned not only kinship but the basic principles of social structure generally. And so I began in 1966 to undertake such a study of modern Hawaiians of Polynesian ancestry. This essay provides an overview and some details of this continuing study.

The first conversation quoted above is an example of the data upon which this essay is primarily based. It consists of what children said to one another, to members of their families, and to me in the course of the relationships that have developed between us over several years. These data have been supplemented by participant observation involving different children and families. The data thus differ from Firth's, which were all obtained by direct observation. Yet the conversation quoted, when compared to the incident described by Firth, indicates that the results can be similar.

Participant observation is necessary in order to develop awareness of speech forms and the social contexts in which they appear. Without this awareness interpretation of speech would be difficult if not impossible. Participant observation is also needed, along with interviewing, to discover all that older children know. Thus I discovered that whereas children four to seven years of age appear to regard all that they know as reportable and thus volunteer it, older children appear to take much of what they know for granted and do not volunteer it.

Speech obtained in naturally occurring situations gives an insight into the organization of experience from the point of view of the participants themselves. Such a method constitutes a kind of ethnosemantic approach. It avoids, however, the difficulties of interpretation that result from artificial conditions of elicitation.

As is well recognized, speech occurs in specific events of social interaction. What is said, how it is said, and by whom reflects the varying relationships obtaining among the participants in a speech event. Social relationships therefore structure participation. They may also be spoken about in the course of interaction. Thus social structure is reflected in verbal interaction in two ways. In this essay data obtained without participation by an outside observer—overheard conversations, for example, like the one quoted above—have been analyzed in terms of the social relationships that structured participation in the event. Accounts given to the researcher by individual children and occasionally by groups of children, which constitute the bulk of data used, have been analyzed in terms of their content—that is, the relationships referred to by the speakers.

Obviously, what was said to the researcher reflected the children's relationships to him or her. Five-to-seven-year-olds, for example, made only fleeting references to lovemaking when talking individually to the researcher. In contrast, children from similar backgrounds competed in mutual joking about one another's alleged sexual exploits in a group studied by Watson (1972, 1975).[1] It is important, therefore, to have data from different audiences and situations in order to study the reflections of social structure in speech. In this study the audiences were other children only (at home and in school), other children and adult members of the family, and the researcher with other children occasionally present. Unfortunately, conversations before the first two types of audience are too limited to allow systematic comparison with the third.

Data presented in the following pages indicate how social structure is perceived by some children four to seven years of age. To see these findings in developmental perspective, comparable data have been analyzed for boys eight to twelve and fifteen to sixteen years of age. The results of this analysis are briefly described here, even though the data must await future publication. A comparable analysis remains to be done for older girls, although some data for girls eight to twelve have been included here.

With these limitations, then, the findings which emerge from a comparison of different age periods are fourfold: (1) nuclear family relationships overlap, and in many cases coalesce with, relationships between nonnuclear relatives (nieces, nephews, aunts, uncles, cousins become siblings); (2) relative age is the earliest and most salient principle of social structure; (3) aloha and respect develop first in relations between younger and older persons; and (4) relationships between persons of the same age and sex take the longest time to evolve.

The principles underlying relations between younger and older persons in and out of the household are well reflected in the child's verbal interaction by age seven or even earlier. But the principles used to avoid conflict among age and sex peers in adulthood, and certain aspects of respect toward elders, do not appear to be formed any earlier than adolescence.

CHILDREN FROM FOUR TO SEVEN
Relatives Outside the Nuclear Family

Children report interaction with aunts, uncles, and cousins as if it were frequent:

> Den we wen back to my uncle's house an my uncle wen go kill one chicken. . . . Me an my uncle wen go eat um las night. [boy, 6]

> I get two bruda and two sista live ova dea wit my aunty. I get ten uncu ova dea. [girl, 7]

Relatives are reported to be involved in visiting and having fun:

> An den my aunty dem came with us . . . an I tow my cousin, "Lani, come swim with us." But she didn' wanted to swim with us. An so when we got all wet she—we wen go throw her inside a wata. [girl, 6]

> Den us wen get us guys pah'ty down my aunty dem house. [boy, 6]

Family outings and parties, which are frequent, typically include many of these relatives, among others. The tendency to associate relatives with a good time led one girl to hide in her uncle's car so he would take her to the show. Unfortunately, she said, she got a "lickin" instead.

The children report special relationships with uncles and grandparents. Several reported running away to grandparents when they got a "lickin" at home. Others reported:

My uncu neva lick me. [girl, 6]

My uncu gon teach my bruda how to drive truck and bundoza [bulldozer]—an car. [girl, 7]

Sometimes a child will go to live with a relative because of special fondness:

My cousin came to ou' house [and said,] "Honey, my mada like you!" Then I wen home . . . muda said, "Go to be' in 'a house [go to bed in the house]." . . . One long time ago I'm sleep ova thea. [Boggs: But you don't sleep at your cousin's house any more.] No, because . . . too long sleep ova thea. Too long fo get up [they are too late getting up for school]. [girl, 6]

Such fondness was one reason to *hanai* (foster or feed) a child in traditional Hawaii. A relative might also *hanai* a child—both now and in the past—when the inability of the child's parents to support all their children coincided with the relative's desire for a child (Pukui et al. 1972:51–53; Howard et al. 1970; Kamakau 1964:26–27). Thus Leilani lived part-time with her aunty and several cousins because her mother and father were separated and the father lacked sufficient income to support Leilani and her six siblings and stepsiblings. Describing her relationship with her cousins, she said:

Byamby I'm gonna look like all thea sistas and I goin be thea sista. If I come jaest like them and by them I goin ha' to live wi' them cause I thea sister awredy. [girl, 6]

Leilani apparently confused her belief that sisters look alike with the fact that living with her cousins would make her their sister in the view of all in the household. Children brought up in the same household regard one another as siblings, regardless of genealogy. Thus one boy refers to his sister's baby as "brother" because the sister and her baby live in his household. Parents reinforce this usage.

Everyone is assumed to have cousins. While children recognize that cousins live at an uncle's or aunt's house, they also are likely to extend or apply the term to anyone who is socially or emotionally close. For example, they use the term "my cousin fren" and one boy said: "Keoki my cousin. My brudda love Keoki's sista.'' The two in this case were not only genealogically unrelated but they also lived some distance apart.

In summary, Hawaiian children interact frequently if not constantly with grandparents, aunts, uncles, and cousins, and they associate these relatives with having a good time. Further, they know that grandparents, aunts, and uncles may take a special interest in a child, providing help and instruction. Shifts in residence or child-care arrangements may also bring a variety of persons into a major role in a child's life. Cousins are felt to be similar to friends and of course are likely to be close friends if the children interact frequently. All children in the household are regarded as brother and sister. These perceptions and attitudes are all consistent with the traditional family systems of Polynesia.

Age and Stratification

Relative age is the most salient feature for differentiating relationships so far as children are concerned. The reason for this, I believe, is the very great difference in status between babies and young children, in conjunction with the prestige of being older and bigger. At the ages of four through seven, the children have just undergone the transition from babyhood to childhood but still lack the prestige enjoyed by older brothers and sisters. Hence, to them, relative age seems very important and sharply demarcated.

Everyone enjoys playing with babies, and this experience is often reported by the children. When a baby is brought into a group, everyone present comes forward to look at, greet, and touch it. Warm and tender feelings are lavishly expressed, responses are made to every move or sound of the infant, and joy is expressed over its accomplishments.

Ou' baby had teet' fo real! My daddy everytime put his finga inside da mout and she bite hah'd, fo real. . . . My mada let us play wit her an den we all go put ou' two fingas insi' she go bite us and den we go say "ow!" [laughter] . . . Good fun! [girl, 6]

My aunty let us hold the baby. I ask her if I can hold her babay. . . . Sometime my sister got to hold her. [girl, 7]

An ou' baby gon come big. . . . She gon rekl [wrestle] us. Even my bruda Ronnie [18 months] he know how to fight my bruda dem fo real. And den . . . my bruda . . . he go hit Ronnie aroun. Den my big bruda, huh? . . . he go faw don. Ronnie scaid. [laughter] Den he wen go carry Ronnie on top his back. Ronnie go bite ova hia an den Ronnie go fall down, konk his head. [girl, 6]

A good deal of verbal play goes on during the interaction with the baby. The baby's name is repeated with variations, and baby talk is used, much of it chantlike. Any accomplishment is welcomed.

Our baby scratch me all around and he bite me. . . . My baby swea'. My sista teach him. [boy, 6]

Beginning at about three years of age children lose this most forward status of being the baby, and a little later they are held responsible for keeping watch over younger siblings. The knowledge of girls, especially, indicates the reality of their responsibilities in caring for younger siblings.

[Boggs: How do you fix a nini (nursing) bottle?] You get one smaw pot an den you put um on da stove [continues]. . . . You make um drip on top you' arm an you say, "Feel da ting hot?" Then you give the bebe. [girl, 7, in group discussion]

Yet keeping watch over younger siblings becomes irksome:

My smaw cousin she everytime come wit me. Everytime when I touch her she cry, cry, cry. . . . She cry too much. Like carry, carry, carry. [girl, 7]

My mada's baby gon follow me. Den I go lick um an my smaw bruda carry um home. Den I wen run play. [girl, 7]

With such experience, one might expect that children would wish to remain babies. They are aware, in fact, that babies can get away with misbehavior:

My baby brother look for trouble. He eat aw da cake. [girl,7]

My mommy try to make him drink the bottle but he throw the bottle at my mommy. He even bite my finger, over here. Sore, when he bite, he bite hard. [boy, 6]

But rather than stressing such advantages of being a baby, the children stress the superiority of age:

I can run fas, nex my baby. My baby go run slow. Me can run fast. [boy, 6]

I know how to catch waves now. [Describes it.] Only me catch the big waves, my bruda catch smaw waves. [girl, 8]

There are claims of being able to do things older children can, claims which are scorned by the older child:

My cousin a smaw shrimp. . . . She say next year she going to school [disbelieving tone].
    Even my other cousins . . . they [so] small they can hardly walk, an they said they can ride my cousin's . . . their sister's bike. [girl, 7]

One reason why children regard older as superior is that older siblings, especially girls, have considerable authority. Nothing illustrates better the role structure among siblings than the interaction which occurs among them while taking care of the baby. Girls and boys have markedly different roles, as do older versus younger children. An older sister issues and revises commands to a younger sister, requests her permission to intervene in the younger one's task, cautions, demonstrates, responds to her requests for information, and corrects. She alone demonstrates such a pattern. She also addresses all siblings collectively and gives explanations. While a younger boy or girl may attempt to explain, he or she is not heeded, whereas an older sister is. A younger sister acts as lieutenant for the older sister, just as the latter does for a parent. She informs her older sister, foresees problems, requests information and advice, shares tasks, and imitates her sister's commands. It is clear that sisters understand their mutual and individual functions, for each is able to step in and substitute for the other.

But in no way does a younger brother share in this authority. Rather, he is often treated as an outcast, required merely to fetch and carry and obey commands. His older sister acts as if he completely lacked competence. The following is an extreme example:

Shalene—oldest girl, 5
Molly—girl, 4
Lei—baby, 11 months
Pam—girl, 2
Junya—boy, 3

Text			*Glosses and Comments*
S	1.	You ən an Pam, an— Lei go on da bed. I gotta ᵍsomeplace. [interruption]	Command and explanation. S is playing mother's role, preparing to go to the store.
	2.	Hurry *ah-ahp!* 'O [go] take Lei on *deah-ah!* [unrelated material]	Urges, repeats command.
L	3.	[murmurs]	Attempt to resolve L's objections (see following).
M	4.	Shalene! Lei no *like!*	Calls attention, reports difficulty.
S	5.	Dis coverum. [pause]	Revises command, requests permission to
	6.	. . . Let *me,* ʸæ? . . . An don' drop her. [interruption]	take over, cautions. S has abandoned make-believe to care for baby.
	7.	Now I gon put *dis* blanket.	Demonstrates.
M	8.	Stop. Do-on't! [steady, high pitch] [yell]	Interdicts one of others.
S	9.	Get that . . . out!	Command to offender.
L	10.	[crying]	Complains.

S	11.	Stupit!	Insults offender.
			Also implies condemnation for offense.
L	12.	[crying]	Continues complaining.
S	13.	'K.	Finishes caring for baby.
All	14.	[crying] Sha*lene*!	Dispute over object.
	15.	Mine.	Same.
P	16.	No-o.	Complains.
S	17.	Come on *to-op*!	Command, direction.
			S may be trying to resolve the dispute.
M	18.	Baby look! Carnəbu,	Calls attention, tries to amuse baby.
		Carn*baw,* carnə*bul.*	Carnival suggests fun and excitement.
		Carnə*bul.*	Plays with words to amuse baby.
S	19.	Go get Lei! [shout]	Command, warning, talks to baby,
		'Oh, 'oh, bəp [baby].	interdicts.
		Stop!	
L	20.	[gurgling]	Pleased.
		[comments on baby's movements, not transcribed]	
M	21.	We'z *Lei* going?	Question, request for information.
S	22.	On hiyah. All you folks,	Gives information requested, calls
		ceyz I gon get right oy ˀ	attention, directs, explains.
		hiya. [pause]	Note that S addresses all, as mother
			does. Direction has to be assumed from
			circumstances.
S	23.	Oh, 'oh. [crooning	Talks to baby.
		tone]	
L	24.	[babbling]	Returns talk.
S	25.	*Aiy yo, hel lo.* [chant]	Talks to baby, calls attention, interdicts,
		Now Junyə Boy, get	corrects J.
		o-off! Look you	Note use of baby talk to instruct in
		droppin the *coo*kies.	greeting. Contrast in tone with J is very
			great. Gloss: "You can't do anything
			right." S directs him to the evidence of his
			own incompetence.
J	26.	Like dis?	Complies, requests approval.
S	27.	Sit down! Gö all the	Disapproves, commands, directs.
		way back. [pause]	
	28.	Si' ahp! Sit like	Directs, directs and demonstrates.
		di-is! [pause]	The emphasis accompanying the
			demonstration implies that he has to be
			shown.
	29.	An *cross* yo' leg—	Directs, insults.
		nobo' + no^n + like see you'	
		peepee.	
J	30.	Not! [matter of fact]	Contradicts S, defends self.
		Is fo' it.	Meaning of his assertion is not clear.
?	31.	ŋaŋ [four times]	Talks to baby, baby talk.
S	32.	Come Moll'! Get off	Corrects M, calls attention, commands,
		dat *blan*⌐*ket.*	directs.
M	33.	⌐I a-⌐-am! Shalene,	Asserts compliance, calls attention,
		What if Lei *fa*-all?	asks about possible difficulty.

S   34. [silence]   Ignores.
          [interaction between M and J]
M   35. *Sha*! Shalene, Jyə   Calls attention, tells on J.
          (Junyə) knock down
          ou^r *kine, box*!
S   36. Get out! *Punk*! Get   Interdicts J, insults, repeats interdict.
          ou-ut! [pause]
J   37. ^m dis free [three] yea's Offers defense.
          ow'.

Younger children may direct complaints about one another to an older sibling, and the latter frequently take on the parental role by accusing or trying to resolve disputes before the complaint reaches a parent. In a dispute over the use of an object, for example, the older sibling will attempt to adjudicate, cajole, direct, or even threaten supernatural punishment if one party does not give up his or her claims.

The attractiveness of the more powerful role is clearly indicated when children play house. The most desired role by far is mother. Second choice is daughter/sister, because she acts as mother's assistant. Aunty is occasionally chosen. But father is never chosen in playing house, at least not in my data. Boys usually play the role of boy or baby, and often not willingly. There is other evidence that boys do take father's role in dramatic play, however, having love affairs and fighting with wives and rivals (Kyle 1968).

Such experience as described above makes age along with sex a major principle for ordering relationships. Children constantly refer to big/small brother/sister, equating size and age. Occasionally it may be necessary to specify further, as in this instance, where size and age are equated:

I get tree big bruda. Da oldes is bigga. He marrie', da bigges one. Tree big one not marrie', only da riu big one. He uny got one bebe. [boy, 6]

The tendency to order everyone by age is illustrated by the following comment:

[Gives ages of all siblings] and I'm seven. My mother is nineteen, my father is thirty-one, my goat is seven, too [laughs]. My cat is only three years old [laughs]. [girl, 7]

The emphasis in studies of early personality development among Polynesians has been upon the "rejection hypothesis": the notion that intrusive demands upon parents are punished after an indulged infancy. Presumably such an experience might create a wish to return to the happy condition of the infant. If one focuses upon the part-Hawaiian child's expressed attitudes at this age, however, a strong desire to be older and bigger appears. A young child among peers would have the lowest status possible if he or she acted like a baby. The age hierarchy of the sibling group provides a better explanation of observed attitudes. In this structure to be older is to have more responsibility, prestige, and authority.

This structure also helps explain the strong norm against acting above one's age, which Mead (1971:116) has noted in Samoa.[2] In my opinion this norm, which is very important in many Oceanic cultures, is a direct outgrowth of the young child's experience with an age-graded sibling hierarchy. In such a structure the child desires to be older but is rebuffed by those whose status he desires to assume. Since he is soon able to act the role of elder with a still younger child, by the time he graduates from such a system he is ready to agree that one should not act above his age. As we shall see, the hazing of younger boys by adolescent males has the same consequence. Through both experiences adults learn to accept and value humility and nonassertiveness. This in turn is a source of dislike for the behavior of other groups, which Hawaiians regard as often proud and assertive.

Order of birth among siblings was an extremely important principle in traditional Hawaiian social structure. It was reflected in the rights and responsibilities of the *hiapo* (firstborn child), the *hanau mua* (senior living member of the senior lineage), and the principle of lineage seniority.[3] It is of interest, therefore, that this principle is experienced during the first years of life and has a direct effect upon the child's personality.

Learning to Participate

In stories told to me about parents, the two most frequent themes are having fun and doing chores. Typical of the former are:

When no mo schoo' . . . we gon down da beach campin an we gon have on pah'ty down da beach an aftadz we gon chop suey's house fo eat an aftadz we gon show and aftadz we gon down da beach an campin again. [boy, 6]

Everytime when my fada come home, dey a'ways like go, my fada my bruda dem. [girl, 7]

Recordings made at home contain several episodes in which parents act spontaneously and jokingly, to taunt, threaten, challenge, and wrestle with young children, types of interaction which I have also frequently observed. (For examples, see Watson-Gegeo and Boggs 1977.) Others in a similar mood tease and contradict what the child says, the child responding with pleasure. Sometimes older brothers or sisters are responsible for the fun:

My bebe gon call my big brudas, my big bruda gon go catch us. [boy, 7]

My sista she pull ou' ea'. Everytime when we was fun she tickle us. [girl, 7]

While such interaction is common, children place more emphasis upon doing chores. As they tell it, failure to perform chores will result in a "lickin."

Everytime we come home my mada tell us to wash the dishes and clean the stove off. [girl, 7]

When my fada come home [he] get mad because my sista no clean the house. [What does he say then?] "Give dem lickin. Wait till you' mada come home, you folks gon get a lickin." . . . I gotta clean the counta'. If I no clean the counta' good my fada gon give me a lickin, too. [girl, 7]

[Boggs: What do they tell you?] "Empty da wubbish can! Honey Boy! Empty da slop." [boy, 6]

The children are eager to claim for themselves ability to perform the tasks of older siblings:

I know how to wash and wipe! . . . But my fada no let me wash an wipe! [pouting] Sista Shalene and my sista Mary, they take turns. [girl, 7]

They describe a system in which everyone has a job to do. Jobs can be traded or shared, but no one is left out.

My mada say, "Wash da dishes" n den one say, "[You] wash da dishes. 'M gon clean da . . . furnitures an all." Ooh, hah'd work we 'ave to do, man! [girl, 6]

My mada cook food everyday. She tahya' cook food. My sista cook food fo her. An my mada watch da bebe fo her. [The baby is sister's. Mother works.] [boy, 6]

By learning to do their chores as part of an interdependent system, children as young as five become participants in the adult world. Parents take these contributions seriously—they are not regarded as tokens to be ignored if the child fails to perform. The family system becomes for the child the basic model of the world. It provides the most absorbing metaphor for dramatic play. Children play house frequently, and even when they play store and school it is the roles of family members and particularly infant care that provide the bulk of the details. A pretended visit to a hospital, for example, is explained by the fact that baby is all alone there. When they play store there is a store baby. The following is a typical recording of playing house:

Carmen—group leader
Ela, Loke, Malia—girls
Moke—boy

Text	*Glosses and Comments*
C 1. Hey, daughtah, you gotta change da baby's clothes, daughtah.	Calls attention, attributes role, commands, frames event. Event takes place in the "doll corner." In these circumstances the action called for frames the event. So does the fact that this is not an action usually performed at home. C often addresses her followers as "daughtah."
E 2. Not me, *her.*	Evades command. E attempts to shift the task to someone else. This is not outside the routine, however, She is doing something else (see below.)
L 3. Ho! Evry*time* I have to do *tha-at*!	Exclamation, complaint. L complains at how often she must do this. At home girls request this task. So this is part of the make-believe.
C 4. Change it! [firm, matter-of-fact]	Asserts authority. C responds to complaint by repeating her command in a tone of voice that suggests you can't fight City Hall.
Ma 5. . . . her washing clothes, das why.	Justifies E's evasion. Ma indicates that having another task excuses evasion of mother's command.
C 6. . . . an you make—I gon wash the dish an you make the two babies go [hums].	Interrupts command to explain. Everyone has a task, even mother. The tasks are appropriate for the roles being played.
? 7. And I gon make the lunch.	Claims task. When mother is assigning work, everyone should have a task.
? 8. I gon iron da clothes. . . . Hεr'z the baby's clothes. Ahyr-r.	Claims task, task talk. Description of what is happening, like a stage aside, occurs because of the metaphor.
E 9. . . . Mommy! Dis goes down fo wash?	Calls attention, attributes role, requests direction.
C 10. ⌈Yes, you . . . wash . . .	Replies, gives direction.
? 11. ⌈Moke's boss. Moke's boss.	Gives direction.
E 12. Aw diis goin down fo a wash.	Task talk or direction.
Mo 13. . . . even you' muu*muu* you didn take care of.	Accusation. "Even" = "also."
? 14. ˡWent down fo wash, you know.	Explains, justifies self.
? 15. Hurry up, you guys, wash da clothes.	Urges others on.

C   16.   Wash da clothes.   Commands, admonishes, asserts status.
            Girl, you betta wash   C reminds with a mild warning. By
            da clothes, eh?   addressing her as "girl" she reminds
                                         her of C's status also.

The children clearly internalize the attitudes and values governing this system. For example, work comes before play:

I don' play, I work. When I pau [finished] I go play. [boy, 7]

[Boggs: What do you do on Sunday?] Play—no, I do my work. Before I play I do my work. Den I go play. I clean out da yah'd, clean my—Robin my bedroom, sweep an mop. You' sons clean da yah'd? [boy, 7]

[Boggs: You get all girls in your family?] My mada no like one boy, he go play, he do nutting. [girl, 7]

Of course there are backsliders:

[Boggs: Why don't you do your work?] I no like. I la-azy. [boy, 7]

This pattern of family organization, which has been aptly described as a "shared function" system (Gallimore et al. 1974) differs profoundly, in my judgment, from other large, poor families where children share in the work. In the Hawaiian system to have a job is status-enhancing. Doing something for the family is a positive value, not something one gets stuck with because no one else has done it. I have not seen any evidence that the same statement can be made for other large, poor families.

Obedience and Respect

Although there are dramatic references to "lickins" in the children's stories, insight into the nature and consequences of parental punishment is provided by other evidence. Home recordings and participant observation indicate that when parents try to get children to do something, such as dress themselves or leave the house, they typically issue a series of commands which at first children ignore or comply with only verbally. Parents will repeat the commands numerous times, escalating only by verbal emphasis, grumbling, and routinely delivered threats ("you guys gon git it"). In this routine escalation no genuine anger is expressed, however, and no punishments follow without signs of genuine anger. No doubt this fact contributes to noncompliance. Before a child is spanked, there is usually a definite series of additional cues from the parent: unmistakable signs of anger, specification of the circumstances in which punishment will be meted out ("if you not *pau* when I come in dea"), and finally a confrontation. The scenario for the final confrontation calls for specification of the command that was violated ("I told you . . ."), followed by accusation and the presentation of evidence, usually by means of a direct question to the accused. The implied answer to the question is intended to incriminate the child. Judgment is then announced, often in the form of an insult ("stupid!"). Physical punishment usually follows immediately, although even at the last moment a scolding may be substituted.

The early stages of attempting to get a child to do something accord with Firth's account of Tikopia (1957:156):

> Since promises of punishment are much more frequent than the act itself children, knowing this, are apt to stand their ground despite all commands made to them. Though these be uttered in most peremptory tones the youngsters merely smile. Repetition is necessary to produce any effect, and so much is this a habit that most orders are given automatically three times over at the start! Much talk and little obedience is the impression gained of family discipline in questions of ordinary restraint.

But, as Firth also describes, punishment follows swiftly upon a parent's anger. Seeing these actions as parts of a single sequence which may or may not be completed clarifies what might otherwise seem to be contradictory statements about the severity and strictness of parental discipline.

Even if they do not obey immediately or at all in many cases, children become quite obedient to parental injunctions as they grow older. There is indirect evidence of respect for authority even at this age:

> [Boggs: What is a bad man?] You say æf words [f-words] an tease li' dat an you no listen to your mother. You no listen to the mother you can have lickin. . . . You got to stay in the house. You like ride your two-wheel bikes an you no can. [girl, 7]

Acceptance of adult authority is also indicated by the children's acceptance of the practice of reporting on one another to adults—what we would call tattling. When children report alleged misbehavior by another child, which happens frequently, the accused does not complain or attempt to recriminate for the act of reporting.[4] Rather, the accused counters by accusing the teller of violating some adult injunction. The message conveyed by this behavior is that it is wrong to disobey adult injunctions and proper to report disobedience. Older children say it is wrong to disobey one's parents, as we shall see. There is no concept of tattling.

If there is objection to parental authority it only appears in make-believe. When they play house at home or in school, children complain about orders given them by parents, request explanations for orders, and escalate requests made of parents. But they rarely do this in real life. The children's reliance upon authority is also indicated in their attempts to play house. As home and school recordings indicate, these attempts are only successful when led by a child whose orders are followed by peers in real-life situations as well. Without such a leader there is only continual dispute over role claims and scenario.

Disagreement among Peers

Boys this age frequently report fighting with their friends:

My fren trow san' everyday at us. Trow san' at us an my baby. [boy, 6]

My fren evytime acting smah't to me. An I wanted to touch him, but I no like. Byamby he scream. [Boggs: What did he do when he was acting smart?] He said—he swea'. [Note that this boy will not use swearwords.] [same boy]

Participant observations indicate that fights, disputes over possessions, and disagreements of every kind are common from kindergarten through second grade. So are insults: being skinny, black, or *haole* (white). Disagreements are as common among girls as boys, although boys do somewhat more fighting.

Recordings made at home and school when no observers were present likewise indicate frequent conflict. Playing with toys or other possessions (such as blankets) produces almost continual disputing over the right to use an object. Ownership, prior use, or not having had a turn yet may all serve as arguments—usually creating further dispute. Likewise manipulating things, such as puzzles. Typically one child will give directions, the other will give contrary directions, and both will claim to know how it is done. From this point on there is contradicting, rapidly escalating to insults and attempts to shut up the other or prevent him or her from proceeding. Each child acts as if he or she were preventing disastrous intervention by the other.

There are also disputes over other claims: being older, bigger, in a higher grade, having fathers who fight. The typical response, especially among friends, boys or girls, is immediate contradiction, a counterclaim, or both. After several stylized repetitions, deadlock is reached. One child may appeal to authority ("mother/teacher/the man say—"). Sometimes a trial by ordeal is suggested, such as the first one to blink loses. This in turn may lead to another argument about who blinked.

Claims to know something that another does not know are temporarily status-enhancing. Girls at the kindergarten of the Kamehameha Early Education Project (KEEP) played an involved game, the goal of which was to make allies by sharing knowledge of the personal name of a parent while keeping this knowledge from selected others. So powerful was this deprivation that girls with great influence would humble themselves in order to be in the know.

Disputes at home between siblings who are more than a year older or younger are not common because of unequal ability, power, and authority. When children are about the same age, on the other hand, means for producing agreement are lacking, at least before conflict has produced injury. Even within the family bickering is frequent among siblings approximately the same age, although it rarely escalates because of the possibility of appeal to an elder authority, which often results in punishment for all concerned.

Both boys and girls expect fighting. This explains, I believe, why they report their own behavior as defensive:

> I fight dat guy ova da beach. I bleed his nose. He was trowin san'. He trow a stone on my head. [boy, 7]

> [Boggs: Why do you fight all the time?] Cause I no like nobody hurt. Cause dey making troubu, dey beat up my fren. [Boggs: What is a troublemaker?] When you walkin by an he say a bad word. Me an Palani jus walking an a boy push me aroun, jis walkin again and he push me aroun. [boy, 7]

> [Questioning me.] You' kids, dey play togeda, dey be frens, they don' kick li' dat? [girl, 7]

The way out of this Hobbesian condition is not clear to the children of this age. Comparison with older children and adolescents, as reported below, suggests that avoidance of fights may result from learning how to evolve rules in games and by transforming disputes into joking. Many games are played by children four to seven years old, among them hide and seek, tag ("chasemaster" and freeze tag), "witch, witch, what time is it?", volleyball, and racing on bikes or on foot. Any discussion of rules among two or more children, however, produces nothing but disagreement, even when the same rules are in fact being described. (This is another example of the desire to gain status by claiming exclusive knowledge.) During play, rules are always cited to support one's own claims to win while denying another's. No consensus is reached in these disputes and rules are not negotiated. For older children it is different, as we shall see.

Joking routines such as the following are practiced, but they do not resolve or avoid conflict as they do in older groups:

> B: He go make dudu in his pans.
> C: I neva.
> B: You tow' me.
> C: Long time, bruda.

Most jokes, like this one, are told to insult. Such jokes are rich and varied (Watson 1972; Watson-Gegeo and Boggs 1977). But they rarely transform competitive feelings into laughter which all share.

There are leaders at this age, as already mentioned. But leaders do not alter the patterns of conflict described here. In the home recordings, leaders were girls: older sisters or cousins. In the kindergarten mentioned earlier the two leaders were both girls, one of whom succeeded the other during the school year. All these girls at home or school were self-assured and bossy and intelligently promoted their own interests. While the older girls did most of the talking by virtue of their age and skill, it is interesting to note that the two leaders who were the same age as their followers relied upon their skill with verbal routines. They were smart talkers, but not the most frequent talkers in the group. This is likewise a trait of peer leaders among older children and adults I have observed.

The absence of boy leaders in our data is probably a result of sampling, since boys have been observed acting as leaders at this age. They are also as skilled as girls at verbal routines. Unlike the girls, however, they model their leadership role upon their view of adolescent toughness and violence.

Although means for heading off conflict among peers are not well developed at this age, the children are skillful at restoring goodwill after a child's feelings have been hurt. Thus Watson (personal communication) provides the following example. This episode begins when Makani (a boy) chokes Kealoha (a girl). Apparently Maile (a boy) had told Makani that Kealoha was telling stories about him outside on the tape-recorder; this was not true, but perhaps Maile had gotten the girls mixed up.

Kona (girl): Ah, see now, Kealoha crying. [tenderly]
?:   Makani, why you do dat?
Kona: Maile, why you tell him ⌈to—
Maile: ⌈I neva ⌉ tell him.
Kona: —why you tell him to choke on Kealoha's neck?

Watson, trying to avoid a fight, tells Maile to go in the classroom. As usual, everybody ignores Watson; Maile moves toward the classroom because another boy, trying to avoid the fight, begins to shepherd him in that direction.

Malo (boy): Hey.
?:   She ⌈really crying
Malo: ⌈Oh, man (sadly) ⌉ I like bust Makaniʌp, kick em.
Kona: [Maile] tell Makani go choke her neck. [explaining]

Several follow Maile, criticizing him and arguing; others comfort Kealoha by sitting silently, eyes on her or downcast, or patting her.

Watson-Gegeo gives other examples involving both boys and girls. The following long and complex episode was recorded at KEEP in 1972 by Violet Mays:

Linda, Kulei, Malia, others—girls
Elroy, others—boys
Carmen—group leader

Text	Glosses and Comments
	[K has just fallen off a chair, along with L, getting milk all over K's dress. A child announces her approach.]
? 1. . . . comi-in! [excited] [laughter]	Announcement.
L 2. æ! ⌈I⌉ sorry, Kulei.	Expresses sympathy, apologizes.
[several others comment simultaneously and squeal with laughter]	
L 3. Sorry, Kulei.	Repeats apology, this time more simply. Deescalation signals a desire to make peace, just as escalation does a fight.
K 4. [pause]	No verbal response. K is not ready to forgive and forget (see below). She keeps L and others on a limb.
L 5. Kulei says "*Tanks, ɛh?*" [laughs]	Jokes. L attributes sarcasm to relieve the strain. Note use of quoted speech and taking role of other.
All 6. [laughter]	Enjoying the situation.
L 7. I sorry, Kulei.	Repeats apology, perhaps because others have laughed at her, thus repeating the injury.
K 8. Now I can't eat my *lunch!* [sadly]	Laments.
? 9. I sorry ⌈Kulei. [subdued]	Expresses sympathy. This is not an apology, since the speaker had nothing to do with K's prospective loss of lunch.
C 10. ⌈Dat's ok⌉ she gon give you some.	Offers reparation. C reassures K and offers reparation on behalf of L, interrupting another to do so.
All 11. [laughter]	Enjoying the situation. Note that this does not conflict with expression of sympathy. No one says, "Don't laugh."
? 12. Oh-h man! Her stannin in *mʌ-ʌd* house.	Comment. Someone excitedly evaluates the situation.
K 13. I sure *am!*	Agrees. K indicates that she shares the evaluation, although her feelings differ.
C 14. Try your pri-ize, Kulei . . . to if da . . . fall down.	Referent unclear.
M 15. [laughter]	Enjoying the situation. M enters

the situation for the first time,
after it is clear. She subsequently talks
more than anyone else.

? 16. Yeah, cause I neva
pull the chɛ' away.

Justifies own act. Someone
attempts to escape responsibility for
the accident.

K 17. I was si'in down. I
was + itin on her an—
[inspires] you guy—
you guys are gonna
have two *faults*,
from my mother,
[prissy] when I tore [?]
it.

Justifies own act, scolds.
K starts to escape responsibility,
then realizes the others are responsible,
not her. She interrupts herself,
calling upon mother's authority.
This introduces a new, serious note.

? 18. Not *we-e*! ᵐwas *dem*.

Escapes responsibility, accuses.
The rush is on to escape blame in
response to K's scolding.

E 19. Wasn' *me*. [laughs]

Escapes responsibility. E's only
individual participation. His laugh
indicates an easy conscience.

C 20. Her!

Accuses L. C fixes sole responsibility on
L, although probably without justification.

M 21. I know her, I know.
I know Lei [Kulei]
fell down ⌈ an—

Supports C. M is C's lieutenant.
She supports C's accusation with
a report that is cut off by L.

L 22. ⌈Carmen!⌉ I spose
gɛrum [get her um]
no *need*. [fast]

Calls attention, claims task. Gloss:
"I'm supposed to get it for her, you
don't need to." Apparently C had
started to get the lunch for K. L is
complying with reparation offered by C.

[conversation led by M, sorting out K's and L's remaining food and
drink. K then returns]

K 23. I *mad* at you, Linda.
[firm and angry] I
really am. I'm not
lying.

Expresses anger to L, emphasizes
very straightforward expression of
feeling, explicitly denying that she is
joking.

C 24. Her mad, you know,
her mad you know.
Her *mad* you know,
Linda. No think I put
down on my nice *food*.

Supports K's expression of feeling.
Referent for last sentence is unclear.

L 25. [pause]

No response.

C 26. I *would* if I was you'
cousin. ⌈I . . .

Continues.

M 27. ⌈If you need⌉ not fo'
cousin. [laughs]

Jokes. M interrupts C with a
remark that she treats as a joke.
Referent unclear.

C 28. As not *fun*ny, daughtas.

Reproves, attributes role. M's attempted
jibe was out of place and brings
a reproof and reminder of her status.

M	29.	I say I like good enough fo' my cousin.	Retracts jibe. Again the referent is unclear, but it sounds like a retraction.
K	30.	[chuckles]	Enjoyment. The first sign that K's mood has changed. Perhaps brought on by reproof to M.
C	31.	She laughin.	Announcement. C points out that K is no longer angry. This takes preference over her disagreement with M.

[L, C, and M then engage in aimless conversation about whether they need a straw while finishing their milk]

K	32.	Well, good, Ruby, us got *fin*is. Thanks fo' dese *fah-ah'ts* [farts]!	Expresses solidarity, jokes. Ruby is not present.
M	33.	Ey! Evybody . . . an dis ting gon dry. . . . Yah, Carmen, da ting can dry, yah?	Calls attention, suggests. M celebrates the happy mood by suggesting a happy outcome to the affair. Note that she first addresses the whole group, then C.
?	34.	Oh, yah.	Agrees. Someone is anxious to go along.
K	35.	^{n}yi-i [you] . . . gotta wash it an den it will dry. Yeah? [Put it by da pan an—	Agrees, explains. K joins in the new mood and expands upon her agreement. She is cut off by L's attempt (not shown) to recall a good time shared with C.

In this incident the primary goal is to restore good feelings and secondarily to escape responsibility for the accident. Adults are not involved in any way, just as the adult was ignored in the episode recorded by Watson. Good feelings are restored by apology, joking, expressions of sympathy, looking after the needs of the one offended, and calling attention to her feelings. The restoration of solidarity is indicated when the one offended returns to the usual routine of eating, makes jokes, and agrees with the suggestion of a happy outcome. The group's leader initiates most of this, offering reparation, accusing the culprit, pointing out the feelings of the one offended, and finally suggesting that she is no longer angry. Others mostly express sympathy. It is noteworthy that there is a minimum of accusation and no scapegoating in these efforts to restore peace.

It may seem contradictory that children can be so sensitive to the feelings of others and yet lack means of preventing conflict. But it is not. Rituals for making peace presuppose, and may even be based upon, conflict.[5]

Death, Monsters, and Animals

Although their relevance is not obvious at this age, attitudes and beliefs about metaphysical or supernatural phenomena eventually come to reflect and reinforce social structure in powerful and pervasive ways. It is therefore of interest to see the beginnings of these attitudes in younger children.

The children at Aina Pumehana school, like those at KEEP, were fascinated by the monsters they saw on television: bats, eagles, Space Ghost, Dr. Smith, King Kong, Spider Man, robots, Dracula—to name a few. They told of the struggles of heroes against these monsters (pronounced "mun-sta"):

> We saw Robin an Batman an da ada girl an afta'dz we saw big, big, big clam shell. . . . Da ting wen eat Robin up an da ting awmos got Robin feet. An afta'dz Robin go li' dat [gestures] an afta'dz da clam sheu wen bite 'im an 'e died. [boy, 6]

Since many children know the details, or think they do, they typically attempt to contribute to the narration:

Alan:	Ah gon teu you guy^s one—'pooky stahry.
	[inspires] Mae—one b^{w}oy, eh?
All:	⌈One man.
Alan:	⌈One man— ⌉one man go kill 'a boy o'a hi'
	[over here], ae? . . . O'a hi', ae?
Boggs:	Yeah! [suspensefully]
Alan:	Da b^{w}oy—da man⌈—'oh—ah—
Jacob:	⌈Took out da⌉ hah-ah't [heart].
All:	⌈An da man
Alan:	⌈An da man—an da man
Jacob:	An da man—an da man—eat da hah-ah't.
Boggs:	Yi-iech! [disgust]
Robert:	Ah know who + s [was] dat.
Boggs:	While it was still live?
Robert:	I ⌈know one⌉ —I know one
Jacob:	⌈Yeah.
Robert:	*Riu'* one.
Boggs:	What?
All:	⌈(whispers) . . . wen go make, Frankenstein.
Robert:	Yeah, Frankenstein. [boys, 7]

Several boys then told how Frankenstein looked for a goat; threw a man down, killing him; carried a girl out; "got drunk"; and "cracked up evrytiin." The narration was also enacted with suitable horrifying gestures and noises. Competition was fierce.

The children I talked to at this age rarely mentioned themes from local folklore. In all the tapes from Aina Pumehana there is only one mention of the scene most local people regard as supernaturally dangerous. I do not know why such references were so scarce, but I do not think it was due to lack of knowledge. Some of the same children recounted such material a few years later, and Watson (1972, 1975) reports traditional local folklore narrated by several girls the same age as my informants. My best guess is that the group studied by Watson provided more audience support for young children narrating local folklore than was provided by me or the unstructured collections of children who recorded for me. Support would be important, because children this young are not expected to narrate such stories at home.

In any case death and the dead are prominent themes in the stories quoted here, as they are in local folklore and in personal experiences narrated to me. For example:

Ann: Mista Steve, you kno' . . . *down* da stɔ̃ [service] station down dea? You know ge' one . . . cah' jis like one *coff*in.
          [material omitted]
Boggs: Yeah.
Ann: An— . . . yestiday I saw on [one] coffin in da cah-ah'.
Boggs: Really?
Ann: Yeah.
Boggs: Down here?
Ann: Yeah. Ah was scaid, ah was rʌnning to my sis*tah-ah*. . . . My sistah tought dat was one, coffin cah' an I . . . go check an I say, "Yah! Das one coffin *cah*'!"
Boggs: H'm.
Ann: Hoo da spooky I rʌn aweh. A—an las' night dey go sleep in da coffin car dah [down] da stehi's [service] station.
          [material omitted]
Moki: The skeleton could come out fo' . . .
          [material omitted]
Moki: Woo! Woo! My feet ah . . .
Boggs: What's that? [pause] Moki?
Ann: Dats da—skeletin. Ge' one skeletin . . . *inside*.

The most complex and unusual story I heard was the following (highly excerpted):

Lis'bet died on top [on] the cross—God—you know where God stay? . . . When she wen go walk on top the cross she die. . . . God gon make Lis'bet walk. . . . [Boggs: How did she get hurt?] No, her spine was all open an one boy he was standing ova thea name Geo'ge. . . . My motha was layin on top the bed an then when she go call—sh wen go like this, "Lis'bet! Lis'bet!" She c'dn' move. So even before she wen go call Lis'bet, Lis'bet was all gone an policemen an fireman an everybody came to look at Lis'bet up in heaven. [girl, 6]

This story appeared to have been rehearsed and may have incorporated elements from a church service. The teacher reported having heard it before I did.

Elements of Christian beliefs appear in some of the stories. For example, one girl reported:

My baby's goin to baptize. Da pries' gonna put 'im inside da wata an gon hol' um.

To which another girl replied, "We put da holy wata on." A boy reported that his father "stay up in Heaven," adding: "He rʌn across the street an he died an now my muda miss him. I miss him." (Actually, the father was in prison.) While Christian beliefs continue to appear in the accounts of older children, traditional concerns loom larger with the passing years, as we shall see. Few of the children attend churches, and even fewer do so regularly.

Speculation plays a key part in the development of attitudes toward the supernatural. There is evidence of this process at work among children five to seven years of age. Thus one girl, more given to asking me questions than any of the children, wanted to know if monsters are really men ("Spider Man take his suit off, he's a man"). It is easy to provoke speculation about where monsters come from. Some are made by masters, others may be hatched from eggs, but none are born the way babies are. There is even speculation about how to avoid death, a major theme when older children talk about the supernatural. Thus the girl whose sister "died on the cross" said:

> And heavens really can kill us. Devils too. . . . When devils come down they kill us an we die. We go up in heaven and heaven ha' go keep us up thea. . . . Devils like babies, yeah? They no like naughty boys an girls but they like goo' boys and girls.

While the children speculate about death and monsters, they appear to speculate even more frequently about animals. Often they draw inferences based upon rather acute observation. Thus one girl, observing that a hen always took her chicks walking, inferred that the chicks learned from their mother how to eat and to climb on a stick. She made other inferences:

> Oua cousin dem go play with um [chicks] . . . da mada was mad, always bite my cousin. We give [them] to da mada back.
>
> The big chickens stay in the cage an sometimes dey get hens wit dem, sometimes dey get mad an den dey jus push um away.

Another girl, looking at a picture of a fish skeleton, observed that it looked like us because it had four fins, like hands and feet, only the bones were skinny, not fat like ours. Another time she reported that her dog "listen what I say" because he did what she told him. A boy observed that a worm was "sneaking" out of a can held by a fisherman.

CHILDREN FROM EIGHT TO TWELVE

As noted earlier, an analysis similar to the foregoing has been carried out for older boys and to some extent for girls. To put these findings in developmental perspective, pertinent results of this analysis are presented below, even though full documentation cannot be included.

From eight to twelve years of age reflective knowledge of kinship develops, along with sentiments integral to it. Relations with age and sex peers are also affected by certain learning experiences that later produce increased affability and cooperativeness. Finally there is the expression of an intellectual curiosity about the world that leads eventually to a transformation of attitudes toward elders from secular respect and affection to something resembling awe. These developments will be briefly outlined here.

Kinship

Domestic roles, as noted earlier, are clearly perceived by the age of eight. Any child from eight years on can give an account of the division of labor in the household. By the age of twelve children are as competent supervisors of younger children at home as adults are—even boys, if they are the eldest. Children this age are fully qualified participants in the domestic world.

By the age of eight children have accumulated considerable knowledge of those relatives who do not reside with them. Peterson (1971:5) reports that twelve girls, aged eight to nine years, "knew 12 relatives at least and 42 at the most with an average of 25 names and relationships known." Cousins and siblings of parents are prominent in these lists: aunts and uncles were recalled by the frequency of contact with cousins (1971:3). Knowledge of mother's side of the family was somewhat but not markedly greater than that of father's side (1971:6). My data from a smaller number of interviews with boys are comparable. Mother's sister is the relative mentioned most often, next to grandparents. Cousins continue to be regarded as close. For example, a member of the audience will encourage a storyteller by calling jokingly, "C'mon cousin!" The prominence of cousins in the individual's experience is interesting, since it matches the importance of generation as a principle in kinship terminology.

Knowledge of kinship also becomes more self-conscious and objective. Thus, while girls of eight and nine interviewed by Peterson did not initially think of aunts and uncles as parents' brothers and sisters, older children did so readily. Similar objectivity is indicated by the following conversation (taken from notes) by two nine-year-olds:

Sharon: Caroline is my cousin on my father's side.
Caroline: My father is her father's cousin, so she my cousin.
Sharon: A cousin is a relative.
             [Taken from notes, not verbatim.]

Children of twelve also differentiate spouses of parents' siblings from the latter when describing aunts and uncles. Honorary or fictive relationships likewise come to be understood as distinct from actual kinship. Leilani, who had been confused earlier about becoming her cousin's sister, told me at the age of nine:

> She is not really my sister. She's my niece, but I respect her like a sister. . . . I respect anyone who treats me nice as a sister. I respect my mother's boy friend like a father. [Taken from notes, not verbatim.]

Affection and Respect

The sentiment of *aloha*—the cement of Polynesian social relations—is most evident from eight to twelve in relationships with parents and younger children, whether the latter are related or not. It is not so evident in relations with peers and with adolescents, at least among boys.

Toward parents boys feel both respect and affection. While I have fewer data for girls, the available data are consistent with the picture for boys. As Mamak (1970) has pointed out, some boys' accounts of their fathers at this age resemble hero worship. Some boys even report fond memories of fathers who are no longer present. Antagonistic attitudes toward fathers are expressed, if at all, only indirectly. For example, one movie that the boys liked involved a shark attacking a father who beat a boy. The boy had earlier befriended the shark. As a matter of fact, this happens to be a theme in Hawaiian folklore.

Children uniformly express affection and friendly concern for those who are more than a few years younger. Despite increasing responsibilities for their care, girls this age seek babies to play with, are proud of becoming aunts, and can always be engaged in serious conversation about caring for babies. Boys this age will pat strange toddlers affectionately, take them by the hand when they are in danger, and play with them. I have never observed a boy this age deliberately haze a much younger boy.

Boys' Relationships with Teenagers

By the age of eight, boys have not experienced protection as babies for several years. In traditional Hawaiian culture, by this age they would have gone to live in the men's house (Kamakau 1964:27). Now they are systematically although informally hazed by older boys, usually their brothers or cousins. This is done on a one-to-one basis on some occasion when the younger boy has shown anger or resentment. There are several far-reaching results of the hazing experience, I believe. Boys with more experience at being hazed appear to be slower to anger. By feeling anger and then suppressing it, the individual learns how to manage it as well as himself.

Hazing reflects the value placed upon toughness and masculine violence. When hazing a younger boy, a teenager will call him "punk," insinuating that he is too small and frightened to fight back. By not fighting back, of course, the younger boy appears to prove the older correct. It may be to counter the image of being a punk that boys begin to lift weights at this age and otherwise try to toughen themselves. They also continue to glorify fighting and engage in sports.

Relationships among Peers

Hazing by older boys also creates a strong sensitivity to assertiveness on the part of peers. Boys this age resent any sign of bossing, forcing, teasing, or claiming superiority by peers. They are at least as prone as younger boys to conflict about a wide variety of things, including the sharing of food and treats and any claim to knowledge. Their feelings about friends are definitely ambivalent. By the time he has reached mid-adolescence, however, the boy has become the typically affable, cooperative young man, ready to accept and help everyone, especially his friends.

This transformation is a consequence of at least three developments, I believe. One is learning not to be resentful when frustrated by older boys. A second is learning how to suggest and apply rules in a group. On one occasion a group of boys ten to eleven years old evolved over two days a set of rules for a group game played with a newly introduced toy: a wind-up time bomb. Rules specified how points were to be counted and turns taken, and they were followed. Eighteen months earlier the same boys could not finish a single inning of baseball because of disputes. Now they played baseball without disruption. A third derives from a prominent feature of Polynesian culture: humor, love of verbal play, and having a good time. By means of joking, which is ubiquitous, the boys appear gradually, collectively, and inadvertently to turn conflict into humor enjoyed by all. At eight years of age they cannot do this very well. By mid-adolescence they are masters of it.

Ways of relating to peers take so long to develop because interaction among peers outside the family in the early years is almost unstructured by adults or older children. Within the family children first learn to adapt to age-structured, hierarchical relationships. When they transfer the attitudes developed there to peers, only conflict and disagreement result. At least among boys, means for resolving this conflict emerge gradually and as a collective result of other culturally structured behavior.

Girls may undergo comparable development, but I was unable to investigate it in comparable detail since between eight and ten there is a growing segregation of boys and girls, except for romantic relationships. Perhaps for this reason my attempts to approach the girls as equals produced amused, silly, flirtatious, or avoidance behavior on their part—even by those who had been friendly with me for several years.

Intellectual Curiosity and Speculation

Boys this age often talk among themselves about the world around them, how things work, and how one can manipulate or control things. Of greatest significance for social structure is their interest in metaphysical (supernatural) forces. Fear appears to lie behind this interest: boys express fear of dying, the dead, dreams of sharks, spirits that leave their graves and walk in the night, cats that are really spirits, haunted caves, whistling at night, and many other things. They are acutely interested in the laws which, they presume, govern such dangers—why they occur, how to avoid them, and what to do should they be encountered. As boys work this out, by speculation and talk among themselves over several years, they arrive at a set of *kapu*s. When somewhat older, they learn that elders may control the powers responsible for such dangers. At this age, however, if they make any such association they do not express it.

TEENAGE BOYS

"Us guys," as they refer to themselves, claim that everyone in the community belongs to a single group (Kanana 1966; Mamak 1970). They attach great importance to recognizing, greeting, and including every peer in whatever activity is going on. According to them all are friends: "Awmos ev'yone in dis whow place is cousins." They are rigidly equalitarian and shun assertiveness of any kind among themselves, thus confirming claims made to Kanana and Mamak that no one was a leader.

The conflict and fighting so common among younger boys are almost totally lacking among the guys, although there is a code duello that is kept alive by a few boys who specialize in fighting. The place of conflict is taken by all kinds of verbal fun enjoyed purely for its own sake. Boys select friends because of an ability to joke and "talk smaht" (humorously) with one another.

At this age the guys are actively withdrawing from participation in the household. Chores are mainly something to get finished so you can be with your friends. School is likewise valued mainly for the opportunity it provides to be with friends. Staying home is boring.

In talk relatives are mentioned mostly in connection with girl friends and fights. Uncles, cousins, and brothers are rather romantically regarded as supporters in the occasional neighborhood brawls which are started by adults. Toward potential in-laws the guys feel respect and embarrassment. There is something like avoidance of them while the guys are going with the girls, and the guys joke about the size of a girl friend's father and brothers.

The earlier respect for parents persists. But there is now a further development in attitudes toward elders, including parents. Most boys appear to have learned by this age that persons, places, animals, and things harbor metaphysical forces that can harm a person if not properly treated, and they take keen interest in learning all they can about these forces. The attitudes involved in *mana* and *kapu* are salient and operational.[6] Even the few skeptics believe it is foolish to take chances. The guys know also that some of these forces are capable of assuming human form and that some older persons, including parents, can control certain of these forces. Because of this knowledge boys are uncomfortable in the presence of elders, in proportion to their age. There is no humor or criticism directed at parents or other old people in their absence. A joking remark about an old woman in a group conversation, for example, brought this retort from one boy: "No good tease old folks. Dangerous!"[7]

SUMMARY

The family experience described here is consistent with what we know of Polynesian kinship systems generally. Children see a lot of aunts, uncles, cousins, and grandparents and may be raised with some of the former as siblings. Relative age sharply differentiates experience with other children. Babies are most favored and indulged, older children direct younger ones. As they grow older, children acquire increased responsibilities and are rewarded with increased prestige. As a result of such experience age becomes an important principle for ordering relationships among siblings. A further result is a strong norm against acting above one's age. Order of birth among siblings is reinforced as a principle of social structure.

The sentiment of *aloha* develops first in interaction with parents, teenage siblings, and those younger than oneself. Young children and infants enjoy entertaining interaction with older members of the family. They develop a sense of participation by learning to do their chores as part of an interdependent system, and they come to internalize the values of working and contributing that govern the system. Such experience combined with dramatic parental punishment—threats fulfilled only in anger—leads to fundamental acceptance of parental authority and reliance upon it.

In interaction among peers outside the family, children transfer the attitudes learned in age-structured sibling relationships; but in the absence of age differences and parental authority, only disagreement and conflict result. Children of the same age are unable to resolve conflict among themselves short of insult or injury, although they are skillful at restoring hurt feelings—perhaps following models observed in the family. Ways of relating harmoniously to peers without conflict are among the latest relationships to develop, not being well established, at least in boys, until adolescence.

Beginning at about the age of eight, major developments affect relations among kin and peers. Domestic roles are already well on the way to establishment by then. While knowledge of individual relatives accumulates, kinship principles emerge to consciousness and come to differentiate categories such as affinal kin versus parents' siblings and real versus fictive relatives. But the most significant development is the result of curiosity about supernatural forces. As boys pursue their curiosity about such matters, they learn that elders know about and may even control such forces. This greatly heightens the respect held for older people, including parents.

Boys become affable and cooperative with peers in adolescence because of several developments: learning not to be resentful when frustrated by older boys in late childhood, learning to negotiate and apply rules in a group, and transforming potential disagreement and conflict into humor by means of verbal play. Skill at this develops throughout childhood and adolescence. By midadolescence verbal play is enjoyed for its own sake and provides one basis for selecting friends.

SYMBOLS USED FOR SOUNDS

ɛ	as in *bet*
æ	as in *bat*
ə	as in *but* (also written as unstressed final *a* in words like *fada*)
ʌ	halfway between ə and *ah*
ɔ	as in *bought*
ah	as in *father*
ö	as in German
ɜ́	higher than ə but less constricted than *r*
ŋ	as in *sing*
ᵍ	superscript indicates sound is partially realized or faint
'	sound is omitted in delivery (the symbol is not used in *fada* because *r* is never present in this word)
⌈	spoken simultaneously with other sounds so marked
⌃	rising and falling intonation
. . .	inaudible or uninterpretable
+	normal word juncture lacking

NOTES

Details of data collection are to be found in Boggs (1972) and Watson-Gegeo and Boggs (1977). Briefly, data from children aged four to seven were obtained from three sources. First were conversations between the author and individual children during class and recess and after school in a first- and second-grade class at Aina Pumehana school from 1966 to

1968 (Boggs 1972). Second were recordings made by three Honolulu mothers of their five-year-old children at home. The mothers were trained to record their children in natural situations in order to study the normal patterns of young children's speech. Third were recordings of spontaneous activity during play periods in the kindergarten operated during 1972-1973 by the Kamehameha Early Education Project (KEEP). The latter two sets of data were obtained under the auspices of KEEP, a research and development effort of the Kamehameha Schools devoted to improving methods of educating Hawaiian and part-Hawaiian children. Richard Day and Violet Mays collaborated in the collection of these two sets of data.

Data from children eight to twelve years old were obtained by conversations with the author similar to those with younger children; participant observation, particularly five two- or three-day camping expeditions; and systematic interviews conducted by Susan Peterson and Alex Mamak, then graduate students at the University of Hawaii.

Adolescent data were obtained entirely by adolescent interviewers, who were trained by the author with Neighborhood Youth Corps support to initiate and record group discussions about the local community and its needs. In pursuit of this goal the boys were encouraged to talk about anything of interest to them. They regularly turned the sessions into typical "talk story" sessions, although never neglecting their task.

I am deeply grateful to my colleagues Karen Ann Watson-Gegeo, who informed me of points raised in John Gumperz' seminar in natural conversation (held in the winter and spring, 1973, at the University of California-Berkeley) and the key idea of verbal routine; Richard Day and Violet Mays for assistance in generating crucial data; and Joan White-horn Boggs, who encouraged me to write such a study. Without their help this essay would not have been written. I am indebted to the University of Hawaii and the Kamehameha Schools for support during portions of the time during which the research was conducted. Certain of the data and ideas contained here were first presented in a paper delivered to the Hawaii Psychological Association in May 1968.

1.   For a comparison of the circumstances affecting performance in this group with those reported here see Watson-Gegeo and Boggs (1977).

2.   For data comparable to those presented in this essay, see Mead (1971:21, 41, 69).

3.   On *hiapo* see Kamakau (1964:26) and Pukui et al. (1972:51–53). On *hanau mua* see Pukui et al. (1972:126–128). On lineage seniority see Kamakau (1961) and Heighton (1971:chap. 2). Attitudes consistent with the institutions of *hiapo* and *hanau mua* are observed in some part-Hawaiian families today. There is no firm evidence, however, that more families held these attitudes in the past. While widespread, the attitudes are not universal. I am indebted to Violet Mays for pointing this out.

4.   Watson-Gegeo (in a personal communication) likewise reports an absence of recrimination for tattling in school.

5.   Traditionally, the resolution of conflict within the *'ohana* ("family") was accomplished by means of *ho'oponopono:* "setting to right" (Pukui et al. 1972:60–62). It involved the expression of love and *aloha* and mutual forgiveness, among other things. See Kamakau (1964:60) and Mays (1973) for other accounts of tradition and modern practices.

6.   For a few salient examples of relevant traditional beliefs and practices see Kamakau (1964:10, 29, 63–64).

7.   Many non-Hawaiians who interact extensively with Hawaiian adolescents may not be aware of this fear of Hawaiian adults, since so far as we know it is expressed only to peers. This is yet another example of the importance of context and relationship in determining the content of communication.

REFERENCES CITED

Boggs, Stephen T.
1972   The meaning of questions and narratives to Hawaiian children. In *Functions of language in the classroom,* ed. Courtney B. Cazden, Vera P. John, and Dell Hymes. New York: Teachers College Press.

Cicourel, Aaron V.
1970   The acquisition of social structures: towards a developmental sociology of language and meaning. In *Understanding everyday life: toward the reconstruction of sociological knowledge,* ed. Jack Douglas. Chicago: Aldine.

Firth, Raymond
1957   *We, the Tikopia: a sociological study of kinship in primitive Polynesia.* 2nd ed. (1st ed. 1936.) London: Allen and Unwin.

Gallimore, Ronald, Joan Whitehorn Boggs, and Cathie Jordan
1974   *Culture, behavior, and education: a study of Hawaiian-Americans.* New York: Russell Sage.

Gumperz, John and Eleanor Herasimchuk
1972   The conversational analysis of social learning: a study of classroom interaction. In *Sociolinguistics: current trends and prospects,* ed. Roger W. Shuy. Report on the Twenty-third Annual Round Table. Georgetown University Monographs on Languages and Linguistics, no. 25.

Heighton, Robert H., Jr.
1971   Hawaiian supernatural and natural strategies for goal attainment. Ph.D. dissertation, University of Hawaii.

Howard, Alan, Robert H. Heighton, Jr., Cathie E. Jordan, and Ronald G. Gallimore
1970   Traditional and modern adoption patterns in Hawaii. In *Adoption in Eastern Oceania,* ed. Vern Carroll. Honolulu: University of Hawaii Press.

Hymes, Dell H.
1962   The ethnography of speaking. In *Anthropology and human behavior.* Washington, D.C.: Anthropological Society of Washington.

Kamakau, Samuel M(anaiakalani)
1961   *Ruling chiefs of Hawaii.* Honolulu: Kamehameha Schools Press.
1964   *Ka po'e kahiko: the people of old.* Special Publication 51. Honolulu: Bishop Museum Press.

Kanana, Sharif
1966   Field notes.

Kyle, Leonard
1968   Paper presented to Anthropology 480(3), University of Hawaii, spring semester.

Mamak, Alex
1970   Field notes.

Mays, Michael P.
1973   *Coming together: a conflict resolution theme in Hawaiian-American families.* Report for the 299 Task Force. Honolulu: Governor's Office.

Mead, Margaret
1971   *Coming of age in Samoa.* New York: Morrow (original 1928).

Moerman, Michael and Harvey Sacks
1971   On the analysis of natural conversation. Paper read at the symposium in honor of Charles Friedrich Vogelin, annual meeting of the American Anthropological Association, New York City.

Peterson, Susan
1971   Group formation and intellectual development among preadolescent Hawaiian girls. Unpublished manuscript.

Pukui, Mary Kawena, E. W. Haertig, and Catherine A. Lee
1972   *Nani i ke kumu* (Look to the source). Vol. 1. Honolulu: Hui Hanai (Auxiliary of Queen Liliuokalani Children's Center).

Watson, Karen Ann
1972   The rhetoric of narrative structure: a sociolinguistic analysis of stories told by part-Hawaiian children. Ph.D. dissertation, University of Hawaii.
1975   Transferable communicative routines: strategies and group identity in two speech events. *Language in Society* 4(1):53–70.

Watson-Gegeo, Karen and Stephen T. Boggs
1977   From verbal play to talk story: the role of routines in speech events among Hawaiian children. In *Child discourse,* ed. Susan Ervin-Tripp and Claudia Mitchell-Kernan. New York: Academic Press.

The Chinese in New Guinea:
The Adaptation of an Immigrant Population

DAVID YEN-HO WU

The Chinese in New Guinea number fewer than three thousand, and they make up only about 0.1 percent of the total population of Papua New Guinea and about 8 percent of the total nonindigenous population.[1] They are thus very much a minority population, but in spite of this for eighty years the New Guinea Chinese have played a significant role in the social-economic history of the country.

Many of the Chinese live in urban centers rather than rural areas in most parts of Papua New Guinea and are now engaged in commercial activities. The Chinese appear to occupy a special place in the PNG social-economic structure; in fact one can describe the Chinese position in an ecological metaphor by saying that they occupy a rather specialized *niche*—the result of a special functional relationship they have had with other groups of people in the same environment (cf. Barth 1961; Hardesty 1972). Barth (1961:448) defines niche as "the place of a group in the total environment, its relations to resources and competitors." Since my discussion in this essay focuses on the social-economic environment rather than on the total ecological environment, I use the term *social niche*.

I shall begin by presenting a historical account of the New Guinea Chinese from the viewpoints of both the outsider and the Chinese to show how the Chinese have adjusted themselves to changes in their social-economic environment and how they have adapted to circumstances and infiltrated new social niches previously not occupied by Chinese. Underlying my discussion is the point that adaptation is a process necessary for the survival of any human group (cf. Cohen 1968). Following the historical account, I shall interpret the Chinese position in Papua New Guinea and the way they have achieved that position.

THE OUTSIDER'S VIEW

The non-Chinese view of the history of New Guinea Chinese is mainly a European view, for the available data from which this history may be reconstructed are obtained from either the official records of the European colonial administrations or the literature written by Europeans in Western languages. As Chinese traders have been active in Southeast Asia since the fifteenth century, it is possible that they reached coastal New Guinea and the Bismarck Archipelago at the same time as the earliest European contacts (Oliver 1961:104; Rowley 1965:56–57). Rowley maintains that some Chinese may have accompanied Malay bird-of-paradise hunters and visited the Sepik River valley long before the Germans claimed it; in any case, Chinese traders had apparently established contacts with the islands off Aitape before the German New Guinea Company was established there.

The arrival of large numbers of Chinese in New Guinea during the last century was closely related to economic development under the German colonial administration, which demanded cheap skilled labor unavailable from the indigenous population. Germany claimed New Guinea as her protectorate in 1884, and the German New Guinea Company was assigned sovereign rights until 1899. When the German New Guinea Company on Kaiser Wilhelmsland (now the New Guinea mainland) experimented with tobacco plantations from 1889 to 1901, hundreds of Chinese indentured laborers were brought in each year, first from Singapore and Sumatra and later from Hong Kong and China, to work as plantation laborers in the present-day Madang and Finschhafen areas. In 1892 there were 1,085 Chinese in the German protectorate (Report 1922:71).

Tropical diseases, hard work, and harsh treatment resulted in hundreds of deaths among the Chinese laborers. Most of these workers stayed only for the contracted period of two to five years, after which time they were repatriated. The arrival of the indentured Chinese laborers on the New Guinea mainland during this period should not, therefore, be considered to be the beginning of Chinese immigration to New Guinea. Only a small number of the laborers stayed after their contracts expired, and still fewer within this small group of laborers settled down in New Guinea and produced offspring. By 1906 there were only 151 Chinese remaining on Kaiser Wilhelmsland, 88 of whom were listed as laborers; the 1911 census for Chinese on Kaiser Wilhelmsland shows 82 individuals, but none of them were listed as laborers (Annual Report 1906, 1911).

Contrary to the general belief that the first Chinese were brought to New Guinea as coolies, a number of Chinese—artisans and traders—had been working for the Germans in the Bismarck Archipelago for some time before the German New Guinea Company experimented with the indentured labor system (Rowley 1958:73). Before Germany annexed New Guinea in 1884, Germans based in Samoa were active among the islands trading in copra and tortoise shell, and some Chinese may have sailed on their ships and helped with the trade.

One of the first was Ah Tam (whose real name was Lee Tam Tuck), who came to New Guinea in the late 1870s with the Hernsheim brothers (*Rabaul Times,* 31 July 1931). By the end of the century he had established himself as an independent shipbuilder and trader on Matupit Island of New Britain. It is said that in 1899 the local native people—the Tolai—began sailing west to acquire the valuable shells they used as a medium of exchange with both natives and Europeans, because they were able to obtain the bigger boats built by Ah Tam (Salisbury 1970:35). At that time there were some thirty Chinese living in the Bismarck Archipelago (Salisbury 1970:33), working for the German firms and the missions as carpenters, housekeepers, cooks, copra buyers, and trading agents. How these people arrived is not recorded, but according to my interviews with Chinese informants, most of the early Chinese came as free migrants from Singapore. This migration might have been related to the fact that since 1894 regular shipping services had been opened between Europe and New Britain via Singapore (Salisbury 1970:32). Chinese newcomers usually worked for some time in Ah Tam's shipyard or store before they were hired by the Germans or became independent traders.

A census of the Chinese population in the Bismarck Archipelago just before 1903 shows that the Chinese were either artisans or traders by occupation. As traders they sailed to the islands and New Guinea coastal villages, either by themselves or accompanied by the Germans, to exchange trade goods for copra with the natives. Occasionally they also recruited natives to work for the Germans. Native villagers of the inland Sepik valley (in the present Kombio census division) recall that their first contact with outsiders was with Chinese who around 1900 brought steel axes, salt, and *lap lap* (waist cloths) to the villages, and people still remember the names—Ah Long and Kasing—of the Chinese pioneers (B. Allen: personal communication). As Rowley (1958:74) points out, the Chinese risked their lives traveling to areas outside European influence, and a number of Chinese were in fact murdered by natives (Schnee 1904:81–85). Some Chinese, however, married native women from the

Sepik area, New Ireland, New Britain, and the Solomon Islands; the distance between these places reveals how extensively they traveled.

The Chinese traders apparently encouraged coconut production by the native people, especially in the New Britain area. Stimulated by the desire to obtain European trade goods, native copra production in the Bismarck Archipelago continued to increase at the turn of the twentieth century, and during the first decade of this century native copra became the major export (Salisbury 1970:33–37).

According to S. G. Firth's account (1973:188–195), large-scale immigration of free Chinese to New Guinea was initiated and promoted by the German colonial administration in New Guinea. Since 1901 Governor Albert Hahl became a vigorous champion of free immigration of skilled Chinese artisans and agriculturists to New Guinea to practice their trades and to open and cultivate land. Individual Germans also endorsed Hahl's view, though with reservations. As Schnee wrote (1904:378–379):

> The importation of foreign, coloured labourers will be unavoidable for the progressive development of the Bismarck Archipelago, because the prevailing economic development of the Bismarck Archipelago depends mainly on the trade with the natives and the coconut plantations . . . ; in both cases only a limited further development is possible [*under the present situation*]. . . . The Chinese are without doubt very suitable labourers and as such they are in general superior to the Malays. However, there are several objections against the importation of Chinese labourers. The Chinese always aim at becoming independent by trading and hence may compete with the Europeans in business. [my italics]

Despite such arguments, Chinese immigration to New Britain began in 1903 and laid the foundation for the later Chinese community, for when the Germans decided to construct a new wharf at Simpson Harbor, they needed Chinese craftsmen to do the work. The Chinese were brought in from Singapore. During the year 1903, the Chinese population in the Bismarck Archipelago increased to over one hundred, a result of "the influx of free Chinese carpenters" (Annual Report 1903:125). The Annual Report (1904:199) states: "Trade, plantation and sawmills in the Bismarck Archipelago are carried on by a personnel of 127 Europeans, 75 Chinese, and 3,865 [native] laborers." The increase in the Chinese population until the war broke out in 1914 is revealed by the annual census figures; however, the annual increase was more a matter of arrivals outnumbering a large number of departures than a steady increase of a settled community (Rowley 1958:76). The floating nature of the Chinese population is demonstrated by the arrival of 260 Chinese from Hong Kong to Rabaul in 1910 and the departure of 174 Chinese from Rabaul in the same year.

Biskup (1970:96) attributes the increase in Chinese immigration to the opening of regular new shipping services between New Guinea and Hong Kong by Norddeutscher Lloyd. Also responsible was the change in port of call of the company's liner from Herbertshöhe (now Kokopo), the German protectorate capital, to its new wharf at Simpsonhafen, which was soon renamed Rabaul. In 1910 Rabaul became the new capital of the German protectorate. Rabaul town was built largely by Chinese. According to German records, Chinese tradesmen were brought in to serve the needs of government and business by Ah Tam for a capitation fee, and Ah Tam himself was granted a thirty-year lease of seventeen acres of land at Rabaul in April 1907 at a nominal rent of a hundred marks per year. Ah Tam's lease land developed into a Chinatown where most of the Chinese lived and to which area Chinese shops in Rabaul were confined, although Asians other than Chinese also became tenants. According to my interviews with old Chinese informants, Ah Tam should not be credited with the recruitment of Chinese laborers and craftsmen from China during the period; this I explain below. Whatever the case, one thing is certain: no Chinese were brought in as indentured laborers, although some became contract artisans.

The Annual Report for 1909 to 1910 indicates the extension of Chinatown in Rabaul and makes special mention of the establishment in town of small Chinese businesses such as tailoring and laundries, despite the fact that the total Chinese population in the Bismarck Archipelago decreased a little that year. It is emphasized in the Annual Report for the next year that mechanical businesses were "entirely in the hands of the Chinese" (1911–1912:440). Most of the Chinese were "employed as mechanics, but many *were* stokers and sailors and some *were* stewards on the ships engaged in the coast traffic. An appreciable number *were* cooks and stewards. There *were* still no Chinese or Malays employed as plantation labourers" (Annual Report 1910–1911:429). The same report for the next year (1911–1912:488) notes that: "The most important section of the non-indigenous coloured population, both in number and economic importance, are the Chinese. There are 926 in the whole Protectorate. Of these 720 are in the Old Protectorate, the remainder are in the two phosphate districts, Nauru and Angaur."[2] The 200 Chinese on Nauru worked as miners, while the 720 Chinese in New Guinea were employed as mechanics, builders, planters, traders, and cooks. "The Chinese now are the only separate traders. Most of these Chinese are not independent traders, but are agents for whites. Their activities are mainly devoted to purchasing copra" (ibid.:440). Although the Chinese population in New Guinea continued to fluctuate, many of them had already settled down as there were "quite a number of Chinese women and children" (ibid.):

Statistics on the occupational distribution for the years 1903 to 1914 (see D. Wu 1974) suggest that as the Chinese population in New Guinea (especially in the Rabaul area) increased, more Chinese had to take up lower-paid manual jobs—the wharf coolie is an example. The proportion of people working as mechanics and carpenters remained roughly the same, while the percentage of people with higher-income jobs such as trading decreased through the years. Thus the speculations of many writers (Biskup 1970:100; Lyng 1919:69; Rowley 1958:77–83; Salisbury 1970:40) on the success of the Chinese in commercial business at the end of the German period actually applied to only a very small portion of the Chinese population.

The Australian military occupation of New Guinea from 1914 to 1921 had the effect of stabilizing the Chinese community in Rabaul, for the traffic between China and New Guinea was stopped (Rowley 1958:77). During this period there were about 1,400 Chinese in New Guinea, about 1,000 of them living in and around Rabaul (Lyng 1919:125). James Lyng, a lieutenant in the army, described the Rabaul Chinatown:

> It is as if a little East-Asiatic township, by some magic power, had been transplanted to New Britain. . . . There are half-a-dozen stores there, several restaurants, tailors, laundries, and bootmakers; butchers, bakers, carpenters, mechanics, etc. . . . Although most of the shops neither impress by size nor cleanliness, but are just what one would expect in a Chinese quarter, there is plenty of excuse for everybody to go there. . . . Over and above all, Chinatown is Rabaul's busy, unruly corner—where people rise early—are always on the move—and go to bed late. While after sunset the European quarter becomes quiet, and the streets look empty and desolate, life in Chinatown moves on—intense—rapid—and wicked. [1919:126–129]

While most Chinese artisans and traders who were essential to the economy carried on their usual work, a number of them had become independent from the European firms and opened their own importing and retailing businesses. In addition, more of them both in number and proportion joined the ventures of the small traders. Chinese success in business caused such alarm among the newly arrived Australians that the administrator Pethebridge took measures to stop Chinese from competing in business with the Europeans (including the Germans, who were supposed to be the enemies). Before outlining the restrictions placed upon the Chinese, I would like to present an account of the kind of "trading" in which they were engaged and which had aroused European jealousy. Again Lyng wrote (1919:57):

> The small European trader, during the latter years, has practically been squeezed out of existence by John Chinaman. One needs only to drive a few miles out of Rabaul, and he will, in less than an hour, pass a dozen Chinese

traders, living mostly in miserable huts put up by themselves, but always with some trays of copra drying in the sun, and generally surrounded by an interested group of natives. His stock of Kanaka merchandise occupies but a couple of shelves, yet he makes money. The native will not go two miles to a white trader when he can sell his coconuts to a Chinaman living but a stone's throw off, and, besides, may pay him a trifle better.

Pethebridge issued a number of orders in 1917 designed not to protect the native producers but to protect the European commercial interests, the majority of which were actually in the hands of the Germans (cf. Rowley 1958:82–83; Salisbury 1970:40–41). The orders on "Trading in Coconuts or Copra in the Gazelle Peninsula," introduced in February and April, fixed the prices to be paid to natives in terms of both trade goods and cash for copra (so that the small Chinese traders could not pay the natives more than the Europeans). In March the "Control of Chinese Trade Order" was introduced, forbidding the Chinese to engage in either the wholesale or importing trades. This order caused such an outcry from those Australian firms in Sydney which supplied the Chinese in Rabaul that it was soon withdrawn. The other regulation which most affected the Chinese concerned the licensing of new trade stations: no new license could be issued within two miles of an existing station. As Salisbury points out (1970:41), this regulation, effective in the Kokopo area, meant that Chinese were kept out of business and the Tolais could sell their copra only to European stations for a fixed price against the rising world market price in copra.

The only change in favor of the Chinese and their position in New Guinea was in their jurisdictional status, previously similar to that of natives. In November 1915 the military administration ordered that Chinese, along with other nonindigenous colored races, be tried in a court separate from that for the natives, and in February 1916 the "Status and Jurisdiction Ordinance" granted the Chinese and other Asians "the status of, and to be subjected to the same jurisdiction as, the white inhabitants of the Territory" (Report 1922:15).

In April 1920, as the first step in prohibiting Chinese immigration, all nonindigenous persons not of European origin over the age of fifteen were required to register their names with the district officer. They were registered as aliens. Although no ordinance was introduced on the matter of Chinese immigration, no newcomer of Chinese descent has been admitted since New Guinea became an Australian mandate in 1921.

Although the Chinese received jurisdictional status equal to that of the Europeans, the treatment they received in practice was nonetheless unchanged. Rowley's statement on the social status of the Chinese in New Guinea during the military occupation can be applied to practices found during the interwar period and even during the 1950s. He states: "The Chinese is not in fact encouraged by the Europeans to think of himself as a citizen of a wider country than that of Chinatown" (1958:79). Lyng also points out (1919:70) that "from a social aspect, the line of demarcation between the different races is naturally far sharper drawn. When the day's work is done each race retires into its own distinct world, the Asiatics having no time for the Kanakas—the Europeans having time for neither."

Such a picture of social segregation among people of different racial origins was still very evident in New Guinea during my visit there in 1971. It is apparent that social and cultural pluralism were encouraged by the Europeans as in European colonies elsewhere: that is, each race should have its own social standing, should live in its own quarter, and should do the line of work suitable to its rank—even the dead should be rested in distinct cemeteries. Moreover, the economic pluralism described by Lyng (1919:69) in German New Guinea actually persisted up until the self-government of Papua New Guinea:

> The functions of the different races engaged in developing late German New Guinea apparently follow certain main lines. The Europeans are the rulers, the teachers, the planters, and the wholesale vendors; the Asiatics are the artisans and the retail vendors; and the Kanakas primitive agriculturists, from whose midst are drawn the lowly labourer, the plantation hand, domestic servant, and cheap sailor.

Since all the official records of Rabaul were destroyed during World War II, I had access only to fragments of information about the Chinese community during the interwar period from such published literature as the *Rabaul Times* and the *Pacific Islands Monthly*. The Chinese position can best be described in Rowley's words (1958:80): "a minority caught between the Europeans and the primitive." Because of their status as Asians as well as aliens, a doubly unwelcome status, they were restricted in their economic activities. They were not allowed to get leasehold land (not to mention freehold land). Nor were they permitted to engage in certain lines of industry or to live in or open stores in certain locations (among them, white residential areas). Whatever they did they would likely draw either criticism or blame, which was often expressed by Europeans in the local newspaper (see the *Rabaul Times,* 1925 to 1942).

Chinese craftsmen and small traders became indispensable for both the Europeans and the natives, however. In addition to a large number of individual contractors, some of the Chinese organized a building company—the Bay Loo Company—hired a European as their manager, and successfully tendered many important construction projects for the administration and private firms in the territory. A shipbuilding company was also established by the Chinese to build boats and do the maintenance and repair work which became essential to the New Guinea islands.

In serving the needs of both communities, the Chinese found a position for themselves in the economic symbiosis between the Europeans who were planners and managers and the natives who were agricultural producers. The part played by the Chinese in the commercial life of New Guinea was that of the so-called trade-store business—"small and not very impressive establishments in all important native villages under European control, where they sell to the natives their very simple requirements and receive in exchange either the products of native industry such as copra, shell, etc., or the wages earned by native labourers" (Robson 1954:29). The Chinese trade stores increased in number between the world wars. In the native markets, however, the symbiotic relationship between the Chinese and the natives could be found in an arrangement in which the Chinese became customers and the natives sellers.

Salisbury (1970:47) maintains that while the New Guinea administration had claimed credit for the development of native markets in Rabaul and Kokopo since the 1920s, this development was actually the result of the demand from the expanding Chinese community for fresh vegetables, fruit, eggs, fish, and fowl. As late as 1961, Salisbury found that Europeans never bought eggs at the native markets and imported canned green beans were the main staple vegetable in European homes. What Salisbury did not mention was that in the markets more than half the produce was of Chinese origin, introduced by Chinese pioneer gardeners.[3] In 1932, for example, when the Kerevat agricultural station—an institution designed to encourage the natives to experiment in cash crop production—produced peanuts for the first time, it was again the local Chinese who bought them (Salisbury 1970:49–50).

During the period 1942 to 1945, when Papua New Guinea was under Japanese occupation, the Chinese lost all their property and were used by the Japanese as forced laborers. When the Chinese returned to Rabaul after the war, they immediately joined in the work of reconstruction. Many of them were hired as carpenters, mechanics, drivers, and clerks, working mainly in Rabaul but also in other places in New Guinea.

The first edition of the *Handbook of Papua and New Guinea* reveals that in 1945 over half the adult Chinese population in Rabaul were listed as artisans and about a quarter had started commercial businesses. It is pointed out in the handbook (1945:29) that "the Chinese now provide practically all the artisan service required in the Trust Territory." Since the early 1950s, to the amazement of European residents, the New Guinea Chinese have shown great economic strength outside artisan occupations. They offered to buy European-owned plantations which had been lying idle since the Japanese invasion, while many European planters were reluctant to reinvest in such plantations because of the uncertain future of the copra industry in New Guinea (see Robson 1954:29).

An article in the *Pacific Islands Monthly* (October 1953:14) described the situation of the postwar Chinese: "They own *huge* capital. As a result, they are now reaching out constantly after properties developed by Europeans, and their readiness to pay high prices, in prompt cash, when chances have occurred in very recent years, has caused perturbation among Europeans."

So puzzled were the Europeans about the source of Chinese wealth that a rumor spread which charged the Chinese with receiving "refugee" money from Red China. This event shows the lack of communication between the European and the Chinese communities up to the 1950s. For years the Europeans had been apathetic toward the Chinese population, whose trade stores were unimpressive and whose role as artisans was considered insignificant. But when a handful of Chinese had accumulated enough wealth to compete with European entrepreneurs, it was taken as a sign of the sudden affluence of the entire Chinese population. In fact, the Chinese had been awarded war-damage compensation for properties destroyed during World War II. Apart from this, the small proportion of the Chinese population engaged in commerce immediately after the war made good profits. In any case, the postwar period was a turning point for the Chinese community in New Guinea: they changed from a craftsman-dominated to a merchant-dominated group.

Three factors account for postwar prosperity in the economic development of New Guinea, especially in the Gazelle Peninsula where the Chinese population was concentrated: the distribution of the war damage compensation fund in New Guinea; the increase of Australian subsidies to the New Guinea administration; and the rise of the world market price for copra. Over two and a half million pounds in compensation funds were awarded to the natives of the Gazelle Peninsula (Salisbury 1970:55). The Tolai people alone were said to have collected more than half a million pounds (Epstein 1970:48). This amount of ready cash, along with the rising returns from copra production during the 1950s, created a remarkable demand for commercial goods. While the Europeans were not prepared to meet the market demand, the indigenous Niuginians were not equipped to engage in commerce; this therefore left an empty niche to be filled. It explains why in 1954 more than half the adult Chinese population in Rabaul were artisans engaged in postwar reconstruction. And yet within a decade less than 20 percent had remained so: many former artisans have gone into the trade-store business. Although the proportion of Chinese engaged in commerce remained roughly the same from 1954 to 1966, the actual number of stores in the Rabaul area increased, and many Chinese stores were opened in other parts of New Guinea as well as in Papua.

In the 1950s the Rabaul Chinese began a large-scale migration to Lae, Madang, Wewak, and elsewhere, seeking jobs and opportunities for commercial enterprises. This was so especially in 1958, when the Chinese were granted the right to take up Australian citizenship: they began for the first time in their history to migrate to Port Moresby, where retail businesses were run by a handful of European firms. In the later half of the 1960s, Chinese migration and business expansion reached the New Guinea highlands. This move followed the introduction of coffee—a new cash crop—to the highlands and the construction of the highlands highway.

Because of growing diversification of the demand for Western goods by the indigenous population, the entry of many sophisticated indigenous people into the trade-store enterprise (see Strathern 1972), and an increase in the European population in the territory, more and more of the Chinese are transforming their trade stores into bigger general and wholesale stores throughout Papua New Guinea. This trend continued until the eve of Papua New Guinea independence.

THE NEW GUINEA CHINESE VIEW

Both formal interviews and long-term participation in the Chinese community of Papua and New Guinea have given me a basis from which to write a history of the New Guinea Chinese from their own point of view. Although a New Guinea Chinese would reconstruct history in accordance with the same time sequence used by others, he inevitably sees things differently. Events which strike an outsider as significant may be obscure to him, while events which an outsider ignores may become very important in the eyes of a Chinese. Here I simply wish to bring up those events that the New Guinea Chinese themselves consider significant. The organization of these events in a time sequence is largely mine.

Chinese immigration to New Guinea was not a planned or organized process: all migrants came as individuals without any assistance from either official or private organizations. However, traditional social organizations in China—family, clan, and lineage—and such territorial groups as neighborhood or village were used as units for recruiting potential emigrants at home. Migration from China to New Guinea, in each case a private arrangement, has been kept well within the structure of the traditional social organization.

Long before the influx of Chinese migrants began in 1903, a number of Chinese pioneers in the Bismarck Archipelago, such as the well-known "Uncle Ah Tam," the Chan brothers, the Chow brothers, and Seeto Dun-Yee, had already worked in Singapore for some years before coming to New Guinea and established themselves as trustworthy employees of German firms, the missions, and the German administration. Uncle Ah Tam was a Hakka originally from Huiyang of Kwong-tung province, while all the others came from the See Yap (Ssu Yi) area, either from Taishan (the Chans and the Chows) or Kaiping (the Seetos). There were also a few Hainanese among the early arrivals, known in local legend as sailors and island traders, most of whom married native women. None of the early pioneers were mentioned as being from Ng Yun (Wu Kwan)— five districts near Canton City—so we may assume that these people were later arrivals.

Once they were established, when more job opportunities came up the pioneers sent messages home asking their brothers or cousins to join them in New Guinea. When the construction of Rabaul began, recruitment through such invitations extended to lineage members and fellow villagers at home. By the time news spread of the "new golden mountain in the South Seas (some said Germany)" where Chinese were welcome, even outsiders who received the right information made their way to New Guinea.

When the newcomers arrived, the established pioneers became patrons for them, acting as leaders as well as protectors; they found jobs for them and sometimes provided them with accommodation. Under such a process of recruitment a large number of Cantonese from Taishan, Kaiping, and Huiyang arrived in German New Guinea. The Seetos, the Changs, and the Choes are still the largest surname groups in the New Guinea Chinese community.

One of the most important figures among the Chinese during the German period was Uncle Ah Tam, who developed his own business empire in Rabaul, an empire which around 1910 included a wholesale and retail store, two shipyards, a hotel, several plantations on New Ireland, a gambling den, a brothel, and an opium house. An illiterate himself, he not only became the landlord for everybody living in Chinatown but many of the newcomers had to seek employment in his shipyards and stores and received unreasonably low pay. Once the employees became acquainted with the new environment and found better jobs they would leave him, and so there were always jobs available for the newcomers at his places of business.

To illustrate both the way a new migrant gets started and his adjustment to new circumstances, I offer here an autobiographical sketch of a

Chinese migrant. It is typical of many first-generation migrants I have interviewed in the field.

> I was a first-year carpenter's apprentice in Taishan before I came to New Guinea in 1910, when I was sixteen years old. As I had been an orphan since I was a boy, I had worked as a cattle watcher, a woodcutter, and a servant. One of our lineage uncles who returned to the village from overseas told me that people were paying ten silver dollars [ten German marks] a month to a carpenter's apprentice in Ah-Pau [Rabaul], a place in Germany, and asked me whether I would be interested in going there. Since as an apprentice at home I received no wage except free board for three years, I was certainly tempted to go to Germany. One of my married sisters paid the fare for me, which cost thirty dollars [thirty marks]. We had about seventy fellow Chinese passengers on the same boat bound for New Guinea.
>
> When I arrived in Ah-Pau, I was hired as a shipwright's apprentice at Uncle Ah Tam's place, where about a hundred Chinese craftsmen were working in two shipyards. I worked for three years without receiving the promised wage, although, like many other workers, I got instead free board and clothing. I then left the shipyard and became a carpenter's apprentice for a lineage brother of mine. Soon, because the war [1914] broke out, I was discharged. The lineage uncle who had recruited me at home invited me to stay in his plantation in New Ireland. For the next three years I did all kinds of jobs in the bush: a sawyer, a woodcutter, a gardener, a fisherman, and so on. I salted fish and sold them to my lineage uncle, who often visited Rabaul and who in turn sold the salt fish to Chinese there. Another lineage uncle then acquired a plantation and hired me as the manager, in charge of some twenty native laborers.
>
> In 1921, having saved up some money, I made my first visit home and my sister acquired a wife for me. I returned to New Guinea alone, but until 1934 I visited home twice more. During that period, I worked sometimes as a carpenter for other Chinese contractors and sometimes as a contractor myself, hiring other Chinese to work for me. At one stage, I also made furniture for sale. Because the *wong-ka* [royal family, which means the government] would not allow us to bring our wives to New Guinea, I married a second wife in Rabaul in 1935. [She is a part-native.] When the *wong-ka* started on the construction of army camps in Lae [in the late 1930s], I was recruited to build houses for the soldiers. When the Japanese arrived we were still working at the army camp.
>
> We fled to the mountains during the war, growing our own crops and vegetables. The Japanese did not harm us, for they occasionally came to exchange canned food for our vegetables. After the war, I continued to work as a carpenter for some years, before I opened my own trade store.

This autobiographical account clearly demonstrates the versatility of the migrants.

Turning to the Chinese population as a whole, I found that the emergence of some of the quasi groups and later the voluntary associations was interesting. During the German period the Chinese had not established any association or community-wide organizations; people relied on their kin, fellow villagers, and people who spoke the same dialect for mutual assistance and cooperation. Evidence for such a generalization is seen in the division of labor in the early years along the lines of speech groups or the migrants' home location. Generally speaking the Hainanese were the sailors, the See Yap people the carpenters, the Hakka the cooks, and the Ng Yun people the mechanics.

During the Australian military occupation the appearance of voluntary associations was gradual in the Chinese community in New Guinea, whereas by the early years of the Australian mandate, despite the small size of the Chinese population, a large number of voluntary associations of various natures had been organized, all with headquarters in Rabaul. The associations functioned more or less like clubs for group congregation, providing the members with company, comfort, recreation, and a place to talk.

At least four types of association can be delineated according to the nature of the association and criteria for recruiting members: the first is the clan association; the second is the locality (or hometown) association; the third is the dialect association; and the fourth is the guild. Most of them are known to Chinese as the Hui Kwan. Two clan associations were formed by people belonging to the Seeto surname and the Chow surname. The Seeto clan association—Kau Lun Tong—still exists in Rabaul today. People who came from See Yap (the Four Districts) organized four different locality associations, and the people of Ng Yun (the Five Districts) formed altogether another association. The Hakka-speaking people formed their own Hui Kwan, the association of Chung Yi Ho (loyalty, righteousness, and peacefulness), which survives today. There were four guilds, organized by seamen, cooks, and two groups of carpenters. The carpenters split into two groups, the pioneers and the later arrivals plus those born locally. During the 1930s the younger group established the Bay Loo Building Company.

The associations did not become involved in political activities within the Chinese community, for they might otherwise have created great factionalism among the Chinese. In 1922 the Kuo Min Tang or Chinese Nationalist Party was officially established, and through this organization the Chinese as a whole expressed its group solidarity and identity. Kuo Min Tang members, along with Chinese schoolteachers, promoted Chinese nationalism and Chinese culture. Through the 1930s about one-fifth of the total Chinese population in New Guinea joined the party, and three branch offices were set up at Kokopo, Kavieng, and Madang. Throughout the years of the mandate until the 1950s, the leaders of the party together with a number of wealthy Chinese merchants became the representatives of the Chinese population; through them, communication between the Chinese population and the administration of the Australian government was facilitated.

Another event which improved the Chinese population's position in the New Guinea social environment was the conversion of many people to Christianity, since the change of status from pagan to Christian served as a sign of conformity to the European way of life and hence helped to reduce, at least in some degree, the hostility of Europeans. Chan Kun, also known as Alois Akun, was the first Chinese student educated by the Vunapope Catholic Mission, and in 1902 he became the first Chinese Catholic "in this part of the world" (Adela 1971:110). Akun's conversion was followed by that of one of the Chow brothers, and then by Akun's own brothers. Like the process of Chinese migration to New Guinea, as members were recruited one by one within the family and lineage structure, so the conversion to Christianity was also through the network of kinship. Thus the Chans and Chows, up to the present at least, have been leading members among the Chinese Catholics of New Guinea. Among the second-generation Chinese Catholics in Rabaul, four priests and eight nuns have been produced.

The Methodist Mission on the Gazelle Peninsula also converted a portion of the Chinese in Rabaul, though fewer in number than did the Catholics. Each mission since the early 1920s has sponsored a Chinese school in Rabaul with funds raised by the Chinese themselves. By offering the Chinese essential education not provided by the administration, the schools substantially increased the chance of the Chinese population's achieving upward social mobility. In addition the missions, particularly the powerful Catholic Mission, acted as patrons and protectors to the Chinese when they suffered from discrimination and from restrictions imposed by the ruling Europeans. The Chinese obtained jobs and construction contracts from the missions, and sometimes they acquired residential as well as agricultural lease land from the missions, which was rather against the wishes of the administration.

On the other hand, the two sects themselves have created hostility between their Chinese adherents. Social demarcation within the Chinese population, shown in social interaction, was noticeable in the late 1930s and during the postwar decade. According to some of the Chinese engaging in group migration from Rabaul to Lae during the 1950s, religious hostility was unbearable and at the same time the Catholic Chinese had seized the better economic opportunities such as stores and business land in town.

From an outsider's point of view, the change in legal status of the Chinese might have been thought to be of great concern to the people themselves. Yet the Chinese in general were insensitive to the manner in which the colonial government was run and the way the colonial law affected them. Although many complained about the unfair restrictions from which they had suffered, they could never explain clearly in legal terms what the law was like. As one old Chinese informant told me: "We had a very hard time in the old days. The Europeans would not allow us to do this or that. When we were poor they blamed us, but when we became rich they blamed us too. If we wanted to open a store in a certain place, we had to pay a European and use his name to get the license." Apparently this old man is referring to an illegal procedure in which a Chinese pays a European to play the "dummy" and become nominal owner of a store. This practice is acceptable to ordinary Chinese, the majority of whom have had little education in Western law. Naturalization is another case: although the Chinese admit the advantages of being able to obtain Australian citizenship, few of them, including the elite Chinese, can explain how this law came to be passed in 1957. Nor can they explain why the government suddenly changed its attitude and treatment of the Chinese. The Chinese themselves never dreamed of fighting for this right and did not even send a petition to the government.

Despite the restrictions enumerated here, Chinese commercial enterprises increased in number during the 1930s. According to reliable informants, there were not less than sixty Chinese commercial enterprises in Rabaul and Kokopo. They included about forty-five trade stores (eight of which were importing and wholesale businesses), two hotels, four restaurants, six tailor shops, two laundries, two bakeries, one construction company, and a few taxi and hire-car businesses. In addition to the early established Chinese enterprises in Kavieng and Namatanai on New Ireland, a number of Chinese had established stores on the New Guinea mainland in Madang, Wau, Solomao, and elsewhere. Most of these stores are small-scale enterprises with capital of only a few hundred pounds.

The Chinese single out three factors which they feel are associated with the boom of Chinese commerce: first, the growth of economic strength and purchasing power among the natives; second, the lack of initiative of European merchants in catering for native customers—Chinese businesses served both the natives and the Europeans, as well as Chinese themselves. Third and most crucial to the Chinese success in commerce was their establishing of stable ties with exporters in Hong Kong and Sydney, so that they became completely independent of the European wholesale firms in New Guinea. Through their Hong Kong agents, New Guinea Chinese businessmen were able to import a large variety of goods cheaper in price, and this enabled them to compete successfully with big European companies. After World War II and since the mid-1950s, prewar Chinese merchants reestablished business ties with their Hong Kong agents.

During my fieldwork in 1971 and 1972 I studied the commercial enterprises run by New Guinea Chinese. In Rabaul alone I counted about 110 small-scale trade stores and about a dozen general stores which also carry wholesale goods, two soft drink factories, three bakeries, two shipbuilding companies, one construction company, six transporting and shipping companies, and three garages. Many of the trade stores were owned by new entrepreneurs who had taken over when Chinese businessmen moved away from Rabaul. In Port Moresby, where Chinese have been allowed to settle since the 1960s, I counted about a hundred stores of various sizes. In addition to these figures, there were another 150 stores distributed elsewhere in Papua and New Guinea (see Figure 1).

CONCLUDING REMARKS

Having provided a brief history of the Chinese in New Guinea, I now wish to discuss early Chinese migration and the adaptability of the Chinese population.

Students of overseas Chinese usually cite "economic pressure"—land shortage, overpopulation, economic depression (see Skinner 1957)—as the main reason for Chinese migration overseas. As S. Y. Wu (1954:2-3) noticed, the American Chinese come predominantly from Kwong-tung province, with more than half the total American Chinese population coming from the See Yap area, especially Taishan. Wu gives as evidence of the food shortage in Taishan the quoted annual rice production, which apparently fell two-thirds short of the quantity required to support the population. Thus more people from this area than any other region in China have had to seek a living elsewhere. Since the New Guinea Chinese are predominantly from See Yap, Wu's assertion is also relevant to the Chinese migration to New Guinea. According to my interviews, all the first-generation Chinese immigrants admit that they came from very poor families and could hardly make a living at home.

The adaptability of the Chinese to conditions in New Guinea can be analyzed from an individual as well as from a group point of view. As individuals, when they had arrived in New Guinea the newcomers were willing to take up almost any job and often through a process of gradual adjustment were able to acquire better positions. Each individual had to rely on himself, his skill, and his ability to compete with others. Those who had relatives to turn to had a special advantage. Those who were adaptable to the environment—physical and social—and could adjust themselves quickly—by acquiring a variety of skills useful in various situations, learning the local language, and building good relations with

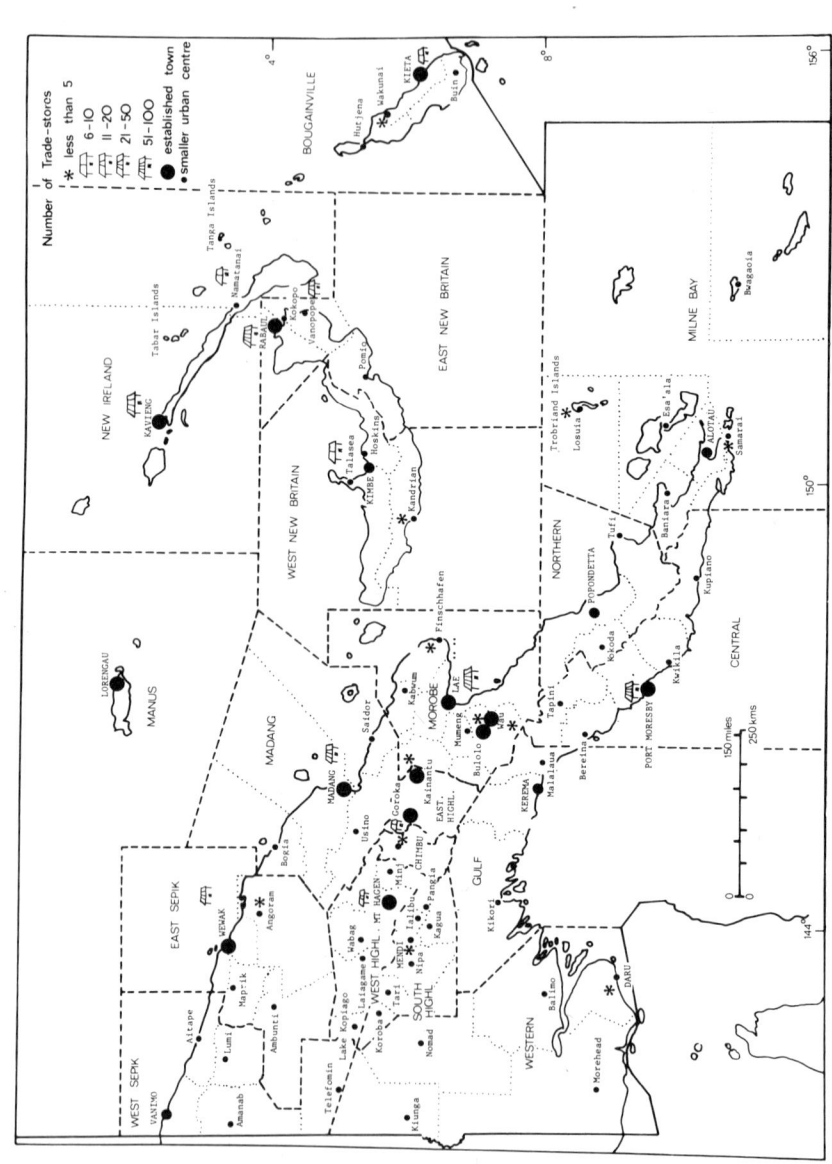

FIGURE 1. Distribution of Chinese Stores, 1971–1972

the natives and the Europeans who held the key to opportunities—were able to obtain better jobs. Otherwise an individual would have to turn to menial work, poorly paid and arduous, or might even have to leave New Guinea. As one informant put it: "Some Chinese arrived hoping to make a fortune, but they had to turn to work on the wharves like horses and cattle."[4]

The ability to take up any opportunities that appeared, and the frequent changing of jobs seen in the autobiographical account of a migrant, indicate the adaptability of the Chinese migrants and show how they have managed to adjust to new circumstances. The lives of the New Guinea-born Chinese also show such characteristics, as the personal histories of many middle-aged Chinese demonstrate. A Chinese man in his early fifties, for instance, had at various times worked as a carpenter, a plantation manager, a sailor, a shop clerk, a shipwright, a bar attendant, and a Chinese teacher; he is now a storekeeper, a ship's master, and a small plantation owner. This man is also a licensed medical assistant.

The way in which voluntary associations in Rabaul grew up and flourished demonstrates the way the Chinese migrants have used organized groups as a means of adapting to a foreign environment. Voluntary associations are commonly found in migrant societies, especially among rural-urban migrants. Such was the case of urban migrants in China itself, where in the major cities the migrants from the same hometown would organize a Hui Kwan for the sake of contacts and mutual assistance. This indicates that the overseas Chinese did not invent voluntary associations themselves but simply resorted to traditional modes of organization in a foreign setting.

Dewey (1970) reports how migrants from rural Java have used traditional ceremonial groups as a means of urban adaptation in New Caledonia. The New Guinea Chinese have made a different kind of adjustment. They did not build traditional religious institutions; on the contrary they adopted a new religion—Christianity. Even though the two sects of Christianity had the effect of dividing the population, there were compensating advantages. The two groups of Chinese who belonged to different Christian churches formed two opposing factions, but instead of engaging in sabotage or overt violence (as did the converted natives on some Pacific islands according to Howard [1970:16]), they expressed hostility in the form of competition: for example, that between the two Chinese schools sponsored by the opposing missions. The students' performances and interschool contests were closely watched and evaluated by parents as well as other people concerned, and consequently this competition had a benign effect on the Chinese population inasmuch as it encouraged achievement and learning. Again it may be conjectured that resentment provoked by outsiders (Europeans, for instance) was contained within the Chinese community and the danger of further oppression minimized.

It is often stated in the literature that the New Guinea Chinese have been a "law-abiding people." One may argue that they are law-abiding not in the sense that they never break the law, but rather in the sense that they never take group action in challenging the regulations set up by the colonial administration or the treatment they receive from society at large. Chinese tolerance or lack of action in the long run arouses sympathy in other people. One elite Chinese points out that the New Guinea Chinese are "silent grumblers," for when they make complaints they make them only to themselves. It is worth noting that nonaggressiveness is emphasized in childrearing among the New Guinea Chinese parents, although space does not permit me to go into the details here.

The final point I would like to comment on is the development and success of Chinese commercial enterprises in New Guinea in view of the fact that the majority of the Chinese population came from the working class. I have already discussed the factors of economic prosperity in New Guinea, factors which are external to the Chinese. Now I would like to point to internal factors.

The first factor is culture. Cultural values such as patience, endurance, frugality, austerity, and temperance were not only emphasized in this immigrant community but were practiced among the majority of the Chinese population. Hard work, for instance, is one of the required conditions for running a trade store; the storekeeper and his family usually work at least fifteen hours a day, seven days a week.

The second factor is the bond within the Chinese family. Once a store has been set up the entire family becomes a corporation. Every member contributes his or her share of the work, yet none of them would make claims on the income. The profits of the family enterprise are usually controlled by its head and used either in business expansion or in investment in other areas, so that in the long run everybody benefits.

The third factor is kinship ties beyond the family, which are essential in business cooperation. Chinese are also able to secure or save up capital by using interlocking credit associations built on the basis of kinship networks.

The fourth factor concerns education. Although the first-generation immigrants were predominantly illiterate in both Chinese and European languages, they paid great attention to getting a better education for their children born in New Guinea. Especially after the war a large proportion of the Chinese families, rich and poor, managed to send their children to

Australia for secondary education. Therefore, beginning in the early 1950s when the Australian-educated young Chinese returned to New Guinea, the English-speaking ability of the Chinese and their knowledge of modern business were greatly improved.

Although many Chinese are now engaged in running stores, it is not correct to say that postwar Chinese investment has been centered solely on commerce, especially in the intermediate trade. As I have indicated, many Chinese are also engaged in primary and secondary industries such as building, construction, and manufacturing. Furthermore, the Chinese are engaged in a very broad range of occupations and professions.

In my historical account of the New Guinea Chinese, I have described how this minority population has adapted during the past eighty years to the changing New Guinea environment. At first they adapted to a rather specialized social niche where they engaged mainly in the occupations of artisan-traders; but gradually, and especially after World War II, their occupations have been diversified. During the past decade there has been a new trend: more and more Chinese have given up their noncommercial professions and become merchants. But because more and more indigenous entrepreneurs have joined in such commercial activities, it is unlikely that the Chinese will remain in a "specialized niche" much longer.

NOTES

Fieldwork for my dissertation research (1974) was conducted in Papua New Guinea from 1971 to 1973. It was sponsored by the Australian National University, where I held a research scholarship, and the Wenner-Gren Foundation for Anthropological Research (grant-in-aid 2573). I owe a great debt to my wife, Wei-lan, for her assistance in the field and constant discussion of the data. I wish to thank Henny Fokker-Bakker, Derek Freeman, Robin Gengos, and Epeli Hau'ofa for the assistance they have given me in preparing the first draft of this study. I am indebted to Karen Ann Watson-Gegeo for her editing of my final draft. I alone, however, am responsible for the ideas expressed here.

1.   The term *New Guinea Chinese* refers to people of Chinese descent who reside in Papua New Guinea; it does not include the Chinese in West Irian. The total Chinese population, according to the 1971 census (information supplied by the Australian Bureau of Statistics, 1 March 1974), was 2,760. However, the number of Chinese youths studying in Australia and absent from home during the time of census taking was not recorded. They numbered about two hundred. And there are an additional three hundred to five hundred persons who are Chinese descendants of mixed marriages between the Chinese and other ethnic groups.

2.   The Old Protectorate included Kaiser Wilhelmsland, the Bismarck Archipelago, Bougainville and Buka in the Solomons, the Admiralty group, and some hundreds of small islands in the former Trust Territory of New Guinea. The whole protectorate included islands other than those mentioned above, for example Nauru.

3.   In 1971–1972, my survey on the variety of native garden produce available at the Rabaul market found at least seven kinds of green-leaf vegetables, two kinds of beans, and three kinds of melons and fruits to be of Chinese origin (see D. Wu,

in press). Moreover, the Chinese bought large quantities of sweet potato and taro for their hired workers as part of their rations as well as large quantities of betel nut for resale in their stores. Besides, only at the Chinese butchers could fresh pork be obtained, which meant that only the Chinese bought native-fed pigs.

4.   The "self-selection" process in the Chinese population certainly benefited New Guinea in its economic development. The German official records on many occasions readily admitted Chinese contributions to economic development in New Guinea, and even Sir John Hubert P. Murray, then governor of Papua, pointed out in 1919 the economic advantages that German New Guinea with its Chinese immigrants had enjoyed, whereas Papuan economic development was handicapped because of forbidding Asian immigrants (Rowley 1958:72).

REFERENCES CITED

Adela, Sister M.
1971   A Challenge to you. Rabaul: Sacred Heart Mission.

Annual Report
1901–
   1913   On the development of the German protectorate in Africa and the South Sea (German New Guinea and the island spheres of the Caroline, Pelew and Marianna Islands). Translated [from German] by H. A. Thomson. Canberra: Archives, Australian National Library.

Barth, F.
1961   Ecologic relationship of ethnic groups in Swat, North Pakistan. In Studies in human ecology, ed. G. A. Theodorson. Evanston: Row, Peterson.

Biskup, P.
1970   Foreign coloured labour in German New Guinea: a study in economic development. Journal of Pacific History (Canberra) 5:85–108.

Cohen, A.
1968   Man in adaptation: the cultural present. Chicago: Aldine.

Dewey, A. G.
1970   Ritual as mechanism for urban adaptation. Man 5(3):438–448.

Epstein, T. S.
1970   Capitalism, primitive and modern. Canberra: Australian National University.

Firth, S. G.
1973   Recruitment and employment of laborers in the Western Pacific before the First World War. Ph.D. dissertation, Oxford University.

Hardesty, D. L.
1972   The human ecological niche. American Anthropologist 74(3):458–466.

Howard, A.
1970   Learning to be Rotuman. New York: Teachers College.

Kotze, S. V.
1921   Südsee Erinnerungen aus Papuas Kulturmorgen. 3rd ed. Berlin: Fonlane (original 1905).

Lyng, J.
1919   Our new possession. Melbourne: Melbourne Publishing Co.

Oliver, D. C.
1961   The Pacific islands. New York: Doubleday.

Pacific Islands Monthly (Sydney)

Rabaul Times (Rabaul)

Report
1922–
  1939   *Report to the council of the League of Nations on the administration of the territory of New Guinea.* Melbourne: Parliament of the Commonwealth of Australia.

Robson, R. W. (ed.)
1954   *Handbook of Papua and New Guinea: 1954.* Sydney: Pacific Publications.
1958   Ibid., 2nd ed.

Rowley, C. D.
1958   *The Australians in German New Guinea: 1914–21.* Melbourne: Melbourne University Press.
1965   *The New Guinea villager.* Melbourne: Cheshire.

Salisbury, R. F.
1970   *Vunamami.* Berkeley: University of California Press.

Schnee, H.
1904   *Bilder aus der Südsee.* Berlin: Dietrich Reimer.

Skinner, G. W.
1957   *Chinese Society in Thailand: an analytical history.* Ithaca: Cornell University Press.

Strathern, A.
1972   The entrepreneurial model of social change: from Norway to New Guinea. *Ethnology* 11:368–379.

Tudor, J. (ed.)
1961   *Handbook of Papua and New Guinea.* 3rd ed. Sydney: Pacific Publications.
1964   Ibid., 4th ed.
1966   Ibid., 5th ed.

Wu, D. Y. H.
1974   An immigrant minority: the adaptation of Chinese in Papua New Guinea. Ph.D. dissertation, Australian National University, Canberra.

In press Chinese as an intrusive language in the New Guinea area. In *New Guinea area language and language study,* ed. Stephen A. Wurm. Language, culture, society and the modern world, vol. 3. Canberra: Australian National University.

Wu, S. Y.
1954   *Mei Kuo Hua-Ch'iao Pai-Nian Chi-Shih: Chia na-ta fu* [One hundred years of Chinese in the United States and Canada]. Hong Kong: S. Y. Wu.

Competing Paradigms and False Polemics in Economic Anthropology

J. I. PRATTIS

It is perhaps a necessary characteristic of new subdisciplines that they are required to go through a process of justification and introspection prior to general acceptance by the academic community. This applies particularly to economic anthropology, where a "thirty years' war" has been waged over the formal as opposed to the substantive nature of non-Western economic systems (Belshaw 1965; Burling 1962; Cook 1966; Dalton 1961, 1969; Goodfellow 1939; Polanyi 1957). Just when the combatants appear to be tiring and attempting a new introspection (Cancian 1966; Kaplan 1968), a new polemic has been taken up (Berthoud 1971; Cook 1969; Edel 1972), though its origins have a much longer history.[1] This is the polemic as to whether exchange theory or production theory should have primacy as the explanatory paradigm in economic anthropology, and presently it has most prominence in French social anthropology (Godelier 1966; Meillassoux 1960; Dupré and Rey 1969; Terray 1972).

Since the time of Malinowski and Mauss there has been an increasing emphasis in anthropology on consideration of reciprocity and exchange as the basic feature of social relationships. A critical response from a number of scholars (Godelier, Berthoud, Cook) who have been identified as production theorists maintains that this emphasis on exchange at best obscures a more fundamental set of relationships and at worst is myopic and wrong. The argument is made that exchange relations are simply observations of specific social relations already defined at the productive level.

Another point of contention is that exchange theory concentrates on the individual actor and that to record an individual strategy is not to explain it, unless the structural constraints are taken into account. The point is made that one can only consider the structural constraints by reference to factors of production: it is the social structure and not the individual that we must look to. The implication is that it is the sociology of production we should study and not the sociology of exchange.

To assess the legitimacy of these claims I propose to examine the theoretical and methodological bases of exchange theory and production theory and demonstrate that the production theory versus exchange theory polemic is in fact false as it is solely concerned with different ontological levels and not different epistemological levels.

EXCHANGE THEORY

The problem which all exchange theorists face was perhaps best articulated by Firth (1964:46): "Here is our great problem as anthropologists—to translate the acts of individuals into the regularities of social process. How do we do it?"

Standard interpretations of social process in social anthropology had largely regarded social process as prior to the acts of individuals. The interest in exchange as a means of integration and articulation in a system, with varying emphases, has looked at the cause-effect relationship the other way around in terms of examining regularities produced by the acts of individuals.

Exchange theory finds its roots in a simple model of social interaction consisting of presentations and counterpresentations between actors A and B exchanging valued goods and services x and y. That is, $A^x \rightleftharpoons_y B$. Whereas Malinowski (1922) was basically concerned with primitive exchange in the Trobriand Islands, Mauss (1954) on the other hand was concerned with the general case of "primitive" exchange inasmuch as it shed light on "modern" exchange. In other words, economic behavior as understood by classical economists was held to be a special class of general phenomena of which primitive exchange was also a part. It is to the laws and structure of the general phenomena that exchange theorists have addressed themselves.

Both Malinowski and Mauss argued for the interpenetration of the social and the economic in terms of the consideration that complex networks of social relations are generated and maintained by the reciprocal transfer of valuables. Mauss was primarily concerned with the simplest expression of exchange (a two-person interactive set) in his discussion of gift exchange. A gift was viewed as a total presentation, a matrix of social and cultural elements of which the material element is only one. The object given is a medium for the transfer of social information, values, and norms. It expresses value commitment, requires a return, and holds both donor and recipient to a contract of interaction much wider and more enduring than the mere exchange of material values.

Latent in these arguments is the assumption that most if not all human interaction is governed by the rules of reciprocity—that if primitive and modern exchange are classes of the same general phenomenon then it might be useful to look to the models of economic exchange for analogies.

Some exchange theorists have used these analogies to a greater extent than others. Homans (1950, 1961) draws on behavioral psychology and marginal utility theory to examine the social processes of actors in small groups. Activities are viewed as responses to different types of reinforcement both positive and negative, as part of the process of exchanging rewards and costs between human beings. From the basic exchange model of $A^x \rightleftharpoons_y B$ Homans argues that an actor will judge how much value he receives from another actor in exchange for values he produces. He will continue to produce x unless he is satiated by y, unless he is cut off from y, or unless the costs of producing x do not provide any marginal benefit to him in the light of resources expended and alternatives forgone. This combination of propositions from behavioral psychology and economics leads one to view social life as a network of social bargainings in which the exchange of rewards is responsible for ranking, interaction, and control.

While Homans overlooked such considerations as the variety of constraints that place things beyond the control of any individual actor and the methodological strictures of behavioral psychology, and while he used a superficial application of the theory of the firm, he did broach the possibility that as alternative modes of interaction were available to actors, choice of one alternative depended on evaluation of the expected costs and payoffs of all alternatives. Homans makes no attempt to extend the range of these formulations beyond the realm of what he referred to as subinstitutional behavior.

Blau (1967), however, uses some of the terms and conditions of social exchange as defined by Homans to conceptualize relationships at higher levels of complexity. His objective is to explain the characteristics of complex structures by deducing them from the principles governing exchange in small groups. In this endeavor he is concerned with a number of distinct levels—microstructure, formal organization, macrostructure, and two types of exchange, direct and indirect. From a consideration of direct exchange in microstructures Blau demonstrates that phenomena such as power and status hierarchies emerge from the characteristics of interpersonal exchange. Four important features are postulated as emerging from the basic processes of social exchange—functional differentiation, integration through interdependence, social ranking, and the differentiation of power and leadership. These considerations are then used to examine how integration in a structure is fostered by the development of norms which in turn make possible the development of authority structures.

Blau assumes that the contributions of members of a group are bound to be differentially valuable and that exchange takes place when resources are differentially distributed. Using these assumptions and the formulations of elementary exchange, Blau accounted for the interactional and ranking patterns in a law enforcement agency. The network of consultations between competent and not so competent agents involved trade-offs of advice for esteem under conditions of different preference schedules of particular agents. Blau used indifference curves and an application of the Edgeworth box to plot the various possible mixes of preference schedules in order to determine the situations and constraints under which an agent would either give or solicit advice and with whom (Blau 1967:174ff). He demonstrated how a system of informal ranking had arisen out of the exchange relations involved in consultations.

He is less convincing, however, when he tries to go beyond the microstructural level. He suggests that principles of profit maximization, diminishing marginal costs and values when combined with inferred data about the preferences of individuals, can be used to generate propositions about group structures of higher complexity. This statement is more of a research strategy, as no real attempt is made to infer the characteristics of macrostructures from propositions about interpersonal behavior. Instead Blau discusses the major properties of macrostructures in terms of exchange being indirect, institutionalized, internalized. Values and norms serve the role of integrating the complex patterns of exchange both within and between macrostructures, and once these values are internalized by the members of a structure then both direct and indirect exchange mechanisms are molded.

While Blau's stated intent is that of accounting for complex structures in terms of the principles governing interpersonal exchange, there still remains a large methodological and theoretical gap between levels of structure.

Barth (1966) develops a processual model of social relations which focuses on interpersonal transactions within an established set of statuses in the context of incentives and constraints on choice. The rights and obligations which define related statuses are expressed in a sequence of reciprocal prestations which are not random over time. The model visualizes actors occupying roles (the product of certain statuses) which define the goods and services to be exchanged. In a transactional sequence a balance is being sought by both actors between costs and payoffs and the role pairs are adjusted in accordance with the require-

ments of reciprocity. If there is a shift in the situation of a particular actor in an already stabilized transaction and role occupancy such that the
return he is receiving is no longer acceptable, roles and expectations will
be redefined so that they are appropriate to the new situation.

Barth's model can be represented schematically as in Figure 1. A and B
interact because each can provide the other with value appropriate to
their relative statuses. B has access to certain resources through A, and
similarly A has access to certain resources through B. In this sense the
relation between A and B is reciprocal. The results of A's and B's respective estimation of the appropriateness of the value being exchanged are

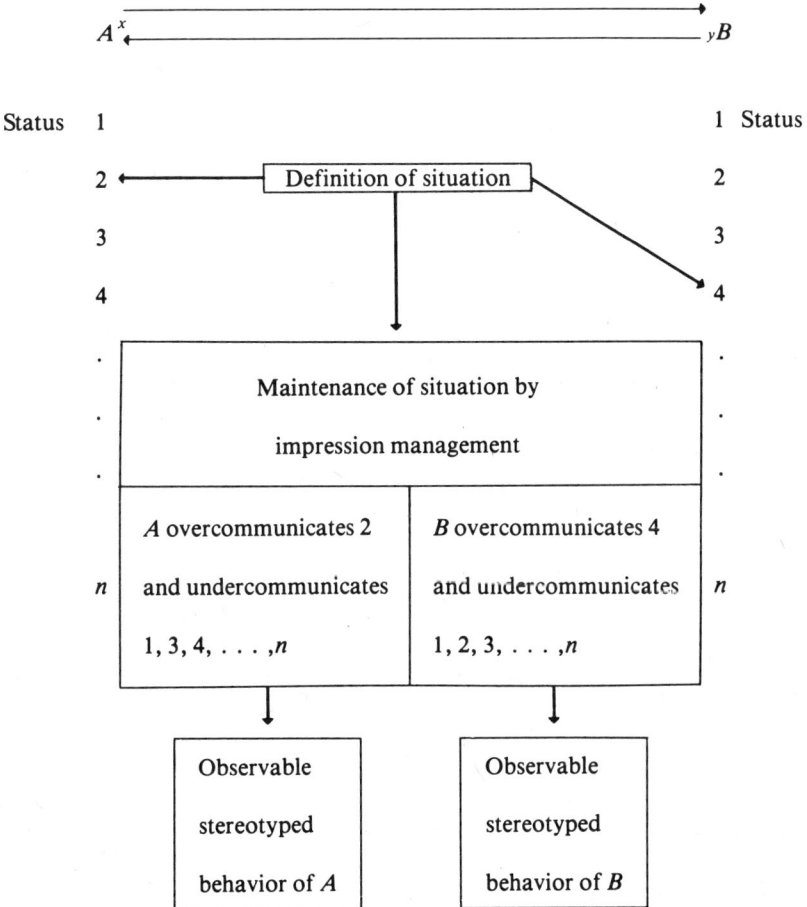

FIGURE 1.   Barth's Transactional Model

that each will select a specific status in which to represent himself during the interaction. As their view of the value being exchanged alters, so do the strategies of impression management they use with respect to it (Barth 1966:4). Before interaction can take place a definition of the situation is required which is maintained and manipulated by impression management, in terms of overcommunicating the relevant and undercommunicating the discrepant with regard to the values being exchanged. Stereotyped forms of behavior are generated from these strategies of impression management.

Barth argues further that each party to a transaction will systematically try to assure that the value gained for him is greater than or equal to the value lost. This implies that in the $A^x \rightleftharpoons_y B$ transaction A feels that $x \geqslant y$ and B feels that $y \geqslant x$. This relationship can hold under conditions of equal exchange and under conditions of unequal exchange where A and B have different evaluations of the prestations involved. It is not generalizable to situations where power is an extraneous variable, as power will permit an actor holding it to define the exchange rates in his own interests. The subordinate actor will receive the exchange commodities that are appropriate to his location in the status matrix and not necessarily in terms of feeling that the value gained is greater than or equal to the value lost.

This lack of concern with power is a serious omission in Barth's work, though it is taken up by Burns and Cooper (1971) in their formal treatment of exchange theory. They discuss the notion of relative power by formally defining the conditions under which actors will influence and control other actors in terms of the relative evaluation of domains that some actors control and others aspire to. The argument made is that evaluations of relative power by actors are the bases for the establishment of exchange relations and for the maintenance of dominance sequences.

While each of the authors discussed can demonstrate that regularities and processes do arise out of interpersonal exchange, the effective theoretical and methodological range of their formulations would appear to be small-scale actor networks. Homans does not attempt to generalize beyond this level, and Blau's attempts to do so are not methodologically convincing. Barth's model requires as givens the situation of the actors, mutually understood values, and status sets as crucial inputs within which variation occurs. This, in addition to the omission of the power dimension, sets severe limits to its range of applicability. Despite claims to an encompassing theory of transaction that subsumes both firm theory and primitive exchange and applies also to levels of complex structure, the exchange theorists discussed here have made explicative rather than theoretical contributions to this direction.

THE POLEMIC

The most critical response to transactional theory has been made by a number of scholars (Berthoud, Cook, Godelier) identified as production theorists. They maintain that an emphasis on exchange obscures a more fundamental set of relationships. Berthoud in his attack upon exchange theory (1971) brings into sharp focus ideas implicit in Cook (1969) and Godelier (1966). He argues (1972:3) that "to posit the primacy of exchange tends to view this particular moment of any economic system as a set of reified relations among products and to forget that these relations are external manifestations (i.e., mere observations) of the specific social relations already defined at the production level."

Berthoud also claims that anthropology should be concerned with making statements about societies, and he is opposed to the use of the individual as a unit of inquiry. He lays the blame for the individualistic bias in economic anthropology upon the insistence that exchange theory has explanatory value. He argues that to record an individual strategy is not to explain it, unless the structural constraints are taken into account. The underlying assumption in this attack is that the productive relationships in a group delineate the field within which exchange may take place.

The basis for this argument is found in Marx's contention that exchange among producers and exchange of productive resources for production clearly belong to the sphere of production and that "the real science of modern economy only begins when the theoretical analysis passes from the process of circulation to the process of production" (Marx 1967:337).

Production theorists view the economy as an integrated process made up of various moments—production, distribution, exchange, consumption—but maintain that the cause-effect interaction between these moments is not equally distributed. A product can be used in a subsequent process either as a means of production or as a means of subsistence. In the first case it remains in the production sector; in the second it becomes a product for the individual's reallocation or consumption and must be replaced in a new process of production. Berthoud makes the point that distribution, exchange, and consumption of products as means of production are directly included within production while as means of subsistence they are direct consequences of production. It is on this premise that the argument is made that production and not exchange is the determinant level of any social structure (1971:14).

Production analysis is the explanation of why a division of labor in production exists in a society and for whom goods are produced. In this analysis of the productive system both the material resources of a society and its organizational principles are encompassed. Thus to study the manner in which an economic system operates and adapts to changing conditions it is argued that it is insufficient simply to trace the channels along which already produced goods are distributed. An alternative conception of the economy as a whole is needed—one that concentrates on the social relations of production rather than exchange.

This response to exchange theory can be considered in a number of ways. While technology and the relationships of production are major factors in determining type of social organization, insistence on the primacy of production factors in a strict determinist manner is "vulgar" Marxism. The role of social science is to explicate the effects of additional factors, social and ideological, that place constraints on behavior. To ignore these factors because of an insistence on strict determinism is not only myopic. It is poor Marxism, for Marx's writings clearly imply that consciousness of class is as important as the reality of class in producing change. The significance accorded by Marx to cognitive and social factors in addition to production factors makes discussion of determinacy problematic.

In methodological terms we can look at exchange and production theory not as epistemological competitors but as different levels of abstraction employed as analytic tools depending on the problem being addressed. It is the problem that stipulates the level of analysis and therefore the relative ability of exchange theory as against production theory. Presumably an analytic concern with political process in Melanesia, where the manipulation of exchange networks is one means of gaining political dominance, would be well informed by exchange theory (Salisbury 1966, 1970; Strathern 1971a, 1971b; Finney 1971). On the other hand, an analytic interest in system level determinants as affected by the relationships of control over the means of production would be more informed by production theory (Frank 1967).

Furthermore, one could argue that exchange theory and production theory have their empirical locus in a consideration of the division of labor but operate along different abstractive dimensions. For Belshaw (1967:35) the division of labor is not merely a segment of society but the whole of it. The transactional nature of interaction between actors who have interdependent needs in his view creates regular social patterns and structures which are articulated and integrated by means of exchange systems (1967:40). The concern of production theorists with the division of labor is in terms of the consequences of different sets of social relationships that control the means of production. Given these positions it would seem that more progress will be made by combining these two levels under a wider theoretical framework than by setting up a false polemic.

There are a number of conceptual misunderstandings in the production theorist's attack. Berthoud defines a product in strictly material terms and is thus able to argue that use of the product in distribution, exchange, and consumption depends on the social relations already defined at the productive level (Berthoud 1971:14). This materialist definition neglects the variety of nonmaterial values that are part of the exchange theorist's concern—among them esteem and compliance.

With respect to the lack of explanatory value of exchange theory, Berthoud (1971:5) argues that to record an individual strategy is not to explain it unless structural constraints are taken into account: "Although individuals present behavioral variations, they are determined by their positions in the power structures (economic, political, and ideological) and their behaviors can only be understood within an analysis of social relations." This is precisely what contemporary trends in exchange theory are attempting to do and what Firth (1939) has long advocated as a research strategy. Work by Salisbury (1969), Cancian (1967), Schwimmer (1972), and Prattis (1973) has been concerned with locating an individual actor within the social structure in terms of his access to resources, information, and power. Similarly Barth's concern with the complementarity of statuses in a transaction places exchange within a wide status matrix. The concern with the framework of social relations is certainly not lacking in exchange theory despite Berthoud's claim to the contrary.

The major thrust of Edel's argument, that exchange models cannot explain the evolution of inequality (1972:1), is clearly wrong. He understands exchange as the reciprocation of equal values whereas the major conceptual contribution of exchange theory is that systems of subordination and superordination are generated by allocation decisions with regard to scarce and valued resources—both material and nonmaterial.

Despite these conceptual misunderstandings, the main point I wish to make is that both exchange and production theory can be conceptualized in terms of an equilibrium model applied at different levels—exchange theory at the level of the actor and production theory at the level of social structure.

MODELS OF EQUILIBRIUM

The notion of levels has frequently been used to legitimize new "brands" of scientific endeavor whereas it should be emphasized that it is simply a means of ordering data (Duncan 1961). There is a tendency in social science to work within a level instead of *with* the level as an integral part of a theoretical system. If it can be accepted that Berthoud's argument amounts to nothing more than a preference for a distinct ontological level and then if it can be demonstrated that both exchange theory and production theory can be subsumed under the same type of model, it would appear that the polemic raised by the production theorists is unnecessary.

The position taken here is that both exchange theory and production theory can be formulated in terms of an equilibrium model. In economics, equilibrium analysis of a system starts off with a number of simple axioms which are combined to form a logically interrelated group of concepts. The basic terms, primary general relations between them, and the dimensions of the system are provided by the concepts. The rules of interrelation described the limits beyond which the elementary concepts do not apply. Given this formulation of equilibrium, dynamic equilibrium is as possible as static equilibrium, since stability and instability both describe properties of equilibrating systems (Krupp 1968:246–248).

While use of this format has yielded very powerful analyses in economics, the use of equilibrium models in anthropology has suffered from a too close (and erroneous) identification with notions of stasis and exclusion of considerations of change and conflict. The old-fashioned functionalist view of societies as tending toward stasis or self-equilibration has obscured the possibility that one can view societies as tending toward equilibrium around a dynamic process or cycle of change. The implications of this view of equilibrium have been explicated for anthropology by Gluckman (1968) and Cancian (1968). Drawing on Nagel's (1967) formal analysis of functionalism, Cancian argues that we can look at an equilibrium model in terms of considering a system S possessing a certain state g which is maintained by the presence of a set of state coordinates. These state coordinates define the g state and can vary, within limits, in response to external and internal events in such a way that the g state is maintained. In other words, the state coordinates determine the presence or absence of g in terms of whether the system limits of variation in the state of coordinates can or cannot be compensated for (Cancian 1968:205).

In this formulation the stability of g is not assumed. In fact the opposite is true: it is assumed that the environment and parts of the system are changing so much that it is impossible for g to persist unless there are specific mechanisms within the system to compensate for these changes. If the mechanisms are inadequate, then the g state will not be maintained. If the compensatory mechanisms operate within the limits, then we can refer to such a system as in equilibrium, and the state coordinates may be described as having the function of maintaining g (Nagel 1967; Cancian 1968). The logical scope of this definitional framework is quite far-reaching because g can be defined in terms of a steady state, rate of change, or cycle of change (Cancian 1968). The definition of the system and the selection of the property of the system to be analyzed depend on the interests of the analyst. No prescription is made concerning the nature of variables or level of system analysis.

If we assume that events are nonrandom, and furthermore that it is our job as social scientists to discern and explain regularities, then equilibrium as defined here would appear to be a reasonable statement about the nature of social life. Because once we assume that there are regularities, then it follows that there must be a degree of systematic interdependence which can be seen to persist within certain limits.

An equilibrium model as defined here provides a useful conceptual framework for dealing with these concerns. Its power lies in the fact that it is neutral with regard to variables, relations, and outcomes, thus permitting one to analyze systems in a manner that need not prejudice outcomes (Krupp 1968:248). The argument so far amounts to little more than the consideration that the prerequisites for using an equilibrium model are simply those of sound methodology. Equilibrium analysis construes a system as made up of relations and conditions. Relations give the system its internal dynamics; conditions determine the scope of the system and provide for the interpretation of special cases. In other words, to use this model one requires specification of system limits and compensatory variation as a statement of antecedent conditions which predict whether or not the defined property of the system will be maintained. It now remains to apply this definitional framework to both exchange and production theory.

EQUILIBRIUM ANALYSIS OF EXCHANGE THEORY

Equilibrium analysis can be applied to exchange theory in terms of both processual and microstructural considerations. With respect to the latter the system dealt with by exchange theorists is a two- or three-person interactive set. The g of this system can be viewed as the maintenance of particular role sets; the state coordinates can be regarded as the conditions and limits under which the role set can expect to be maintained. For Homans, equilibrium is a state of the system which in particular circumstances grows out of interactions within the elementary group and is amenable to explanation by the combined use of sociological and psychological propositions. In his discussion of social control he argues that in a group where members have achieved a maximum level of satisfaction, full equilibrium exists in that a slight change within the social system—network of activities, interactions, and so forth—would be followed by further changes tending to reduce the impact of the initial change (Homans 1950:296).

Whether or not one accepts the explanatory power claimed by Homans for these propositions, the structure of his conceptualization can be

clearly viewed in terms of specifying certain limits within which a particular state of the system can be predicted. Similarly Blau's (1967) analysis
of interaction and ranking in the federal law enforcement agency could
be viewed as a statement of the conditions and prestations necessary to
produce and maintain an informal hierarchy of roles.

Barth's (1966) analysis dealt initially with two actors who have defined
an exchange situation by means of impression management according to
certain statuses expressed as roles. The values exchanged in a progres-
sional sequence of transaction are evaluated by the actors according to
some overarching principle. What Barth initially arrives at is the argument that prestations must be appropriate to the framework within
which the actors are located according to differential status, so that specific types of exchange can be anticipated as normative. This is simply a
statement of the conditions of prestation and impression management
which are requisite to the maintenance of the role pair initiated by the actors.

Barth's application of the transactional model to relationships on
board a Norwegian fishing vessel (1966:6–11) is stated in explicit equilibrium terms, though Barth does not seem to see the implications of this.
His analysis was of the development of new role expectations between
skipper, net boss, and crew as a function of the consequences of a change
in exploitative technology. In fact what his analysis did was to specify the
limits beyond which variations in technology, work pattern, authority,
and privilege could *not* go without redefining the situation and thereby
causing a change in the structure of the role set—skipper:net boss:crew.
This is simply a statement of the limits of variation of a set of state coordinates necessary for the maintenance of a particular property of the
system under consideration.

The processual aspect of Barth's and Blau's theoretical concerns is in
terms of the generating capacity of the interpersonal exchange situation
for other structures of higher orders of complexity. Although their formulations in this regard are not very satifactory, one could view the processual link between levels of structure as the property of the system to be
analyzed. Consistent with the dictates of equilibrium analysis, Blau's
concern with different levels of functional differentiation, integration
through interdependence, social ranking, and power differentiation, and
Barth's consideration of the changing constraints on an actor's definition of the situation, would be construed as the state coordinates which
maintain the system's processual property. While the translation of these
conceptual concerns into empirical boundaries would present severe
operational problems, given the present conceptual status of exchange
theory I would submit that exchange theory in its "generative" domain
suffers from the lack of elementary methodology. A concern with equili-

brium analysis and the specification of the limits and conditions under which "generation" is posited to occur would do one of two things. It would either place exchange theory on a firm methodological base or demonstrate that the concern with generative properties is not a feasible avenue for inquiry and thus direct research endeavor elsewhere.

EQUILIBRIUM ANALYSIS OF PRODUCTION THEORY

The theoretical concerns of production theory can be subjected to the same analysis briefly suggested for exchange theory. That is, one can apply equilibrium analysis to production theory in terms of considerations of both process and the maintenance of a structured set of relations. This requires, however, that one take the premises of the argument made by Berthoud et al. back to the theoretical set from which they originated.

Marx's analysis of capitalism sought to answer questions about the unequal distribution of wealth and the evolution of inequality. He was also concerned with the origins and future of the system as a whole and about the nature of wages and profits, matters which could not be illuminated by concentrating on exchange alone. It was the consideration of the relationships of production which provided a method for approaching these questions in terms of accounting for how labor produced more value than it itself cost. In these terms Marx conceptualized society as being made up of superstructures grafted onto one basic structure—production (Marx and Engels 1959:398, 410–411). The different stages of human organization identified by Marx (1964:52) were distinguished one from the other by the different manner in which crucial elements of the productive process stood in relation to each other.

Given this oversimplified picture of the Marxian framework one may see how an equilibrium model, as discussed here, might be used to express the formulations in a systematic way. There are two ways in which this might be done. In the first case one could posit as the g factor the dynamic sequence of stages in economic organization and as state coordinates the progressive evolutions of such factors as division of labor, alienation, property, capital, and money. Given the state coordinates as specified, one could expect shifts in productive organization. In this formulation the property of the system is the dynamic process of productive forces that is involved in shifts from one level of socioeconomic organization to another—for example, primitive → feudal → capitalist → communist, where it is the arrows that are defined as g.

The other possible approach is to look at a particular form of socioeconomic organization as the g state (cf. Gluckman 1968) and consider as state coordinates those elements in the superstructure which *inhibit* the inherent contradictions and shifts in the relationships of production that could generate a change in the g state. In examining the capitalist stage, for example, and assuming that the development of class consciousness is the key to the shift out of a capitalist mode of production to the communist mode, one may look to such factors as increasing differentiation of labor and rewards, stratification within class, and racism as state coordinates which maintain g by inhibiting the development of class consciousness and the recognition of a common position vis-à-vis the factors of production.

The point to be made in this brief examination is that the theoretical base upon which the production theorists draw for their polemic is consistent with the definitional framework of an equilibrium model as outlined by Nagel (1967) and Cancian (1968).

CONCLUSION

The major conclusions to be drawn from this exercise concern the neglected systematic power of equilibrium analysis, the conceptual status of the production theory versus exchange theory polemic, and the groundwork for further research.

The discussion of equilibrium models pointed out that the nature of the system analyzed, its property, and the variables designated as state coordinates were in no way predetermined. This means that specification of the system under scrutiny as (1) a two-actor interactive set, (2) a level of socioeconomic organization, or (3) a processual change from either microstructure to macrostructure or (4) from one level of productive organization to another in no way precludes the application of equilibrium analysis. The equilibrium of the system can be defined as centering on a property which can be a steady state, a rate of change, or a processual change. The use of an equilbrium model simply requires thorough methodology in terms of specifying the limits of variation of attendant variables under which the designated property can be predicted.

Though there are many operational difficulties in translating conceptual limits into empirical boundaries, both exchange theory and production theory can comply with this definitional framework. This being the case one can reject the polemic raised by production theorists: it is based on false premises. The demonstration that production theory and exchange theory can be subsumed under a common set of methodological assumptions indicates that they are not epistemological competitors. Furthermore, the argument made with regard to respective domains of applicability—small-scale actor networks as against levels of socioeconomic organization—implies that exchange and production theory are complementary approaches on different ontological levels.

While there are empirical limitations and conceptual inadequacies in both exchange and production theory, there is no methodological base for the type of polemic raised by Berthoud et al. Perhaps a quote from Aaron's discussion of Marxism (1969:171) may serve as a stricture for both groups of theorists:

> The theory, founded on historical materialism, of the capitalist mode of production constitutes the main point of Marxism. . . . Marxism claims scientific dignity only as a theory of capitalism. As a theory of every social formation it affords a research program, or orientation of curiosity, guiding ideas and countless intuitions or suggestions.

By implication, exchange and production theory are research strategies which if raised to the stature of dogma or primacy, ill serve scholarship. The next step to take appears to be the development of a theory that bridges the gap between the levels served by exchange and production theory, a step which may well involve some form of synthesis between the two. Such a theory cannot be developed by a false polemic that confuses ontology with epistemology. It is the bridging of the gap between levels of structure that constitutes the main challenge in economic anthropology.

NOTE

1. Edel, in a paper presented to the American Anthropological Association in 1972 at Toronto, argued that the issues raised by Godelier, Berthoud and Cook have a history in past debates between Marx and the classical economists, Dobb and Sombart, Sweezy and Bettelheim. (See Edel 1972).

REFERENCES CITED

Aaron, R.
1969   *D'une sainte famille à l'autre: essais sur les marxismes imaginaires.* Paris: Gallimard.

Barth, F.
1966   *Models of social organisation.* Royal Anthropological Institute Occasional Paper no. 23. London.

Belshaw, C. S.
1965   *Traditional exchange and modern markets.* Englewood Cliffs, N.J.: Prentice-Hall.
1967   Theoretical problems in economic anthropology. In *Social Organization,* ed. M. Freedman, Chicago: Aldine.

Berthoud, G.
1971   On production, a Marxian conceptualization in anthropology. Paper presented at the annual meeting of the American Anthropological Association, New York.

Blau, P.
1967   *Exchange and power in social life.* New York: Wiley.

Burling, R.
1962   Maximization theories and the study of economic anthropology. *American Anthropologist* 64:802–821.

Burns, T. and M. Cooper.
1971   *Value, social power and economic exchange.* Stockholm: Samhallsnetareforlage.

Cancian, Francesca
1968   Functional analysis of change. In *Theory in anthropology,* ed. R. A. Manners and David Kaplan. Chicago: Aldine.

Cancian, Frank
1966   Maximization as norm, strategy and theory. *American Anthropologist* 68:465–470.
1967   Stratification and risk taking, a theory tested on agricultural innovations. *American Sociological Review* 32:912–927.

Cook, S.
1966   The obsolete anti-market mentality—a critique of the substantivist approach in economic anthropology. *American Anthropologist* 68:323–345.
1969   The anti-market mentality re-examined. *Southwestern Journal of Anthropology* 25:378–406.

Dalton, G.
1961   Economic theory and primitive society. *American Anthropologist* 63:1–25.
1969   Theoretical issues in economic anthropology. *Current Anthropology* 10(1): 63–102.

Duncan, O. D.
1961   From social system to ecosystem. *Sociological Inquiry* 31:140–149.

Dupré, G. and P. Rey
1969   Refléxions sur la pertinence d'une théorie de l'histoire des échanges. *Cahiers internationaux de sociologie* 46:133–162.

Edel, M.
1972   Exchange and production: a controversy in anthropology and political economy. Paper presented at the annual meeting of the American Anthropological Association, Toronto.

Finney, B.
1971   Bigfellow man belong business in New Guinea. In *Melanesia: readings on a culture area,* ed. L. L. Langness and J. C. Weschler. New York: Chandler.

Firth, R.
1939   *Primitive Polynesian economy.* London: Routledge.
1964   *Essays on social organisation and values.* London: Athlone Press.

Frank, A. G.
1967   *Capitalism and underdevelopment in Latin America.* New York: Monthly Review Press.

Frankenberg, R.
1967   Economic anthropology. In *Themes in economic anthropology,* ed. R. Firth. London: Tavistock.

Gluckman, M.
1968   The utility of the equilibrium model in the study of social change. *American Anthropologist* 70:219–237.

Godelier, M.
1966   *Rationalité et irrationalité en economie.* Paris: Maspero.

Goodfellow, D. M.
1939   *Principles of economic sociology.* London: Routledge.

Homans, G. C.
1950   *The human group.* London: Routledge.

1958   Social behavior as exchange. *American Journal of Sociology* 62:597–606.
1961   *Social behaviour: its elementary forms.* London: Routledge.

Kaplan, D.
1968   The formalist-substantivist controversy—reflections on its wider implications. *Southwestern Journal of Anthropology* 24:228–251.

Krupp, S.
1968   Equilibrium theory in economics and in functional analysis as types of explanation. In *Economic anthropology,* ed. E. E. LeClair and H. K. Schneider. New York: Holt.

Malinowski, B.
1922   *Argonauts of the Western Pacific.* London: Routledge.

Marx, K.
1964   *Selected writings in sociology and social philosophy.* New York: McGraw-Hill.
1967   *Capital.* Vol. 3. New York: International.

Marx, K. and F. Engels
1959   *Basic writings on politics and philosophy.* New York: Doubleday.

Mauss, M.
1954   *The gift: forms and functions of exchange in archaic societies.* New York: Free Press (original 1925).

Meillassoux, C.
1960   Essai d'interprétation du phénomène économique dans les sociétiés traditionelles d'autosubsistance. *Cahiers d'études africaines* 1(4):38–67.

Nagel, E.
1967   A formalization of functionalism. In *System, change and conflict,* ed. N. S. Demerath and R. A. Peterson. New York: Free Press.

Polanyi, K.
1957   The economy as instituted process. In *Trade and market in the early empires,* ed. K. Polanyi et al. Glencoe, Ill.:Free Press.

Prattis, J. I.
1973   Strategising man. *Man* 8(1):46–58.

Salisbury, R.
1966   Politics and shell money finance in New Britain. In *Political anthropology,* ed. M. J. Swartz et al. Chicago: Aldine.
1969   Formal analysis in anthropological economics: the Rossel Island case. *Game theory in the behavioral sciences,* ed. I. R. Buchler and H. G. Nutini, Pittsburgh: University of Pittsburgh Press.
1970   *Vunamami.* Berkeley: University of California Press.

Schwimmer, E.
1972   *Exchange in the social structure of the Orokaiva.* London: Hurst.

Strathern, A. J.
1971a   Cargo and inflation in Mount Hagen. *Oceania* 41:225–265.
1971b   *The rope of moka.* London: Cambridge.

Terray, E.
1972   Historical materialism and segmentary lineage based societies. In *Marxism and primitive societies,* ed. E. Terray. New York: Monthly Review Press.

Ecology, Structuralism, and Fishing Taboos

JOHN J. COVE

Discussions of Lévi-Strauss' structural method inevitably end up on the issue of linkages between models and the empirical. We may agree that categories of thought can be understood through oppositions. If we cannot determine which elements will be opposed in a particular context, however, testing becomes problematic. This essay is concerned with developing a combined ecological and structural approach as one way of overcoming the dilemma. Using fishing taboos from two societies, it will be argued that the items prohibited are ecologically correct symbols for the activity and that the relationship between those items can be understood by the ecological stressing of certain oppositions.

While doing research in eastern Cornwall, I was told of fishing taboos which were prevalent in the nineteenth and early twentieth centuries. They referred to the avoidance of clergy, women, and rabbits. My informants could not explain why these things were taboo, except that they had been regarded as bad luck for fishermen. Before analyzing these taboos, it will be necessary to outline the context in which they occurred. The problem here is to determine what relation taboos have to fishing activity in Cornwall.

The major species fished in nineteenth-century Cornwall were pilchard, herring, and mackerel. All three were migratory and schooled off the coast at different times of year (Crouch 1935:133). Due to variations in water temperature the runs might be as far as twenty miles offshore, and in some years they might not occur at all (Noall 1970:14). Two types of gear were used to exploit these resources. The first was a form of seine, an enclosing net set by circling a school. The second was the drift net, a type of entangling barrier.

Pilchard was the most important resource commercially, and fishing could be characterized as highly competitive. Fox (1943:22–23) mentions that there were periods of open warfare between drifters and seiners. Drift net fishermen felt that seining did not permit sharing in the pilchard runs. Thomas (1893:85–86) describes one set made off the town of Falmouth where thirteen million pilchard were caught, that set comprising half the annual landing for that area.

Seine fishermen argued that they had to maximize their chances given competition from the drifters. The seines used were open-bottomed, which meant that they were effective only when worked in shallow waters. Drift nets, however, could be set regardless of water depth. A second difference was in possibilities for territorial control. As an enclosing device, a seine must be set quickly and cannot catch fish after the enclosure is complete. A drift net, on the other hand, can be left indefinitely. The implication of these differences was that drift net fishermen could often set further offshore and block or scatter runs before they reached seining grounds.

The size and seasonal nature of the pilchard runs also led to problems with access to market. Catches were sold to pilchard stations which cured and shipped to continental markets (Jenkin 1932:146). Due to limitations in processing facilities and labor, the stations frequently could not purchase every catch. In such periods catches would either be dumped or sold for fertilizer (Crouch 1935:120).

The environment and technology, reinforced by competitive elements, led to a high degree of uncertainty for fishermen. Not only were times and locations of runs problematic, but catching and market were also unsure. A number of strategies appeared to be directed to this problem. Uncertainty about time and location of runs was reduced to some extent by information search. Seiners, who were restricted in range of exploitation, had a shore-based crew component which acted as lookouts (huers). Their task was to watch for runs and direct their boats to interception points (Jenkin 1932:171–175). Drifters spent considerable time at sea in search.

The information available did not provide a useful basis for evaluation. Lookouts could only see a restricted area of the coast. The signs used to detect runs (birds, ripples, water color, activity of other boats) could not be used to give accurate estimates of fish quantities.

In relation to competition over runs, agreements on fishing times and areas were made in some communities (Cornish 1884:140). Attempts to attract investment in nets and boats by pilchard station owners was a means of ensuring preference over other fishermen (Rowe 1953:265–266).

The problem of uncertainty was also expressed and managed in local beliefs. It was thought that one of the factors responsible for successful fishing was the goblin Bucca, who had the power to keep fish out of one's nets. By stating their lack of control over nature in this way, fishermen were provided with a way of influencing it. Offerings to Bucca, if accepted, were thought to bring fish into the nets. These offerings can be seen as a form of maximization—an attempt to create the best possible state of nature. Fishing taboos can be regarded as the opposite side of the same coin. Avoidance of certain actions was thought to result in avoidance of the worst possible fishing conditions, a minimax strategy:

Alternatives

		Use/follow	Not use/violate
Strategies	Magic	Success	Success or failure
	Taboo	Success or failure	Failure

As Malinowski pointed out in his analysis of Trobriand magic, it is a form of irrational action but it is not used irrationally (1948:29–30). In a comparison of offshore and lagoon fishing, he argued that magic was used only under conditions of uncertainty (Malinowski 1938:17). Taboos are a similar type of strategy, at least in the contexts in which they occur (Steiner 1956:146–147). The fact that magic and taboo are irrational means is at one level immaterial. They are concerned with the same problems as information search and fishing agreements and are created by the same conditions.

Taboos are strategy rules concerned with avoiding the worst possible conditions or outcomes. They are more likely to occur in contexts where these conditions and outcomes can vary and individuals have little or no information for determining what will happen. It will be argued later that conditions of high uncertainty in fishing are created by particular combinations of environment, resource, and technology.

In Cornwall the objects specifically tabooed were clergy, women, and rabbits. The most obvious common characteristic is their "normality" in nonfishing contexts. Fishermen married, they went to church, they hunted and ate rabbits. To make a point of specifying these items as unlucky can be seen as a transformation of the normal into the abnormal. After a brief discussion of the taboos, analysis will focus on the normal/abnormal distinction to locate parallels in fishing activities.

The taboo on clergy applied to the behavior of both ministers and fishermen. Ministers were prohibited from coming near the boats, and fishermen thought that even meeting a clergyman on the way to their boats would bring bad luck. Once at sea, neither minister nor church could be mentioned, except by using substitute terms ("white choker" and "clighty" respectively). These terms were used frequently since particular churches were good landmarks for navigation and setting nets (Nance 1924:473).

Contact with women followed a similar pattern. A fisherman meeting a woman after leaving his home was required to return home and start again to avoid misfortune. If he met a woman the second time, he could not go out fishing that day. In some parts of Cornwall meeting a woman with an empty basket was considered dangerous. As with clergy, women were not allowed near the boats (Harris 1900:7; Nance 1924:474).

Although meat was eaten at sea and skins were used for clothing, it was considered unlucky for the crew ever to mention the name of a land animal except through substitution of the term "four legger." Rabbits and in some places cats were considered particularly dangerous and mentioning them at sea was taboo. If the rule were violated, fishing stopped and the boat returned to port for the remainder of the day (Harris 1900:18).

Breaking of any of these taboos, unless followed by the preventive measure of not fishing for the day, was thought to result in misfortune. Damage to boat or nets was thought to follow such violations automatically.

Given the range of objects that could be taboo, the central question is why these three items—clergy, women, and rabbits—were selected. For purposes of analysis, it will be assumed that these items share common characteristics which are inappropriate in some way to a fishing context. Further, it will be assumed that these items can be understood as symbols and it is at this level that they should manifest their inappropriateness (Lévi-Strauss 1963a:2–3).

The type of fishing done in nineteenth-century Cornwall can be seen as emphasizing differences in nature. The categories of land and sea were strongly opposed: fishing required separation from the land and normal patterns of social life. The idiom used to contrast land and sea was sexual. The sea was thought of as the major source of food and wealth and was spoken of as being fertile. In comparison, the land was regarded as barren.

Separation from the land stressed another opposition, that of man and woman. Division of labor made fishing a male activity. As a result, male/female relations were structured out of one portion of nature. Further, men were part of both land and sea, while women were only part of land.

In the same way that land/sea were contrasted sexually, man/woman were contrasted economically. Men were the producers while the women were nonproducers, although women's labor entered into the conversion of fish to commodity for they did the curing both for home consumption and in the pilchard stations.

These oppositions can be stated as an equation:

[sea:land :: man:woman] :: [fertile:barren :: productive:nonproductive]

There are two categories in this equation, objects and properties. By substituting objects for properties, one can state what fishermen should avoid. The land symbolizes contexts that should be avoided (barren). By avoidance of landlike conditions, fishermen avoid being like women (nonproductive).

Clergy, women, and rabbits share the characteristic of being land things. So, however, do a wider range of objects. The three take on special significance in that they reflect inherent contradictions in reality. In the same way that men are of the land and the sea is sometimes barren, the taboo items have properties they should not have. Women and rabbits are of the land, yet are symbols of fertility. Clergy are men, but are not of the sea and are not productive. The taboos express the inconsistencies in the equation when it is applied to reality. It is thus as anomalies that clergy, women, and rabbits are powerful symbols. By converting contradictions in reality to taboo, fishermen are recognizing what should not be and avoiding what they cannot.

The explanation developed for the Cornish fishing taboos is based on two ecological factors: (1) high level of uncertainty and (2) stress on particular oppositions. To test the conclusions, it should be possible to predict where such taboos will occur and what will be taboo.

To limit the range of fishing contexts, the uncertainty characteristic can be used. Two major environmental factors would seem to be important—territory fished and mobility of species. If the territory exploited were relatively small (a river), then locating the resource should be less difficult. Similarly, if the species fished were sedentary, location would be less problematic. If they are migratory as well as mobile then the difficulty is compounded, since when as well as where is involved.

Although it can be assumed that the gear used in any fishery will be adapted to environment/resource, frequently different types of gear can be used successfully. Following Von Brandt's suggestion (1964:2–3), gear will be classified here by associated activity: hunting, active trapping, passive trapping, and gathering. Implicit in this classification is the relative importance of information. As information requirements increase, so should the level of uncertainty.

Territory, resource mobility, and technology, as shown in Table 1, can be used to determine variations in level of uncertainty. Thus it is predicted that fishing taboos should only occur in contexts fitting those ranked from 6 to 13 in level of uncertainty.

The oppositions stressed in the Cornish fishery are just one of a number of possible equations. The original equation was derived from primacy of marine resources, territory fished, and division of labor. Given alternative resources, different territory, and other criteria for division of labor a wider range of equations could be developed. Each of the logically possible equations should result in different anomalies and hence in different taboos.

The Cornish equation itself can be used to generate additional taboos which might be found in similar types of fisheries. Each pair of oppositions can be examined as in Table 2 to determine possible anomalies. Similar oppositions and anomalies can be developed from other equa-

TABLE 1.   Fishing Contexts and Expected Uncertainty Levels

Territory [a]	Species [b]	Activity [c]	Uncertainty Level (Low to High)
Small	Sedentary	Gathering	1
Large	Sedentary	Gathering	2
Small	Mobile	Passive trapping	3
Small	Mobile	Active trapping	4
Small	Mobile	Hunting	5
Large	Mobile	Active trapping	6
Large	Mobile	Hunting	7
Small	Migratory	Passive trapping	8
Small	Migratory	Active trapping	9
Small	Migratory	Hunting	10
Large	Migratory	Passive trapping	11
Large	Migratory	Active trapping	12
Large	Migratory	Hunting	13

[a] Factors such as climate and type of coast may also be important.

[b] Size of species fished and characteristics such as pelagic, demersal, and anadromous could also be used.

[c] A number of combinations have not been used since they imply unlikely technological adaptations.

tions. The anomalies specify the range of items from which taboos should be selected in a particular fishing context.

We turn now to the second ethnographic example, the Nootka of North America. As with other northwest coast tribes, the Nootka were traditionally a fishing people. Although they used a wide variety of marine resources, the most important were salmon, herring, and sea mammals. Except for the gathering of clams and mussels, fishing was exclusively a male activity: women were restricted to curing and preparation (Swan 1870:11).

Pacific salmon are anadromous and hence spend different parts of their life cycles in fresh and salt water. While living in the sea salmon tend to migrate in scattered schools over routes covering hundreds of miles. There are seasonal concentrations in the coastal rivers and streams, however, when they return to their place of origin to spawn.

Primary exploitation of salmon took place during spawning season.

TABLE 2.   Stressed Oppositions and
           Anomalies

Oppositions	Expected Anomalies
Sea/land	Landmarks
	Distinctive land features (mountains, forests)
	Amphibians
	Prolific land species
	Land species used for food
	Nonproductive areas at sea
	Least prolific sea species
Sea/women	Contact with women while engaged in fishing activities (pubescent, pregnant, or menstruating women)
	Women having contact with fishing gear
	Women's activities associated with fish (curing, cooking)
Man/land	Nonfishing males (old men, men in occupations not associated with the sea)

The technique used for river fishing was the fixed trap, with a variety of different types of trap for particular conditions (Drucker 1951:16–18). Some offshore fishing was also done, especially for spring salmon, but this was for immediate consumption and tended to be a dietary supplement.

Herring were second in importance as a food resource. They are also migratory and concentrate in coastal inlets to spawn. Fishing was carried out from canoes using nets and rakes during the spawning runs, and roe was collected by placing fences across the spawning grounds (Drucker 1951:35).

Sea mammals such as seal, sea otter, sea lion, and whale were not a major food source for most Nootkan groups. Drucker (1951:36) argues, however, that these animals ranked next to herring in importance due to their prestige value. Exploitation was by offshore hunting, the harpoon being the primary implement.

Salmon, herring, and sea mammals differed in the uncertainty of catch. Uncertainty associated with sea mammal hunting was a result of size of territory, species mobility, species number, and potential danger. Salmon and herring fishing had the problems of seasonality and quantity. Exactly when runs would occur and how large they would be were uncertain. Yet, in a matter of weeks, the Nootka had to catch and cure sufficient food to last the winter. Years in which runs were poor were not uncommon, and annual runs sometimes did not occur (Drucker 1951: 37).

This uncertainty was reflected in Nootkan beliefs. Fish and sea mammals were thought to have immortal souls (Sapir 1921:351). Care was taken not to offend the spirits of sea mammals, for it was believed they could refuse to be caught again. Prayers were offered to ensure favorable fishing conditions (Drucker 1951:53, 174–176). Taboos were concerned with avoidance of actions or objects which would be seen as offensive by the various species sought. Again the taboos operated as a minimax strategy—minimizing chances for the worst possible state of nature (when fish avoid the fishermen).

In summary, the ecological parameters for the Nootkan fisheries are shown in Table 3. From the Cornish analysis, it will be assumed that there are two sets of oppositions—properties and items. For properties of the resource and environment we can differentiate between anadromous and nonanadromous species. In the sea mammal fishery, the properties are similar to those obtaining in Cornwall. Exploitation is primarily concerned with the scarcity or abundance of the resource. For salmon and herring an additional property seems to be relevant. Given a technology adapted to rivers and inlets, the availability or nonavailability of the species is important. Unless those species leave the sea, their abundance or scarcity is immaterial. In fact the Tsimshian have a myth which illustrates the difference between abundance and availability (Boas 1916:158–160); in this myth a widow and her daughter were starving although they could see salmon jumping at the mouth of a brook. Given limited technology, the resource could not be exploited unless it moved upstream.

The items stressed and related properties are presented in Table 4. It was anticipated that the Nootkan fishing taboos would refer to items having inappropriate characteristics or properties. Using HRAF data an attempt was made to classify taboos using the oppositions given in Table 4.

For the salmon fishery there were five taboos which related to the land/sea opposition. Three referred to activities on the beach (noise, fire, shredding cedar bark). Given that the beach is common to both land and sea, it would appear that the taboos are prohibitions on productive activities in an anomalous zone. Two taboos were concerned with contact between salmon and land-based production (cutting salmon with other than mussel shells, sliming salmon on the ground or wood.)

TABLE 3. The Nootkan Fisheries

Resource	Environment	Fishing Territory	Gear	Division of Labor	Level of Uncertainty[a]
Salmon	Sea/river	River	Trap	Sexual	8
Herring	Sea/inlets	Inlets	Trap	Sexual	9
Sea mammals	Sea	Sea	Hunting	Sexual	7

[a] Uncertainty level taken from Table 1.

TABLE 4. Items Stressed in the Nootkan Fisheries

Fishery	Stressing Factors	Items Stressed	Equivalent Properties
Salmon	Territory	Land/sea	Scarcity/abundance
	Resource	River/sea	Availability/nonavailability
	Division of labor	Man/woman	Productive/nonproductive
Herring	Territory	Land/sea	Scarcity/abundance
	Resource	Inlet/sea	Availability/nonavailability
	Division of labor	Man/woman	Productive/nonproductive
Sea mammals	Territory	Land/sea	Scarcity/abundance
	Division of labor	Man/woman	Productive/nonproductive

Two of the salmon taboos were classified as associated with the sea/river opposition. The first taboo was on sea dwellers going upriver to fish without purification. The second was the prohibition on using the terms for cod, dogfish, and crab—all of which are nonanadromous, the crab being amphibious as well. The final taboos which could be classified by the oppositional schema were based on division of labor. Menstruating women and pubescent girls could not eat fresh salmon.

The remaining seven salmon taboos were unclassifiable given the information available: (1) dogs and cats eating fresh salmon, (2) carrying salmon by their tails in baskets, (3) cutting off salmon heads, (4) chewing spruce gum, (5) deformed salmon, (6) giving fresh salmon to other tribes not on the same river, and (7) leaving spring salmon uncooked overnight.

For sea mammal hunting there were seven taboos listed. Two referred to noise and fires (land/sea). One was on women entering whaling canoes (man/woman), and one was on contact between fishermen and pregnant or menstruating women (man/woman). Three other taboos were unclassifiable: the use of the term for hunting, eating before or during a hunt, and contact with offal. No taboos were given for the herring fishery, though Drucker states that observances for herring were similar to those for salmon (1951:177).

The results from the Nootkan case are inconclusive. Only 57 percent of the taboos given in the literature were accounted for by the model. A comparison of Cornish and Nootkan fisheries indicates that differences in control over resources and organization of labor should be taken into account. Such refinements coupled with better knowledge of "items and symbols" should improve prediction.

The overall analysis is suggestive at a more general level. One of the problems with structural explanation has been difficulty of evaluation. This difficulty appears to come from two sources intrinsic to a structuralist approach. The first is the notion that the object of analysis be treated as a "thing in itself" (Lévi-Strauss 1963b:206-231). This implies that understanding is not a result of discovering relations between the object and others, but rather through its internal organization. Secondly, structuralism is concerned with relations between internal elements rather than the elements themselves (Lévi-Strauss 1962:53). Without being able to specify those elements or relate the "thing" to other social phenomena, prediction becomes impossible. Some anthropologists, therefore, have asserted that structural models cannot be evaluated by positivist criteria (Prattis 1972).

If structuralism is not concerned with elements or external relations, other approaches are so concerned (Leach 1960:386-387). Since the problems to which they are addressed differ, there are no logical reasons why they cannot be combined with structuralism. An ecological approach is just one such orientation. Recent work in myth by Ackerman (1973) and Cove (1973) indicates that structuralism can be usefully combined with structural-functionalism, so that predictive models can be developed.

Many anthropologists feel that structuralism has replaced other approaches. I would argue, however, that we should treat structuralism as would a *bricoleur:* it is but one item in our collection. Rather than letting that item limit what we can do, we should let our projects determine the items. A good *bricoleur* is someone who can combine different means at his disposal, not just use one well.

NOTE

This essay was originally written for the symposium "Theory on the Fringe: New Directions in Theoretical Anthropology," SUNY (Oswego), 7–9 May 1972. My thanks to Drs. Charles Ackerman and Derek Smith for their help and suggestions.

REFERENCES CITED

Ackerman, C.
1973   To'uluwa: man of the Pleiades. Unpublished manuscript.

Boas, F.
1916   *Tsimshian mythology.* Washington, D.C.: Bureau of American Ethnology.

Cornish, T.
1884   Mackerel and pilchard fisheries. *Fisheries Exhibition Literature* (London) 6:104–146.

Cove, J.
1973   Survival or extinction: a solution to the problem of famine in Tsimshian and Kaguru mythology. Unpublished manuscript.

Crouch, J.
1935   Essay on the natural history of the pilchard. *Annual Report of the Royal Cornwall Polytechnic Society* 3:65–107.

Drucker, P.
1951   *The northern and central Nootkan tribes.* Washington, D.C.: Government Printing Office.

Fox, C.
1943   The present position of the Cornish pilchard industry. *Annual Report of the Royal Cornwall Polytechnic Society* (new series) 10:21–36.

Harris, J.
1900   *Our cove.* Truro: Joseph Pollard.

Jenkin, A.
1932   *Cornish seafarers.* London: Dent.

Leach, E.
1960   Lévi-Strauss in the Garden of Eden: an examination of some recent developments in the analysis of myth. *Transactions of the New York Academy of Sciences* 23:386–396.

Lévi-Strauss, C.
1962   *La pensée sauvage.* Paris: Plon.
1963a   The bear and the barber. *Proceedings of the Royal Anthropological Institute*
          93:1–11.
1963b   *Structural anthropology.* New York: Basic Books.

Malinowski, B.
1935   *Coral gardens and their magic.* London: Allen and Unwin.
1948   *Magic, science and religion.* Garden City: Doubleday.

Nance, R.
1924   Taboo names in Cornwall. *Journal of the Royal Institution of Cornwall*
          21:470–477.

Noall, C.
1970   *Cornwall remembered.* Truro: Tor Mark Press.

Prattis, J.
1972   Science, ideology and false demons. *American Anthropologist* 74:1125–1128.

Rowe, J.
1953   *Cornwall in the age of the industrial revolution.* Liverpool: Liverpool University
          Press.

Sapir, E.
1921   The life of a Nootkan Indian. *Queen's Quarterly* 28:232–243, 351–367.

Steiner, F.
1956   *Taboo.* London: Cohen and West.

Swan, J. G.
1870   *The Indians of Cape Flattery at the entrance to the Strait of Fuca, Washington
          Territory.* Washington, D.C.: Smithsonian.

Thomas, W.
1893   *Romance of the Cornish cove.* London: Houlston & Sons.

Von Brandt, A.
1964   *Fish catching methods of the world.* London: Fishing News (Books).

Structural Analysis of Chol Mayan Pronouns

JOHN J. ATTINASI

A systematic approach to language regards grammar as a set of categories which are available to speakers for linguistic expression and are in turn utilized by hearers for linguistic interpretation. Language concerns a structurally bounded sphere of thought and perception; thought and perception are themselves limited renderings of the flux of existence. It follows that the grammatical categories of language are selections of various aspects of experience, primarily for communication but also for expressive, directive, metalinguistic, and poetic purposes, and for purposes of social or phatic communion as well.

Categories are meaningless if viewed in isolation. It is only the internal structure—the number, nature, and contrast of oppositions within the category—which gives grammatical meaning. And it is the internal structure which provides the link between the sense or comprehension of the grammatical system and the extensional reference to extralinguistic reality. To assign labels such as "present" to verbal morphemes without an explanation of the oppositions involved in the category of the encoding of time (tense) is an error. Serge Karcevsky expressed it in 1929 as follows: "Un morphème n'est qu'une marque sur la ligne phonique d'un croisement de rapports, et rien d'autre" (quoted in Hamp et al.:1966:5). The category of singular in Chol has a much different meaning from the category of the same name in languages where singular and plural are equally marked oppositions, for in Chol the singular form is unmarked with regard to number. In still other languages (such as Navajo or Tagalog) singular is opposed to dual and to plural in a three-way opposition. The basis of these differences is the structuralist notion that a grammatical category has meaning only in terms of the contrasts between its constituent oppositions.

A consequence of the structural theory of oppositions is the problem of the motivation for discrimination of categories and oppositions within categories. Saussure viewed the grammatical system as an isolable set of internally established relations, similar to the display and capability of movement of chessmen at any given instant in a game. He also viewed the symbols that comprise language as arbitrary. Both these views share arbitrariness as their chief characteristic; but each differs in the way motivation is deleted from the system. In the former instance, motivation is admittedly disregarded to give investigatory power to the analysis. The grammar is assumed to be a closed system in order to explore the way a limited number of morphological elements and syntactic procedures account for the practically unlimited number and referential power of utterances. In the latter instance, arbitrariness is a point of view concerning the origin of the linguistic symbol. This question has remained intriguing and largely undecidable since the time of Plato's *Cratylus* (Jakobson 1965; Benveniste 1966).

Since mid-century, a wider scope of structural investigation has resulted in greater numbers of less easily defined categories and oppositions. More complex categories in art and social relations have been analyzed. But rather than utilizing networks of multiopposition categories, there has been a predilection to limit oppositions to strictly binary functions.[1]

In the treatment of the Chol pronouns that follows, a three-dimensional model will be used to illustrate the structure of the oppositions which intersect to characterize the meaning of the pronoun morphemes. Whether the categories have perceptual and cognitive reality to the speaker of Chol is a legitimate and interesting question, though no attempt at its verification is made here.

THE THREE DIMENSIONS

The dichotomies *langue/parole,* code/message, and competence/performance are roughly equivalent ways of noting the distinction between the abstract repertory of language ability (in the case of *langue,* socially possessed; in the case of competence, individually possessed) and the actual production of linguistic utterances. The utterance or "speech event" is a finite string of audible speech. The speech event contains participants and a topic, or reference. The participants may be the same as the reference or different from it. From these aspects of the speech event are derived the categories of contrast in the pronominal system.

TABLE 1. Pronominal Morphemes

Number	Clusion		
	+		−
	Speaker	Hearer	Imperson
− Plural	k	a	i (y, ∅)
	hon	hat	hin
	on	et	
+ Plural	lo:	la	ob [o']

The three dimensions of pronoun contrast are the following:

1. *Address* is the relationship between speaker and hearer. Alternative terms for this relationship are encoder/decoder, producer/receiver, transducer/interpretant, first person/second person, addresser/addressee.
2. *Clusion* is the relationship between the participants of the speech event (speaker and hearer) and nonparticipant referents ("imperson," erroneously called "third person" in traditional grammar).
3. *Number* is the relationship between marked plurality and the absence of plural marking.

Table 1 shows the pronominal morphemes which concatenate to form the intersection points of these three dimensions. This information deserves to be treated in more detail.

Address

The grammatical category of address is essential to any theory of language because all speech originates from a source of production, the addresser, and is interpreted by a receiver, the addressee. The interpretant receiver may be the same as the addresser (talking to oneself); the intended receiver may not be visible (as in writing or in cries into the darkness); the addressee may be at a different social or conceptual level of reality (prayer, ritual, dream speech). But clearly these are cases marginal to the majority of speech events that originate from a speaker and are received by a hearer. The speaker and hearer and the persons of the speech event reference and constitute the marked half of the opposition "clusion." This marked category itself requires a dichotomous marking since speech event reference can include either participant. The category of address distinguishes these two participants in a one-dimensional linear way (see Figure 1).

Speaker	Hearer
+ Address	− Address

FIGURE 1.   The Pronominal Dimension of Address

Clusion

The dimension of clusion with its terms inclusion/exclusion is implicit in the definition of the category of address and intersects with it. The speaker and hearer are included in the speech event. When they are referred to by the speech event, the reference is *personal.* When no reference to the participants is made, the reference of the speech event is *impersonal* (even if the referent is human).

The marked term of the opposition contains a further distinction, address, and is marked by a full set of pronoun morphemes used exclusively for this purpose. In contrast the unmarked term "imperson" is more limited in that it contains no opposition of address and seems to be restricted formally as well. There is no full, fixed, and exclusive paradigm of morphemes that marks the paradigmatic slots formed by the intersection of the contrasts. Instead there are numerous alternatives roughly paralleling the demonstratives and topicalizers and "zero" positions often filled by clitics for prosodic continuity. The morpheme /hin-i/ is listed with the imperson free pronoun to retain symmetry with /honon/ and /hatet/. In the corpus of data, however, /hini/, iliyi/, išiši/, eba:nel/, and variants of these appear with equal frequency. Similarly, /hin-ob/ is listed as the imperson plural free pronoun, though neither this nor any other markedly pluralized form is frequent. The most frequent is the derived demonstrative /e-ba:n-e/ (< √ba:n/ "alone, single, sole"). If these various forms are semantically differentiated demonstratives, it is not certain according to which criteria discriminations are made. Nor is it yet clear in which environments no imperson pronouns (zero forms) appear. The following rule for such pronoun deletion in the imperson is tentative and optional:

$$\textbf{MPR·ZIMP} \begin{bmatrix} i \\ \\ imperson \end{bmatrix} \rightarrow \emptyset \ / \begin{bmatrix} negative \\ or \\ modal \end{bmatrix} \underline{\qquad}$$

Read: The /i/ of the imperson pronoun is deleted optionally in negative sentences and after modals.

Ordered prior to the deletion rule is the glide rule, MPR·GLY. These two rules account for the following phonetic renderings:

MPR·GLY
MPR·ZIMP
/mač-i-om/ ⎯⎯⎯⎯⎯⎯⎯⎯⎯→ [mač.yom] "he doesn't want to, no good"

MPR·ZIMP
/mač-i-kuč/⎯⎯⎯⎯⎯⎯⎯⎯⎯→ [mač.kuč] "one can't support it, impossible"

no rule
operation
/mi-kehe-i-kuc/⎯⎯⎯⎯⎯⎯⎯⎯⎯→ [mi.ke.he.ʔ i.kuc] "he begins to carry it"

MPR·ZIMP
⎯⎯⎯⎯⎯⎯⎯⎯⎯→ [mi.ke.e.kuč] "he begins to carry it"

An alternative or corollary to these solutions may be that there is a semantically mediopassive conjugation allowable with nearly every verb, formed by the omission of all pronouns. If this were so, the qualitative difference between person and imperson would only be more emphatically drawn.

The display of the two dimensions treated so far creates a plane, with the dimension of clusion perpendicular to the linear dimension of address. Figure 2 illustrates this display.

Number

A third dimension is added to the paradigm by the category of number. The marked half of the opposition encodes plurality. The unmarked half encodes no special information with regard to number. Both the persons and the imperson participate in the category of number. The defective form of the imperson is again manifest in this category. The persons utilize special morphemes: /la/ for hearer plural and omniperson and /lo:/ → /lohon/ for speaker plural. But the imperson has no special morpheme. Instead it makes use of the usual pluralizer for human referents: /ob/, [oʔ]. In many instances the imperson marks no plural, leaving plurality unmarked.

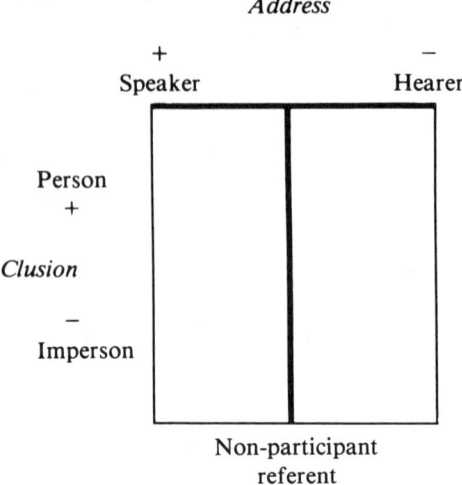

FIGURE 2.   The Pronominal Dimensions of
Address and Clusion

Beyond Distinctions: The Omniperson

These three binary oppositions yield six intersecting points which are the personal and imperson pronouns, in both nonplural and plural form. A seventh pronoun class exists in Chol: the omniperson, which does not participate in the either/or oppositions of the pronominal dimensions. Rather it neutralizes the distinctions, encompassing all the dichotomies like a dialectical synthesis. Its position is thus a point in the center of the three-dimensional display of the pronominal categories (see Figure 3). Formally, this pronoun class is a combination of the nonplural speaker morphemes and the position 10 hearer plural morpheme /la/:

Free:	honon-la
Bound:	k . . . -la
Ergative:	-on-la

This formal relationship is mirrored by the reference of the omniperson, which is primarily that of an inclusive plural: "speaker plus hearers" (as opposed to the exclusive plural /honon-lohon/ "speaker and speaker's group"). The reference is wider than that signaled by the morphemes, however.

Although the morphemes /k/ and /la/ do not indicate it, the speaker's group and a singular hearer may also be referenced by the omniperson. The extension of the reference of this form is also applicable to nonparti-

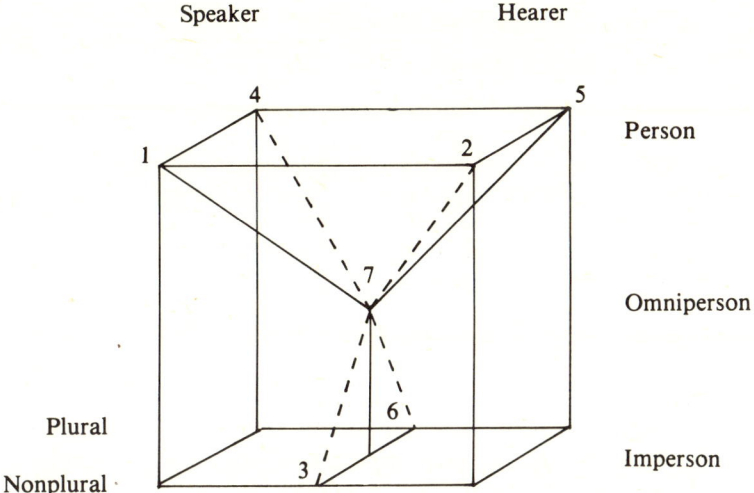

FIGURE 3. Chol Pronoun Box

cipants of the speech event (imperson), justifying the position of the omniperson as beyond all distinctions in the three-dimensional system of pronouns. The omniperson can also be used as a general pronoun to refer to no special person. This form appears frequently in general reference to nouns habitually possessed (body parts, kin terms) and in general metalinguistic use (informant interviews). This pronoun is glossed in Spanish by an infinitive or a reflexive verb form:

mi k-p' ʌk'-la   "*sembrar, se siembre,* to
                                       plant, it is planted";
                                       literally, "we-all plant"[2]

It would appear that the omniperson is beyond all distinctions, those of clusion and number as well as that of address. Figure 3, a three-dimensional paradigm, illustrates the relationship of the pronominal categories to one another.

THE THREE PRONOUN SERIES

The pronominal morphemes concatenate to form three sets of pronouns, each with syntactic properties special to the series.

The Free Pronoun Series

The free series of pronouns (see Table 2) does not require any particular concatenational formula. These pronouns are composed of a

TABLE 2.   The Free Pronouns

Components	Pronouns	Gloss
hon-on	→ honon	"I"
hat-et	→ hatet	"you"
hin-i	→ hini	"he, she, it" (imperson)
hon-on-lo:-on	→ honon-lohon	"we" (exclusive)
hat-et-la	→ hatet-la	"you-all"
hin-ø-b	→ hin-oʔ	"they"(imperson plural)
hon-on-la	→ honon-la	"we-all" (omniperson)

radical element (which itself seems to be formed from /h/ and a characteristic sign of the person or imperson) and a characteristic morpheme. This analysis is at a much deeper morphological level than any other analysis, since no productive mutability of the component morphemes is possible. These pronouns are thus treated elsewhere as stable morphemes, even though by the present analysis and by a consideration of their syllabic form they may be considered multimorphemic words.

The Bound Pronoun Series

The bound pronoun set (see Table 3) is used for the pronominal referencing of roots. This includes possession of nominals and the referencing of the subject of verbs (except the past forms of intransitives). The nonplural forms of this series are prefixed to the root, or to the derivational-plus-root sequence, filling position 4 of the verb phrase morphotactics. The suffix portion of this series fills postroot position 10, occasionally preceded by a clitic in position 9.

When the bound omniperson is used for noun possessives and in verb phrases that are utterance-final, the following rule operates to advance the plural suffix /la/ to a position preceding the prefix part of the discontinuous morpheme /k . . . la/:

TABLE 3.   The Bound Pronouns

Position 4	Position 10	Gloss
k		"I, my"
a		"you, your"
i ([y], ø)		"he, his; she, her; it, its" (imperson)
k	lohon	"we, our" (exclusive)
a	la	"you-all, you-all's"
i ([y], ø)	ob	"they, their"
k	la	"we, our" (omniperson)

MPR · PLADV

$$k - X \sqrt{} \ Y - la \rightarrow la\text{-}k \ X \sqrt{} \ Y \ / \ NP, \underline{\qquad} \text{utterance final}$$

Read: The plural morpheme /la/ of the discontinuous omniperson bound pronoun /k . . . a/ advances, becoming /la-k/.

This rule may also apply in the case of the discontinuous speaker plural bound pronoun. The instances of this are rare in the data and occur only with nominals. The plural advance rule might be modified; or, better, another rule might be written:

MPR · EXPLADV

$$\begin{bmatrix} k- \\ bound \end{bmatrix} \ x \ \sqrt{} \ y- \ \begin{bmatrix} lohon \\ plural \end{bmatrix} \longrightarrow lohonk \ x \ \sqrt{} \ y \ / \ NP$$

Read: The plural of the exclusive plural /k . . . lohon/ advances, becoming /lohon-k/ in nominal forms.

A rule concerning the bound pronoun /k/ operates when a root begins with /h/:

MPR · HK

$$\begin{bmatrix} -syl \\ -int \\ -cen \\ -hi \\ -flt \\ -nas \end{bmatrix} \rightarrow \begin{bmatrix} +int \\ +hi \\ -chk \end{bmatrix} \ / \ \begin{bmatrix} +int \\ -cen \\ +hi \\ -chk \\ bound \end{bmatrix} \ \underline{\qquad}$$

Read: /h/ becomes [k] following the bound pronoun /k/.

This rule may be thought of as feeding obligatorily into the geminate segment rule or into one of the paired /k/ rules which themselves are derived from the more powerful and widespread geminate segment rule.

PR · GEM

$$[\alpha\text{---}] \qquad\qquad\qquad [\alpha\text{---}]$$
$$\begin{matrix} \cdot \\ \cdot \\ \cdot \end{matrix} \rightarrow \emptyset \ / \ \underline{\qquad} \begin{matrix} \cdot \\ \cdot \\ \cdot \end{matrix}$$

Read: Any segment can delete if followed by a segment like itself. More simply, geminate segments may become simple.

Ordered following the HK rule is a pair of morphophonemic rules that account for the behavior of the bound pronoun /k/ before many interruptants:

$$
\text{MPR} \cdot \text{KDEL} \begin{bmatrix} +\text{int} \\ -\text{cen} \\ +\text{hi} \\ -\text{chk} \end{bmatrix} \rightarrow \quad \emptyset \quad / \begin{bmatrix} \underline{\quad\quad} \\ \text{bound} \end{bmatrix} \begin{bmatrix} +\text{int} \\ +\text{hi} \end{bmatrix}
$$

Read: Before certain high stops, the bound pronoun /k/ deletes.

$$
\text{MPR} \cdot \text{KDEINT} \begin{bmatrix} +\text{int} \\ -\text{cen} \\ +\text{hi} \\ -\text{chk} \end{bmatrix} \rightarrow \begin{bmatrix} -\text{int} \\ -\text{hi} \\ -\text{flt} \end{bmatrix} / \begin{bmatrix} \underline{\quad\quad} \\ \text{bound} \end{bmatrix} \begin{bmatrix} +\text{int} \\ +\text{hi} \end{bmatrix}
$$

Read: Before certain high stops, the bound pronoun /k/ becomes deinterrupted to [h] (or [x]).

The application of these rules must be stated in prose. The k-deletion rule is more frequent in the western dialects, and the k-deinterruption rule is more frequent in the eastern dialects. If the stop is either /k/ or /k'/ following the bound pronoun the rule almost always operates, probably always in the eastern dialects. Before any other high stops, the rules operate optionally in the eastern dialects and not at all in the western dialects.

The rules just presented are ordered in the following way:

$$\text{MPR} \cdot \text{PLADV} > \text{MPR} \cdot \text{HK} > \text{MPR} \cdot \text{KDEL}$$

or

$$\text{MPR} \cdot \text{KDEINT} > \text{PR} \cdot \text{GEM}$$

The output of these rules can be seen with three examples: /k-hol-la/ "head" (literally "our-all's head"), /k-kʌč-la/ "we-all tie," and /k-k'aš-el-la/ "we-all pass through." These are shown in Table 4.

TABLE 4. Rule Operation on Bound Pronoun Forms

Morpho-phonemic Canon	Rules					Phonetic Output
	PLADV	HK	KDEL	KDEINT	GEM	
k-hol-la	la-k-hol					→ [lak.hol]
k-hol-la	la-k-hol	la-k-kol			la-kol	→ [la.kol]
k-hol-la	la-k-hol	la-k-kol		lah-kol		→ [la:.kol]
k-hol-la	la-k-hol	la-k-kol	la-kol			→ [la.kol]
k-kʌč-la	la-k-kʌč		la-kʌč			→ [la.kʌč]
k-kʌč-la	la-k-kʌč			lah-kʌč		→ [la:-kʌč]
k-kʌč-la			kʌč-la			→ [kʌč.la]
k-k'aš-el-la	la-k-k'aš-el		la-k'aš-el			→ [la.ka.šɛl]
k-k'aš-el-la	la-k-k'aš-el			la-h-k'ašel		→ [la:.k'a.šɛl]
k-k'aš-el-la			k'aš-el-la		k'aš-e-la	→ [k'a.še.la]

The Ergative Pronoun Series

Ergative systems utilize the same pronouns for the grammatical patient in transitive sentences and the grammatical argument in intransitive sentences. True ergativity requires that the primary and obligatory argument in transitive sentences be the patient, and that encoding of the agent be optional or secondary in some other way. Most ergative systems exhibit "split ergativity" (Silverstein 1973), wherein the ergative function is shared with other morphemes.

The direct-object function of the Chol ergative series of pronouns is somewhat different from the true ergativity of languages like Georgian and Eskimo. In Chol transitive sentences, the agent is expressed primarily (using the bound series pronouns) and the expression of the patient is always secondary. Never can a typically ergative sentence like "hit me" (that is, "I am hit") occur, with no overt expression of the agent. But often sentences with implicit expression of the patient are encountered:

mi-k-ʌk'-en   "I give (it [to you, him, them])"

The argument-of-intransitive-sentence function of the Chol ergative series of pronouns exhibits a split in ergativity along lines of tense. The argument of nonpast intransitive sentences is expressed with the bound series; the argument of such sentences in the past tense is expressed by the ergative series. In the following examples, the argument "you" of the event "going" is encoded by the ergative pronoun /et/ only in the unmarked past (3) and comparative past (4) sentences. In nonpast sentences (1 and 2) the bound pronoun /a/ encodes the argument.

1. Bound: mu-iš-a-ma:l-el   "you will go now"
2. Bound: mi-a-ma:l-el   "you go"
3. Ergative: ma'an ti-ma:l-i-et   "you did not go"
4. Ergative: ȼa-iš-ma:l-i-et   "you have gone"[3]

In the special progressive aspect syntax, the ergative pronoun encodes the argument in all sentences, transitive and intransitive. This syntactic form is similar to predicate complement syntax /ti + USTEM/, which utilizes only the bound series of pronouns in the independent sentence.

The ergative pronouns are also utilized in the existential predication of arguments with lexical roots:

1. /wʌ'- č-an-on-la/   [wʌ.č'a.non.'la]   "we are here"
2. /č'u:-ana-on/   [č'u.wa.na.'hon]   "I am a mayordomo"
3. /k'išin-et/   [k'iš.ni.yet]   "you are drunk"

This function may also be thought of as split. Predications with no roots attached—that is, predications of specific arguments when the predicate is known through context or previous statement or question ("who is a mayordomo?")—are encoded by using the free series of pronouns. In complete predications containing both argument and predicate, as in the preceding examples, the ergative series of pronouns is utilized.

The various pronominal functions are tabulated in Table 5. Formally the ergative pronouns are suffixing. They occupy position 8 of the verb phrase morphotactics, and the plural morphemes identical to those of the other series in form and distribution occupy position 10[4] (see Table 6.)

TABLE 5.   Pronominal Functions

Function	Free	Bound	Ergative
Existential prediction			
Without root	x		
With root			x
Possessor of object		x	
Possessor of transitive event (agent)		x	
Recipient of transitive event (patient)			x
Argument of intransitive event			
Nonpast		x	
Past			x

TABLE 6. Ergative Series Pronouns

Position 8	Position 10	Gloss
on		"I, me, I am"
et		"you, you are"
ø (clitic)		"he, she, it, him, her, he is, she is, it is"
on	lohon	"we, us, we are" (exclusive)
et	la	"you-all, you-all are"
ø	ob	"they, them, they are"
on	la	"we-all, us-all, we-all are"

IMPLICATIONS FOR SOCIOCULTURE

Each culture structures and assigns meaning to the natural environment, sometimes in similar (universal) but often in divergent (relative) modalities. Discriminations which encode experience divide or "map out" semantic space, fitting every possible configuration of sense experience into categories embodied in and symbolized by linguistic signs. In this way the Heraclitean flux receives interpretation. Mankind settles a fundamentally indeterminate universe. There is no experience that cannot be interpreted by ethnocentered classification; there is no action that cannot be referred to within the finite scope of verbal categories of tense, aspect, and mood. For the system here under discussion—the pronouns—all combinations of personal and nonpersonal participants in speech events and narrated events are categorized as intersections of the dimensions of the system diagrammed in the Chol pronoun box (Figure 3).

The distribution of morphemes in linguistic environments indicates that these distinctions—clusion, address, and number—are the main foci of Chol intension and interpretation. These are supplemented by the category which transcends all distinctions and is used for abstract, general, infinitive, and inclusive reference—the omniperson. The three pronoun series are derived mainly from formal considerations of the basic inventory of pronominal morphemes (Table 1), their combination, frequency, and use. The distribution of the free and bound series, and the rules of morphophonemics, are strictly formal and do not mirror salient symbolic features of the system. Only the distribution of the ergative series presents formal evidence of the cognitive distinctions encoded by the three dimensions of the system. This occurs fundamentally in the past of intransitives wherein the ergative pronoun signals the overt neutralization of the agent/patient distinction, a fact which underlines the semantic structure of Mayan verbs. Transitive verbs are possessed actions and intransitive verbs are activities which occur at personal loci; but no verb is semantically an action initiated by a personal actor. (In the nonpast this neutralization of agent/patient is logical for intransitives, but covert.)

More important, the limited paradigm of the imperson pronouns in all three series indicates that the dimension of clusion is motivated from within the linguistic competence of Chol and is not a mere *hoc est pocus* artifact of the linguist. The pronouns which reference the participants of the speech event form a paradigm of limited and invariant formal shape. On the other hand, the imperson pronouns are nonexistent in the ergative series, optionally deleted in the bound series, and unsystematically diverse in the free series.

This radical distinction between the participants of the speech event and the nominal argument of narrated events is further supported by the concept of personal or participant knowledge. A Chol values personal knowledge as highly as he values personal effort. Intermediaries, vicarious experience, work performed for another's benefit, material objects not personally constructed, and observation without participation are all less valued than personally performed, immediately realizable works. To speak of ideas or events which are narratives or hearsay, a special clitic particle /bi/ is used. This particle only occurs in reference to the imperson; its general meaning is "this is not my personal knowledge."

Intersecting with these notions, the fundamental concept of the participants in the speech event, speaker and hearer, is valued as highly in the wider sphere of social relations as it is within the linguistic structure. Without /t'an/ "the power of speaking," a Chol is unable to address the ancestors or seek favors from God. His state is described as /kisin/ "bashful shame" and spiritual impoverishment. To make up for his spiritual and verbal deficiencies, he employs /š-resal/ (a woman prayer who prays in Spanish), /trinsipal/ (an old man experienced in the words and ways of Chol prayer), or/šiba:/—whose prayers in "unintelligible" Chol dronings are accompanied by blowing, clinking glass and steel, and other nonverbal sounds. These sacred realms exhibit structuralist reversals which reinforce the secular values of personal speaking and hearing: the use of intermediaries for sacred purposes corresponds to their lack in secular domains; the nonverbal noises and the speechless oral production of blowing and droning in the most private kind of curing which occurs at night corresponds to values of speaking and hearing. These values flourish not only in daily activities unrelated to religion but also in daytime public cults performed either in Spanish or Chol.

The social activity of the Chol is seen primarily as speaking—not just "saying something," /ʌl/, but "speaking to someone," /peːk-an/. In telling me of his fearlessness toward strangers one man said: "This is why we have a mouth, so we can speak to anyone at all." Here value attaches to the relationship of addresser and addressee in the speech event, not to topic. At the end of a conversation the Chol say: "Well, we've spoken to each other, /ȼa-š peːk-ʌ la-k-bʌ/, *ahi nos platicamos.*" The value of speaking is emphasized again at the penultimate good-bye, in which the correlative statement to the Euro-American "I'll *see* you" is "soon I will *talk to you*," /mu-š to peːk-an-et/.

Lastly, it may be seen that not only are the dimensions of clusion and address fundamental to Chol language and culture, but also that the concept of number as it appears in the system of pronouns is replicated in other areas of perception and speech. For all lexical roots, whether nominal or verbal, plural is a semantically (and formally) marked category. This means that the presence of a pluralizer such as /ob/ for human nouns signals that there is necessarily more than one of the referent. The absence of this marking does not indicate anything with respect to the number of the referent; there is not necessarily more than one of the referent, but there may be. In clearer terms, the absence of an overt marking indicates that there is no statement of number being made. When any lexical number indicator is used, such as a numeral or the quantifier /kabʌl/, no plural marker is used normally. In situations where the speaker's attitude is added to the narrative statement, the addition of a plural morpheme carries overtones of mood:

kabʌl š-kal-ʌl	"a number of girls, many girls"
kabʌl š-kal-ʌl-ob	"too many girls, lots of hussies"

For nonhuman nouns the plural is never noted by a morpheme, but only by numerals or by /kabʌl/ (or occasionally, and only in the eastern dialects, by the repletive suffice /tak/).

The claim which may be made from this evidence is that the Chol perceive references without numerical specification and only with additional ratiocination do they append numerical considerations. Thus, whether there is one or many of the object (/otot/ "house," for instance), the perception concerns the distinctive characteristics of the Chol concept of (what the English philosopher would call) "houses," as opposed to trees, rocks, and chickens. From our own point of view it may be instructive to look at a painting and note our perception of what distinguishes painting from photography, writing, or nature. Note that the notion of number, "one painting," does not enter the semantic field until there are several considered. At that point the distinction "one painting of several paintings" becomes necessary to and inextricable from the perception. For the Chol even this situation retains its purity: it is as if every root word were inherently a collective. More precisely, every root is "unmarked" with regard to the semantics of number.

The addition of conceptions concerning number are elaborated for the Chol and reflect the mathematicality of the ancient and modern Maya. The ancient Mayan civilization used its complex numerical system chiefly for astronomy and calendrics. The contemporary Mayans conjoin mathematical classification with other perceptual—chiefly spatial and textural—considerations. Returning to the unmarked perception of the referent of a Chol linguistic symbol, we see that the encoding of any concept of number engages a wider semantic apparatus. "One painting" requires the further notion "one-*flat* painting," /hun-k'e-bonol-pisil/. Similarly, "one chicken" is "one-*animal* chicken," /hun-*koːt*-mut/, and "one house" is "one-nonspecific-object (residual) house," /hum-p'eː-otot/.

This last argument concerning number, coupled with the first argument concerning clusion, embodies and perpetuates in a negative way what the argument concerning address states positively. If the imperson were to be deleted from the pronoun paradigm on formal grounds, and the plural deleted on the semantic grounds that it invokes another entire system, what is left is the key triangle of speaker, hearer, and omniperson, indicating the highest values in the ethnography of Chol speech. From linguistic statistics it can be learned that these three pronoun types—speaker /honon -on k-/, hearer /hatet -et a-/, omniperson /hononla -onla k- $\sqrt{}$ -la/—are the most frequently encountered in speech. From observed behavior and stated norms emerge similar notions which underline concerns with immediacy in all experience, with the supreme value of the speech event, and with abstract principles and comprehensive symbolization. This world view receives repeated iteration and reinforcement with every sentence spoken in Chol, not only from the lexical content of the utterance but from within the grammatical system as well. It is instructive to see that concepts of grammar are not different in kind from more general concepts of ethnology, and that within a given community the elucidation of one will never be complete without the integrated elaboration of the other.

NOTES

1. The predilection for limiting oppositions to binary functions may be more a postulate of the investigator's culture or an artifact of his or her technology than a characteristic of the object of investigation.

2.   In this general use the omniperson is as near to a truly infinitive form as is overtly possible to the Chol. (The production of bare roots is not always possible.) The more frequent phonetic form [mi.lak.p'ʌk'] is derivable by the rule MPR · PLADV.

3.   Phonetic renderings for these examples are: (1) [mu.ša.ma:.'lɛl], (2) [ma.ma:.'lɛl], (3) [ma.ʔan.ti.ma:.li'yet], (4) [ȼaš.ma:.li.'yɛt].

4.   There may be a slightly different accent pattern in the ergative series, which shifts accent from final to penultimate syllable when the plural is derived from the ergative series rather than the bound series:

> mi-k-sub-en-et-la   [mi.ksu.bɛ.ñɛt.'la]
> "we-all [bound] tell you [ergative, nonplural]"
> mi-k-sub-en-et-la   [mi.ksu.bɛ.'ñɛt.la]
> "I [bound] tell you-all [ergative, hearer plural]"
> mi-sub-en-on-la   [mi.su.bɛ.'ñon.la]
> "He (they) [bound] speak to us-all [ergative, omniperson]"

REFERENCES CITED

Benveniste, Emile
1966   Catégories de langue et catégories de pensée. In *Problèmes de linguistique générale*. Paris: Gallimard (NRF).

Hamp, Eric P. et al.
1966   *Readings in linguistics II*. Chicago: University of Chicago Press.

Jakobson, Roman
1965   Quest for the essence of language. *Diogenes* 51:21–37.

Silverstein, Michael
1973   Hierarchy of features and ergativity. Mimeographed manuscript, Department of Anthropology, University of Chicago.

Meta-Anthropology: The Elementary Forms of Ethnological Thought

S. LEE SEATON

KAREN ANN WATSON-GEGEO

The primary objective of Durkheim's *Elementary Forms of the Religious Life* was to establish a theory of religion with Australian ethnography serving as the crucial experiment. But the longer-ranged secondary objective was to renovate the theory of knowledge. As noted by W. E. H. Stanner (1967:227), the epistemological concern was obscured by the impact of Durkheim's revolutionary theory of religion on the one hand and controversy over ethnographic materials on the other.

In this essay we wish to reverse the order of priorities: to place the development of the theory of anthropological knowledge first, to take ethnology as our medium, and to regard ethnography as our ultimate goal. It is our contention that ethnography and ethnological theory may only be integrated as an "anthropological science" through the medium of culture theory. What has been absent from the conceptual reviews of culture theories published so far is a fundamental conception of the enterprise of theorizing about theory—in a word, *metatheory*.

It is only at this abstract level of analysis that cross-theoretical communication is unbiased by adherence to *particular* paradigms of culture theory. For instance, using a distinctly materialist conception of culture to discuss an idealist perspective is simply an intellectual version of ethnocentricism. Our preference is for a self-consciously comparative metatheory which emphasizes the operational consequences of selecting one theory over another. Such a metatheory has been offered by philosopher Stephen Pepper under the title *World Hypotheses* (1966), originally published in 1942.

1.0   METATHEORY IN ANTHROPOLOGY

First we shall take a look at metatheory in anthropology to date. As usually interpreted, ethnography is the descriptive science of culture, and ethnology uses ethnographic data as the factual materials for building theory.[1] When we wish to analyze theories themselves, however, we need to move to a third level of abstraction. As we shall use it here, *meta-anthropology* is the study of ethnological theory and hence the study of the theories of culture. More generally, meta-anthropology is a component in the developing interdiscipline of metatheory. It is our intention to examine seven basic topics as initial steps toward increasing metatheoretical consciousness and communication among anthropologists.

The seven topics are: (1) the role of metatheory in anthropology; (2) the state of the art in contemporary meta-anthropology; (3) the introduction of a suitable metatheoretical architectonic for culture theory; (4) the identification of inadequate culture theories; (5) the identification of adequate culture theories; (6) the critique of culture theories; and finally (7) the critique of meta-anthropology.

A metatheory is a theory of theory, though the apparent simplicity of such a definition is deceiving. Before we can assess the role of metatheory in anthropology, two implicit problems of the basic definition must be resolved. First, the meaning of "theory" is less than self-evident, yet as the key term in the definition some understanding of the use of theory as an analytical device is needed in order to make the definition meaningful. Second, a theory *of* theory invites a basic confusion in levels of abstraction. The very idea of a metatheory is problematic because it involves an apparent violation of Russell's theory of logical types (Russell 1908), that is, self-reference.[2]

1.1   The Meaning of "Theory"

The terminological confusion surrounding the words *theory, model, framework,* and so forth is a matter of record. Without attempting to legislate terminology we may note that all usages agree that (1) findings, results, or conclusions are expressed in propositions or statements and (2) that such propositions stand in some coherent relation to one another. Granted that there are important dimensions in doing science which may not be propositionalized (that is, may remain tacit), public knowledge itself exists only in statements in some kind of language.[3] Of course there are many different languages available to scientists, including the formal languages of mathematics, computer languages, and natural languages. Whatever the language, doing science has as its aim the production of a collection of propositions embodying knowledge.

But a collection of propositions, even if true, is not necessarily a coherent set. Coherence implies that there must be a focused interrelatedness to the collection. For example, such orderliness may emphasize the logically consistent integration of propositions involving substantially different foci, such as the "synthetic theory of biosocial evolution." Whatever the emphasis, the important thing is that the propositions are somehow connected to one another. Just how tight the network of propositions becomes depends upon the substantive and conceptual linkages that are established or are assumed to exist, and evaluation of the network is governed by the standard of logic adopted.[4]

1.2   The Meaning of "Metatheory"

A metatheory, then, may be defined as a coherent set of propositions *about* a coherent set of propositions. In this sense a metatheory is analogous to a metalanguage, a language used to discuss another language.[5] A language may be subject to several alternative metalanguages; mathematics, for example, includes ordinary language, symbolic logic, and set *theory* as metalanguages.

As long as the metalanguage and the object language are dissimilar, no type-theory violation of self-reference can occur. When the metalanguage is indistinguishable from the object language, however, confusion may easily lead to paradoxes of self-reference. To untangle this complex of levels of abstraction and interlevel and reference, we shall review the sequence of events described by Gregory Bateson as formative in his discovery of the "double-bind" theory of schizophrenia (1972).

Bateson recalls that in 1952 he visited the Fleishhacker Zoo in San Francisco "to look for behavioral criteria which would indicate whether any given organism is or is not able to recognize that the signs emitted by itself and other members of the species are signals" (ibid.:179). Witnessing two monkeys playing at combat, he concluded that the monkeys must be able to signal the message that "this is play." Proceeding to analyze this kinesic statement, Bateson came to the "realization that this message contains those elements which necessarily generate a paradox of the Russellian or Epimenides type— a negative statement containing an implicit negative metastatement" (ibid.:179–180).[6]

Type theory is designed to preclude such self-referential statements as Epimenides' famous paradox of the liar: "I am lying." To exclude paradoxical statements necessitates the inadmissibility of *all* self-referring statements, including those which are obviously true. Further, "consider the view that every valid theory must be obtained from observed empirical data. This is a theory about theories and their validity," yet it "does not seem to conform to its own criterion as to what constitutes a valid theory, at least unless it can itself be shown to have been obtained as a generalization from observed empirical data" (Fitch 1967:156).[7]

Self-referential principles, such as the *argumentum ad hominem,* depend upon the proper insistence that a theory abide by the standard it sets for others.[8] A metatheory must be able to refer to theoretical principles which it adheres to and uses in analysis of object theories. Failure to appreciate this requirement underlies many conflicts between theorists who are literally talking past each other. To be adequate, a metatheory must exist at a clearly different level of abstraction from the level of object theory. If it does not, we are led inevitably to a form of the Mannheim paradox in the sociology of knowledge: if social factors determine the character of knowledge, then the knowledge that knowledge is determined by social factors is determined by social factors.[9] No matter which way one turns, there is an infinite regress. Figure 1 illustrates the relationships of metatheory (in this case, meta-anthropology) to other levels of abstraction in anthropology.

To ensure the significance of interlevel analysis, the metatheory and the object theory must adhere to the same standards of discourse. Moreover, it is apparent that there exists a "natural" heuristic between some theories and certain metatheories. Set theory, for example, has largely replaced symbolic logic in metamathematics even though the two metalanguages are logically equivalent.

The key to productively pairing metatheory and object theory is the identification of the pragmatic nature of the object theory itself. That is, why do we theorize and conceptualize about the specific subject matter projected by the theory itself? Note that this does not call for a prior metatheoretical analysis. Rather than "question begging," the task is to address ourselves to what the theories themselves are saying. We should properly ask of an object theory: What is its raison d'être? Let us now address this question to culture theory.

1.3 Culture Theory

As we have defined "theory," a culture theory must be a set of coherent propositions about culture. Lest one despair at the thought of yet another assault on the problem of what we mean by "culture," note that we need only concern ourselves with the existent usages of the term, not their possible ethnographic validity. We are therefore interested in what theorists claim for the concept of culture, not its utility to ethnographers in the field. Further, although Louis Schneider and Charles Bonjean introduced their recent collection of papers on the idea of culture in the social sciences with the thought that "the various social sciences share few concepts as pervasive and as durable as the concept of culture"

Meta-anthropological theory

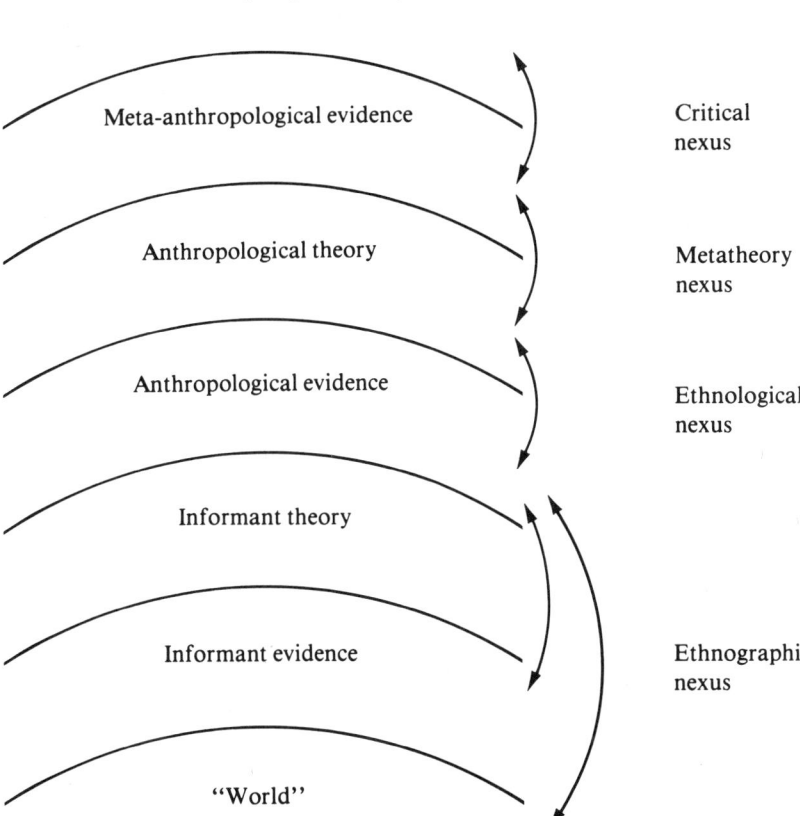

Meta-anthropological evidence   Critical
                                                 nexus

Anthropological theory   Metatheory
                                                 nexus

Anthropological evidence   Ethnological
                                                 nexus

Informant theory

Informant evidence   Ethnographic
                                                 nexus

"World"

FIGURE 1.   Levels of Abstraction for Meta-anthropology

(1973:vi), we need not be immediately concerned with nonanthropological usages of the concept.

The provision of the last paragraph hardly simplifies the search. Given the inclusiveness of the massive conceptual survey of Kroeber and Kluckhohn (1952) as well as the obvious dynamic of anthropological thinking about culture, one may wonder if any "object" exists for culture theorists other than their own specifications. Yet James A. Boon's anthropological contribution to the Schneider and Bonjean volume does give a point of reference. He comments (1973:1) on how the culture concept has significance: "For the concept of culture allows anthropologists to deal with human phenomena in a way that is at once (ideally) descriptive, holistic, and comparative. As a concept it is both complex and ephemeral, therefore continuously controversial, yet tenacious to a degree which suggests it is indispensable.''

Whatever the operational definition of culture in the field, few ethnologists are likely to challenge Boon's suggestion that any adequate concept of culture must be "descriptive, holistic, and comparative." That is, the concept must generate a theory that permits accurate description of everything significant to the totality of human existence. In essence, the criteria implicit here are *scope* and *precision* within a comparative structure. These we shall further develop in Section 3.3.

2.0   CRITIQUE OF CONTEMPORARY META-ANTHROPOLOGY

In adopting a specific metatheoretical approach to the analysis of culture theory, we are explicitly rejecting a number of alternative approaches: namely, historical, biographical, and ad hoc frameworks of several kinds. We shall briefly lay out our reasons for rejecting these approaches, concentrating on one example of each. Thus Marvin Harris' *Rise of Anthropological Theory* (1968) is an example of the historical conceptual approach: he incorporates a spirited critical review of culture theory within an imaginative historical treatment. Abram Kardiner and Edward Preble's *They Studied Man* (1961) is an example of the biographical approach: they rely upon biographical sketches to develop critiques of theory. And David Kaplan and Robert A. Manners' *Culture Theory* (1972) is an example of an ad hoc approach.

2.1   History

The reasons for explicitly rejecting these alternative approaches lie in our conception of the nature of scientific criticism and metatheoretical communication. Although we regard as quite important the diachronic treatment of the development of anthropology as both a discipline and a system of thought, history provides neither a guide to criticism nor a language for metatheory. Thus, to take an example, Lamarckian transformism may have played a valuable role in shaping the intellectual climate for the comprehension and acceptance of social evolutionism. Epistemologically and empirically, however, Lamarckian culture theory is inadequate.

The importance of differentiating the heuristic value of particular theory from its truth value is further illustrated by the Lamarckian case. As portrayed by Harris, "with the first of Lamarck's publication in 1801, the consequences of the general evolutionary outlook irresistibly swept biological thought along toward its great nineteenth-century synthesis" (1968:36–37). And yet, as a theory of agricultural eugenics with many implications for Soviet social planning, twentieth-century La-marckianism was a disaster. Harris comments that the "magnitude of this error cannot be overemphasized" (ibid.:237). Clearly, scientific criticism cannot be bound to historical period. The language of meta-theoretical discourse must be atemporal: Lamarckian theory may have been in some sense "beneficial" to the development of a theory of evolution in the nineteenth century, but this does not mean it was ever an adequate theory or ever true.

2.2 Biography

The rejection of history as an organizing concept for meta-anthropology nevertheless focuses attention on the role of time in theorizing. In biographical approaches time is measured in terms of the life cycle of the theorist. Earlier versus late formulations are distinguished and turning points are identified. Kardiner and Preble's sketch of Franz Boas is replete with such characterizations, as, for instance, in the following commentary (1961:131) on Boas' attitude toward general theory in anthropology: "An early optimism regarding the formulation of laws of cultural development is found in his famous paper, 'The Limitations of the Comparative Method in Anthropology' (1896)." But later: "Extreme skepticism and a dread of making mistakes qualified most of his work from around 1910 on. The enormous complexities in the study of man and society and the problems of cultural relativism seemed to him to present overwhelming obstacles to any useful generalizations in ethnology" (ibid.:138). Intervening between these two "contradictions in doctrines" was Boas' "enthusiastic period" (ibid.:131–132).

The question to be raised is this: How do such periods affect the treatment of Boas' historical particularism? Boas' critique of social evolutionism was principally methodological and never involved the rejection of evolution as an explanation of culture change. Boas was trained in mathematics, and his optimism for general theory was tempered by consideration of the sampling issue raised by Sir Francis Galton with respect to E. B. Tylor's pioneering work in anthropological statistics. The latter-day critique of Kroeber's "epicureanism" may be understood in the same methodological light. Kardiner and Preble report Boas' complaint that Kroeber was satisfied "with less than a 'high degree of probability for a conclusion' " (ibid.:132). The phraseology is still the mathematical; the target is still unsupported general theory. What justification is there for periods of "optimism" and "pessimism"?

When an artist's works are collected into periods such as Picasso's "blue period," it is to ensure the integrity of the object of criticism. But dividing the topics and methods of an artist informs us only as to his or her concerns and ambitions. The critical evaluation of the works remains timeless. An early promise may never be delivered; a problem left unresolved at one time may be returned to with success later on. Furthermore, to focus on periods in a single artist's or scientist's lifework is to focus on the individual and not on art or theory. After all, it is with culture theory, not life history, that we are concerned. A fundamental problem in culture theory such as "Galton's Problem" may remain a barrier to particular styles of analysis until someone else points out a solution. The basic problem of using biographical sketches as a basis for analyzing theory is simply that, unlike life, there is no natural sequence in dealing with theory. There are massive discontinuities in theory (and art) which span several lifetimes. The life cycle implies a "shape of time" largely inappropriate to critical discussions of cognitive processes of the human intellect (cf. Kubler 1963).

2.3   Ad Hoc Approaches

The final approach to meta-anthropology which we regard as inadequate is typified by the recent Kaplan and Manners essay in the "Foundations of Modern Anthropology" series (1972). The metatheoretical survey of culture theories is presented in a chapter entitled "Theoretical Orientations." The authors take considerable pains to isolate and justify the concept "theoretical orientation" as an appropriate collective noun (ibid.:32–34). A theoretical orientation is said to be an approach to "selecting, conceptualizing, and ordering data in response to certain kinds of questioning" (ibid.:34). Such an approach is recognized as different from a theory itself: theoretical orientations "may help to generate theories; they are not in themselves theories" (ibid.).

Our criticism of this approach to culture theory lies in its failure to treat higher levels of abstraction with the same concern as is demonstrated for ethnographic data. Thus, having acknowledged the role of theoretical orientations in shaping specific culture theory, it is startling to read that the four approaches identified "do not, of course, exhaust the theoretical orientations utilized by anthropologists. To be sure, there are others" (ibid). Even in an introductory text, admissions of conceptual incompleteness imply a casual attitude toward abstract issues.

That such relaxed attention to metatheory is directly consequential for the character of the survey itself is illustrated by Kaplan and Manners' treatment of French structuralism, probably the most significant theoretical development in contemporary anthropology. First Lévi-Strauss' "structural analyses" are dismissed as a "special version of 'functional' analysis" and "structuralism" is relegated to a chapter on "formal analysis." There is no apparent recognition of structuralism as a *theory* of culture and not just another way of looking at data.

The four theoretical orientations identified by Kaplan and Manners are evolutionism, functionalism, history, and cultural ecology. Inspection of this typology reveals a mixture of levels of abstraction in their categorization, the clearest example of which is their constructed category, "cultural ecology." Having begun with an odd collection of social and cultural anthropologists they term "cultural ecologists," the authors struggle to bring order out of "old" versus "new" cultural ecology. In fact, there is a certain sense of cultural ecology as a residual category into which stray anthropologists might be fitted. Finding White, Frake, Vayda, Geertz, Leach, and Gluckman in a single category is surprising to say the least. Not finding the godparent of ecology, Gregory Bateson, even mentioned is incredible, save for the obvious ad hoc involved in the category in the first place.

3.0 THE WORLD HYPOTHESIS ARCHITECTONIC

If the existing approaches to meta-anthropology are unsatisfactory, then an alternative formulation is necessary. We think that Stephen Pepper's metatheoretical *world hypothesis* architectonic (1966) is the most attractive alternative. Pepper's neglected work provides a rich analytic perspective without entailing commitment to particular philosophical paradigms in anthropology. Furthermore, Pepper introduces specific criteria for evaluating a theory—scope and precision—which are analytic means for making critical judgments on theory while avoiding interpretation or explanation of culture itself. In the following paragraphs we shall present the idea of world hypotheses and then critically survey culture theory in anthropology.

3.1 World Hypotheses and Root Metaphors

The term *world hypothesis* is almost self-defining in that it refers to a hypothesis about the world itself. A cultural world hypothesis is a general theory of culture, unrestricted with reference to either locus or level of application. Theories which deal only with components of culture such as enculturation or kinship, or are limited to certain culture areas or levels of sociocultural development, are excluded under this definition. As intended by Pepper, "the peculiarity of world hypotheses is that they cannot reject anything as irrelevant" (1966:1). Which is to say we shall be dealing only with theories which claim to be comprehensive approaches to the ethnology of total cultures. To be comprehensive, it should be noted, does not require that every aspect of a culture be covered. That which is covered, however, must be deemed sufficient for a complete description of the culture.

Every world hypothesis is based on a fundamental association between some well-understood concept and a view of the unknown character of the world. Pepper termed this analogy the *root metaphor* basis of the world hypothesis (1966:84–87). Only four root metaphors are identified by Pepper as generating adequate world hypotheses: form, machine, event, and organism.

3.2 The Evidential Modes of Collaboration

Every metaphor, no matter how intuitively satisfying, requires further support if it is to be employed as the foundation for theory. In particular the association implied by the analogy must be collaborated by evidence. The operational characteristics of ethnographic evidence need not concern us here. It is important, however, to recognize that two basic evidential dimensions pertain to ethnological theory.

The first of these dimensions goes by the familiar name of *data*. Data may be distinguished as of two epistemological varieties: analytic and synthetic (see Quine 1953 for more on this distinction). Essentially, evidential data are multiplicative corroboration in that they rest on social agreement on empirical findings (Pepper 1966:51–60). In this sense, data constitute the core of paradigmatic science (Kuhn 1962:176–187).

Conceptually orthogonal to data is collaboration derived from the logical convergence of evidence. That is, a theory may stress the interdependence of conceptual components and it is the consistent integration evident in the structure of the theory which offers support for the overall hypothesis. Einstein's theory of relativity was initially supported only by such convergence because data were lacking (Holton 1967–1968). For this mode of evidence Pepper coined the useful term *danda*. Danda is therefore the affirmation of the constructive side of Ockham's razor (the principle of parsimony). That is, concepts should not be multiplied beyond necessity *and* those concepts should be interdependent (mutually supportive).

As with data, the danda dimension has two basic features: dispersive and integrative. If a theory contends that the world is not dominated by specific forms, then the danda for that theory will reflect conceptual dispersion and no total reduction of concepts to any particular characteristic form. Conversely, the integrative feature applies to possibilities for radical reduction. It was this very feature, resulting in the reduction of Maxwell's several electromagnetic equations to a single equation, which marked the specific contribution of the special theory of relativity.

3.3 Theories of Truth

Differences in reliance on the principal forms of evidential collaboration imply alternative conceptions of the nature of truth. Thus data rest on the idea that a tie between empirical experience and propositional constructions may be established through public observation and replication. Danda, on the other hand, emphasizes that the step-by-step demonstration of a theory's logical properties is itself the only means of *validating* the theory's propositional integrity. One of the chief attributes of a world hypothesis is its specific theory of truth.

3.4   Criteria for Conceptual Adequacy

Obviously the only point to doing meta-anthropology is to make a critical evaluation of existing culture theories. To be critical means to identify explicit criteria to be used as standards for conceptual adequacy. As noted, metatheoretical standards must pertain both to the metatheory itself and to the object culture theories. We must therefore reject standards which apply only to certain theories: for example, the requirement that a theory be capable of formalization should apply only to formal theories. Pepper's criteria of scope and precision are necessary properties applicable to any theory or metatheory. To reject either criteria would jeopardize the significance of theorizing in the first place.

A world hypothesis must be sufficiently precise to distinguish differences which make a difference. That is, the resolution of its conceptual focus must be able to make consequential discrimination. A world hypothesis must also have a realm of application which will encompass the totality of entities subject to its predicates—it must be logically complete. An adequate world hypothesis or theory will be reasonably precise and comprehensive. A world hypothesis may be judged inadequate if it fails one or both of the critical tests. For example, elite theory generally fails the test of precision, primarily because of its indeterminacy in definition. Group theory, which has proved so useful in sociology, can be charged with lacking scope when applied outside pluralistic societies.

As might be expected, there is a built-in antagonism to the relationship between the criteria. Theories which respond to operationalization will likely suffer a loss of scope. That is, as a theoretical concept is rendered more precise, the scope of its conceptual salience and generalizability will usually decline. Conversely, expanding the scope of a construct will cost in precision. The formulation of "political culture," for example, has been expanded from its original ethnocentric bias as *The Civic Culture* (Almond and Verba 1965) to encompass virtually every aspect of attitudinal politics, thereby destroying its precision (for a critique see Kim 1964 and Pye 1973). In general, theories with great precision will stress integration but lack scope. On the other hand, theories of adequate scope will stress differentiation but be dispersive to the point of indeterminateness (Pepper 1966:143–146).

3.5   Adequate World Hypotheses

The world hypotheses chosen by Pepper are constructs, so that multiple individual philosophies qualify under each category. Thus *formism* has as its archetype Platonic idealism but also subsumes scholasticism and realism. The source of this basic treatment of the world as *form* is the simple commonsense perception of the similarity of things. Epistemologically, formism asserts a one-to-one mapping (isomorphic) function between the identified form (a triangle, for instance) and the subject at hand (say, society). The character of this correspondence becomes the test of truth. If society is not hierarchically stratified, then the correspondence is inaccurate and the hypothesis false. Of course perception offers us many different forms of similarity, the geometric configurations of circle and triangle being among the most popular for social theorists. While offering vistas for subtle differentiation, however, the multiplicity of forms runs the constant risk of being reduced to some ultimate form.

When some specific form is identified as the atomic or primal structure which serves as the basis or origin for all other forms, then formism collapses into *mechanism*. The root metaphor of mechanism is the *machine,* from levers to electromagnetic fields. The primary categories of mechanism, like those of formism, are spatial. But in mechanism it is location and relation, rather than shape, which define space. Precise measurement of position becomes the principal task of analysis. Only certain components of perception yield to measurement, however. Thus although mass and charge can be measured (but not simultaneously), qualities such as color and sound, although perceived, remain largely outside the scope of measurement. Hence the major challenge to mechanism is a lack of scope.

Formism and mechanism share a common preference for abstraction (measurement implies abstraction). This preference is expressed in their reliance on the concept of *law.* In mechanism laws rest on a causal test of truth. Formists also speak of laws, resting on logical rather than causal truths. The nature of these two theories of truth, the causal and the logical, is in accordance with our classification of truth theories, since both are *analytic* with reference to data. The world hypotheses differ in terms of danda, as formism is dispersive (many forms) and mechanism is integrative (ultimate reduction to a single causal principle).

The principal motive for seeking analyticity is to remove the vagaries of perception as barriers to certainty. There are those who do not share either the interest in certainty or the reduction to simplicity. In place of analyticity, these theorists would substitute synthetic insight based on experience: certainty is replaced by authenticity.

Thus whereas formism and mechanism offer something permanent as the basis for knowledge, *contextualism* stresses the reality of change. This emphasis on change marks a shift from the spatial concerns of the first two world hypotheses. Change takes time, and therefore temporal dimensions replace spatial dimensions. The basic root metaphor is no longer a "thing" but an *event,* and more specifically an event in the sense of a historic event. "By historic event, however, the contextualist does not mean primarily a past event, one that is, so to speak, dead and has to be exhumed. He means the event alive in its present" (Pepper 1966:232).

Contextualism, then, seeks to represent events as developing acts. The stance of the contextual researcher is that of involvement, not analytic alienation. As participant, the contextualist's theory of truth is strictly *operational* (hence the identification of contextualism with pragmatism). Of course the contextualist may abandon an event to write up his or her verified hypotheses at any given moment. The findings, however, remain contingent, tentative, and relative (for some other observer-participant may trace the event differently). By his or her own standards the contextualist accepts this as a proper limitation on claims to knowledge.

What does threaten the contextualist is the identification of permanent structures. If event after event exhibits isomorphism, the contextualist's postulate of change is disputed. If the form of events is constant, then contexts do not in fact differ. It is only this claim implying the nonidentity of events which justifies the lack of precision in contextual analysis. Without the claim, the breadth of scope is insufficient to offset the needs for greater precision.

Organicism, the final world hypothesis with an adequate balance of scope and precision, shares with contextualism the temporal concern. Rather than stressing the duration of change, here the emphasis is on the process of change, particularly change as metamorphism. Organicism is based on the root metaphor of the *organism,* understood as a life process, not merely as cellular. Where the stress is on individual organisms, the life process of prime interest is likely to be the *life cycle.* Where the concern is for collectivities of organisms, the dynamics of population are the focus.

In contextualism an event is broken down into its parts, the historic sum of which is the event. In organicism the organism is likewise separated into constituent components, but there remains as integral role for the whole. This key ingredient of integration (gestalt property) is the problematic core of organicism. It is fundamentally related to the discussion of growth. As simple increase in size, growth is explained in terms of additive "parts." But growth as increasing differentiation (adaptation, specialization, and so forth) is meaningful only as an attribute of some whole (Bertalanffy 1967:76–77). Not being consequential to any single

Data

		Analytic	Synthetic
Danda	Dispersive	*Formism* Correspondence	*Contextualism* Operationalism
	Integrative	*Mechanism* Causation	*Organicism* Coherence

FIGURE 2.   Adequate World Hypotheses with Truth Theories

member, however, the concept involves transcendence. At this point precision is jeopardized. Yet without the part-whole transcendence, organicism retreats into mechanism. Even if organicism abandoned the part-whole transcendence, it would never become true mechanism. Because each organism retains its characteristic life matrix (process, cycle, and so on), the organic laws applicable to it are relative to the specific entity involved. Thus the theory of truth associated with organicism is organic *coherence* (Pepper 1966:310–314). Obviously, life implies the minimal coherent integration of parts in a compatible whole.

Contextualism and organicism share a common preference for synthetic data. Their respective truth theories place authentic perception rather than agreement at the foundation of knowledge. They differ from each other in that contextualism relies on step-by-step procedures to arrive at an authentic description of phenomena. Organicism rejects such incremental or iterative methods in favor of comprehensive perception of the whole. Figure 2 displays the four adequate world hypotheses in association with their truth theories in terms of the two evidential dimensions.

3.6   Inadequate World Hypotheses

So far we have dealt only with world hypotheses for which the balance of scope and precision is relatively adequate. To dramatize the significance of choosing among alternative world hypotheses, it is useful to consider what happens when one critical dimension is emphasized to the exclusion of the other. After considering the problem at the level of world hypotheses, we shall turn to the varieties of ethnological theory produced by inadequate world hypotheses.

As mentioned earlier, scope and precision stand in an antagonistic relation. If scope is sought without regard to the requirements of precision, the resultant world hypothesis is *animism,* the personification of objects. Conversely, if precision is taken as the supreme criterion, then the product is essentially *mysticism*. The critique of each is put by Pepper as follows: "Animism is a world theory chiefly inadequate for the indeterminateness of its interpretations and lack of precision; mysticism, chiefly for its lack of scope and its lavish use of 'unreality' " (1966: 119–120).

Animism as a world hypothesis (and not as a specific form of primitive religion, although the two have much in common) is a theory which takes its root metaphor from the idea of the *person*. Surrounded by other human beings, one may conjecture that the whole of the world is essentially personal. The world hypothesis is then created as a product of the process of *personification*. The ultimate character of personhood is spiritual, and the notion of spirit underlies the fundamental criterion of truth in animism. As there are no public rules governing spiritual abstraction, the concept easily becomes muddled and eventually empty. However, the lack of a check on such hypostatization permits increasing conceptual refinement without substantiation. In time, the generality and complexity of such categorical elaboration produces an ontological fallacy that if the concepts are widespread they must be real. The conceptual consequence of animism is an authoritarianism in which truth is determined by adherence to a dogma of infallible authority (Pepper 1966:123). An ethnological product of animism is culture theory based on racial determinism.

Distinct from the perception of other persons is the experience of another state of *existence*—not merely another self or spirit, but the immediate and direct impression of experiencing truths which transcend ordinary understanding. Today in the West we tend to associate mysticism with the procedural schools of meditation and so to emphasize the exotic quality of mysticism. The experiential character of the root metaphor is actually much less exotic and a good deal more everyday than that, however. "The ordinary common 'fact' of the root metaphor is the common emotion of love" (Pepper 1966:133).

In the Western tradition of mysticism the reality of love tends to be expressed in terms of sympathy, that is, fundamental powers of attraction. In place of the multiple spirits of animism, mysticism emphasizes the unity of all experience. Rather than personification, the mystic operates within a sublimated world of peace and harmony. Ultimately that world permits no distinctions of significance. The mystical experience itself is only a small part of the total experience of any individual, however, even the mystic. Faced with the complexity of human experience beyond the scope of sympathetic reduction, the cognitive claim of the mystic is to treat these aspects of experience as unreal. Paradoxical as it may sound, it is the mystic who makes greatest use of such terms as "only apparent," "superficial," and "illusion." The only test of truth available to the mystic is the immediate emotional (affective) experience (Pepper 1966: 135). Of particular importance are revelation and beauty. All apparent evidence is ultimately reduced or is reducible to such affective dicta. An ethnological manifestation of mysticism is the theory of the evolution of consciousness, especially that associated with Pierre Teilhard de Chardin.

No complete listing of inadequate world hypotheses can be given. Not only would the list be too long for publication, but in principle there is no limit to the number of inadequate hypotheses. For example, although geographical determinism does make a balance of scope and precision, its root metaphor *place* is obviously inadequate as it includes no dimension of time. Even elementary knowledge of the passing of the seasons, let alone total climatic changes, is sufficient to acknowledge the importance of such a dimension. However incomplete the inventory of inadequate culture theories, the specific problems associated with animism/racism and mysticism/consciousness are important enough *sui generis* to warrant our attention.

4.0   INADEQUATE CULTURE THEORIES

As a preface to the following sections which consider specific culture theories, we may reiterate the relationship between culture theory and world hypothesis. A world hypothesis is a metatheoretical construct covering perhaps many different specific culture theories. Note that it is theories instead of theorists which are considered. The world hypothesis does not itself, either logically or historically, generate a culture theory. Rather, the world hypothesis architectonic is a *conceptual* typology, a classificatory framework. Its validity rests on its usefulness for scientific criticism and creativity. For if culture theories are properly classified by type of root metaphor, the architectonic should yield insights into the nature of the typed theories as well as into the differences among them.

4.1   Animism: Racial Determinism

As a culture theory racial determinism rests on the proposition that the variation in culture is a function of the variation in *race*. It is difficult to summarize the doctrine of cultural racism for two related reasons. First, "race" continues to be a highly problematical term even though its scientific usage has been greatly restricted compared to nonscientific usages. Second, those culture theories which elaborated racial determinism to the fullest have virtually disappeared from scientific discourse. Therefore to comment usefully on racial determinism as an inadequate culture hypothesis, we need to place the concept of race in its proper time reference and to recall a form of theorizing largely forgotten (repressed?) by modern anthropologists.

In 1850 Robert Knox stated the fundamental tenet of racial determinists: "Race is everything; literature, science—in a word, civilization depends on it" (quoted in Harris 1968:99). Such a theory that would reduce all cultural differences to a single cause—race in this case—is uncommon today. Even other social theorists such as Hume, Hegel, Comte, Marx, Morgan, Tylor, and Spencer, who all conferred considerable importance on race to account for cultural differences, never proposed such radically deterministic hypotheses.

A consequence of single-cause explanations of phenomena is the ease with which one can turn a causal principle into a definition. Thus if race causes culture then differences in culture are prima facie evidence for differences in race. One effect of this obvious fallacy is the need constantly to invent new races to account for cultural differences which come to be pointed out in previously homogeneous culture areas. Monogenesis is replaced by an ever-expanding polygenesis. Perhaps if this were the only implication of racial determinism, the only charge to be leveled at it would be its inelegance and hypostatization.

Yet in terms of its animistic base and its social history, the theory is fundamentally inadequate. A race is typically defined as "a group of mankind, members of which can be identified by the possession of distinctive physical characteristics" (Brace and Montagu 1965:269). Although modern anthropologists have little use for such phenotypical characteristics as skin color, these were the very attributes of interest to racists. Given that human evolution is controlled by genotypical factors and that phenotypes are essentially secondary qualities, racism is a form of personification. Hence the idea of a "race" is essentially animistic.

In racial determinism, a group of persons sharing some superficial characteristic is treated as a spiritual entity—that is, a race. If language is regarded as one of a group's physical characteristics, the personified group may be labled a "nation" or "folk." In general, little real discrimination was practiced among these terms—one suspects that if very precise measurements had been made, the results would have destroyed the mirage of racial roots for nationalism. In fact racial determinism is dependent upon the imprecision of its animistic foundations. As the synthetic theory of biosocial evolution is showing, precision in genetic analysis simply will not support racism.

4.2 Mysticism: Evolution of Consciousness

Pierre Teilhard de Chardin's theory of the evolution of consciousness rests upon his revelation of the *noosphere,* or sphere of consciousness evolution, and its meaning for the human future. The noosphere is the "growth outside and above the biosphere, of an added planetary layer, an envelope of thinking substance" (1964:157; see also Teilhard 1959). For Teilhard, the transcendent truth of the universe is that it evolves progressively toward consciousness and human beings represent the highest expression of this evolution (ibid.:12–14).

Teilhard's theory grows out of his conviction that biological evolution is essentially over. Biological evolution has been replaced by psychic evolution, with the world's "evolutionary capacity . . . *concentrated* upon and *confined to* the human soul" (ibid.). The past and present variety of human cultures produced by adaptive radiation and described by Teilhard as layerings at various stages of development are in fact coming together in unity. This Teilhard calls *planetization,* "the growing coextension of our soul with the world" (ibid.:17, 115).

Culture takes a central role in the coming challenge to human nations, now that evolution is a matter of "the surrounding environment"—that is, learning (ibid.:162)—rather than of the genes. To survive the challenge, we must all come to see ourselves as part of the "whole" and "must strive to break down every kind of barrier that prevents separate beings from uniting" (ibid.:46). This is the concept of monism, or the Grand Option. The universe converges toward its center, at which is "the fundamental impulse of Life . . . the one natural medium in which the rising course of evolution can proceed" (ibid.:54). That impulse is love. Thus, as with mysticism in general, love becomes the criterion for truth. Those who have experienced the transcendent meaning of the universe should form a "conspiracy" of love. The evolution of consciousness therefore becomes the "specific evolution of the moral value of our actions" (ibid.:17; italics removed).

Actually, the evolution of consciousness is the mystic experience on a mass level. For the goal of progress is the omega point, the "universal center" from which radiations of energy constantly emanate. These radiations were "hitherto only perceptible to those persons whom we call 'mystics' " (ibid.:122). As the planet cools toward its ultimate end, emanations from the omega point will "warm the earth psychically" until mankind detaches itself from the earth to join "the one true, irreversible essence of things" in the "supreme synthesis" (ibid.:122–123). The omega point, this final metamorphosis which Teilhard likens to the experience of death, is the mystic peak experience. It ushers in a new state of existence characterized by peace, beauty, and harmony.

Teilhard's evolution of consciousness shares with other varieties of mysticism a lack of scope. It fails to account for biosocial interaction in evolution by ignoring the social in favor of the strictly physical and strictly psychic. It also fails to account for the nonconscious elements of human culture. Even as animism logically implies authoritarianism, so mysticism denies the meaning and propriety of cultural diversity to the point that it envisions, and seeks, the end of culture.

5.0 ADEQUATE CULTURE THEORIES

We now turn to a discussion of the four root metaphors—form, machine, event, organism—as they apply to adequate culture theories. The task before us is not the construction of a taxonomic structure, for Pepper's architectonic is the classification system to be used. Given a framework, the task of classification is replaced by the work of *identification*. That is, into what class does a particular theory fit? For the job of identification to be properly completed, every theory surveyed must be classified without excessive distortion to either the theory or the taxonomy. We have found it useful to divide the world hypotheses into two types (see Figure 2) which reflect the degree of empirical differentiation permitted by the culture theories identified with the world hypothesis.

In general, each world hypothesis generates two culture theories: one which emphasizes the differentiation of cultures and one which stresses their relative uniformity. This empirical dimension, data, is distinct from the characteristic danda of given world hypotheses. Subclassification by degree of empirical differentiation does not change either of the modes of collaboration. In the following paragraphs we shall deal initially with those theories which stress differentiation of cultures.

Once identification has been completed, the taxonomy will serve as an index to the metatheoretical characteristics already discussed in terms of the architectonic. Of particular importance will be the areas of inter-theory integration and theory criticism. Since Pepper's framework is itself formistic metatheory, the question of immediate conceptual integration is structurally answered by the implicit conceptual pluralism underlying formism. Therefore the discussion of direct integration (that is, without an intermediate metatheory) takes the character of the critique of meta-anthropology as defined here. We shall consider several alternative criticisms of meta-anthropology after examining the surveyed culture theories in the critical terms of the architectonic.

Table 1 displays the adequate culture theories in anthropology as they are classified according to Pepper's four root metaphors.

5.1   Formism—Structuralism

As indicated in Table 1, anthropological theories of culture subsumed under the term structuralism are examples of formism. Three varieties of structuralism which are complete enough to be considered culture theories are those of Benedict, Radcliffe-Brown, and Lévi-Strauss.

5.1.1   *Cultural Configuration.*   Although Ruth Benedict is perhaps

TABLE 1.   World Hypotheses in Anthropology

Formism	Contextualism

Structuralism:
    structure/opposition
	Culture history:
	    trait/history

1. Culture configuration
    (R. Benedict)
	1. Historical particular
	    (F. Boas)

2. Social structure
    (A. R. Radcliffe-Brown)
	2. Culture historicism
	    (A. L. Kroeber)

3. Cognitive structure (C. Lévi-Strauss)	

Functionalism:
    function/satisfaction
	Diffusionism:
	    trait/diffusion

1. Functionalism
    (B. Malinowski)
	1. Kulturkreis
	    (W. Schmidt)

2. Social organization
    (R. Firth)
	2. Heliocentrism
	    (W. Perry, G. Smith)

	3. Multicentrism (C. Wissler)

not commonly regarded as a structuralist, her configurational approach to culture is typological and therefore formistic. In *Patterns in Culture,* she characterizes culture as "a more or less consistent pattern of thought and action" (1934:46). The patterns in a culture taken together constitute its "configuration" and each culture is to be studied as a "whole configuration" (ibid.:52). The configuration of a culture is to be abstracted from the ethnographic data.

Other metaphors in which she discusses culture are geometrical: "In culture . . . we must imagine a great arc on which are arranged the possible interests provided by the human age-cycle or by the environment or by man's various activities" (ibid.:24). A culture's identity depends on its selections from the arc. The configuration of culture is also described as a "complex interweaving of cultural traits" (ibid.:37), so that culture traits are the units of cultural form. Even individual socialization is a matter of learning to live according to "cultural forms" (ibid.:232).

The primary demonstration of Benedict's theory is her illustration of the concept of cultural configuration by applying descriptions of contrasting kinds of culture configuration to ethnographic data from three societies. Borrowing from Herbert Spengler's *Decline of the West* she contrasts "two great destiny ideas," the Apollonian of the classical world and the Faustian of the modern world (ibid.:53). The Apollonian seeks order, peace, consciousness, and impersonality. The Faustian on

TABLE 1.   *(Continued)*

Organicism	Mechanism

Systems theory:
    system/metabolism
1. Cybernetic
    (G. Bateson)
2. Information
    (R. Rappaport)
	Cultural materialism:
	    technology/integration
	1. Technoeconomics
	    (J. Steward)

Social evolution:
    survival/evolution
1. British
    (E. B. Tylor)
2. American
    (L. H. Morgan)
	Cultural materialism:
	    technology/conversion
	1. Technoenergism
	    (L. White)

the other hand is possessed of a strong sense of self and will and believes that only through conflict can one come to understand the meaning of existence. In addition to these two configurational types she also introduces a third which is opposed to the Apollonian, borrowing this time from Nietzsche: the Dionysian seeks annihilation of order, personal mystical experience, and the unconscious. Benedict never clarifies the relationship of the Dionysian to the Faustian, though they do not seem to be identical. Since the Zuni are taken to illustrate the Apollonian and the Kwakiutl the Dionysian, it may be that the Dobu are Faustian.

As with formism in general, Benedict rejects the possibility of ultimate forms and argues instead for a multiplicity of forms. There are no ultimate forms in culture, for "the possible human institutions and motives are legion on every plane of cultural simplicity or complexity" (ibid.:37). (Note the implicit hierarchical principle here.) Her seeming rejection of cultural typing is in fact an argument not against types but against type as a "fixed constellation of traits" rather than an "empirical characterization" (ibid.:238). In line with the dispersive danda of formism, she states that "categories become a liability when they are taken as inevitable and applicable alike to all civilizations and events" (ibid.). She prefers to regard the Apollonian, Faustian, and Dionysian configurations as "directions" rather than types (ibid.), though she uses cultural type elsewhere.

Finally, despite Benedict's Boasian emphasis on culture change there is an implicit permanence to the culture configurations she identifies. For underlying the concept of configuration, as with all structural notions, is the principle that "each people further and further consolidates its experience, and in proportion to the urgency of these drives the heterogeneous items of behavior take more and more congruous shape"—so that institutions do become traditional in a "well-integrated" culture (1934:46, 37).

5.1.2 *Social Structure.* In contrast to Benedict's formism, which would give us the sense of a culture's personality, Radcliffe-Brown's structural-functionalism seeks to classify societies according to the structure of their social systems. As with formism in general, Radcliffe-Brown's method is to work by analogy, by "perceived similarities and differences" (1948:36). Social structure is defined as "an arrangement of persons in institutionalized roles and relationships" (1958:176) viewed synchronically. A social system is said to persist (that is, remain the same entity) over time if its structure persists (1948:81-84).

Function is defined as the "total set of relations that a single social activity or usage or belief has to the total social system" (1948:85). As defined here function is automatically bound to the notion of structure, for it involves the "*continuity* of the structure being maintained by a *life-process* made up of the activities of the constituent units" (1952:180).

For Benedict, culture traits were the units of cultural configuration. For Radcliffe-Brown, social groups and how people are arranged in them are the units of analysis. In practice the "arrangement of persons" is assumed to be stratificational: having identified "social groups," the analyst looks next for hierarchical "arrangements into social classes and categories" (1958:168). In essence, then, social relations are assumed to be oppositional.

Opposition, in fact, is a key term throughout Radcliffe-Brown's discussions of social structure. He defines social relation in terms of opposition: "A social relation exists between two or more individual organisms when there is some adjustment of their respective interests, by convergence of interest, or by limitation of conflicts that might arise from divergence of interests" (ibid.:199)—that is, a kind of dialectic. In fact, in his explanation of totemism Radcliffe-Brown discusses the dialectic which was to intrigue Lévi-Strauss later: "The resemblances and differences of animal species are translated into terms of friendship and conflict, solidarity and opposition. In other words the world of animal life is represented in terms of social relations similar to those of human society" (1958:116). Thus, underlying totemism is a more profound social problem: "how opposition can be used as a mode of social integration" (ibid.:127).

As with other formists, Radcliffe-Brown rejects the usefulness of classifying social systems on the basis of a single form and also assumes that social systems vary in their structure. Traditions and norms are the logical outgrowths of the structure of the social system, and are developed in the dialectic of social relations.

5.1.3 *Cognitive Structure.* Whereas for Radcliffe-Brown the forms of social structure are the explanation for culture, Claude Lévi-Strauss is interested in social structure only as the reflection of an underlying structure for human thinking. He argues that primitive or savage thought is analogical—that is, the savage seeks to establish "homologies between natural and social conditions" on a variety of levels (1962:73) in order to work out cultural problems. The analogical process is the one-to-one mapping relationship typical of formistic theories, as we have seen; and as Lévi-Strauss wishes to recover these processes in cultural data, his own method is essentially analogical as well. He postulates a homology between language and all other aspects of culture such that the methods of structural linguistics are amenable to the study of all social relationships (1967:205).

The dynamic element in formism is the dialectic, and Lévi-Strauss argues that human thinking is essentially dialectical. From the "remains and debris" of experience, the "bricoleur-like" savage thinker builds up structured sets and "progresses from the awareness of oppositions toward their resolution," whether in constructing a myth, a social structure, or a kinship system (1962:21–22; 1967:211). In fact, the "material out of which a whole culture is built" consists of "Logical Relations, oppositions, correlations, and the like" (1962:67). The process is strictly logical, analytical, and detached from affective considerations.

Carrying Radcliffe-Brown's analysis of totemism one step further, Lévi-Strauss argues that the connection between the human relationship to nature and the characterization of social groups "is indirect, passing through the mind," so that it is "not the resemblances, but the differences, which resemble each other"; in other words, "the resemblance presupposed by so-called totemic representations is between these two systems of differences" (1962:13, 77; italics removed). The purpose of totemic representations and mythic constructions is "to provide a logical model capable of overcoming a contradiction" (1962:226). But, with other formists, Lévi-Strauss' model is also dispersive. The possible resolutions to such contradictions are "theoretically infinite," meaning that in each case a large number of different "slates" can be generated, leading to a "spiralwise" layered growth of the system (ibid.).

Thus Lévi-Strauss assumes a variety of formal relationships or oppositions available to human thinking. His analysis is aimed at discovering for each cultural group the homologies, analogies, or forms used in the dialectic. In spite of their diversity such forms show a degree of permanence—not only because they are sufficiently abstract to bear changes in content, but also because of the timeless character of the "savage mind": its object is to grasp the world as "both a synchronic and a diachronic totality" (1962:263). Regarding the human mind as essentially a "closed system" (ibid.:269), Lévi-Strauss' structuralism thus hovers at times on the brink of identifying final forms, and thus of becoming mechanistic.

5.2 Formism—Functionalism

A second set of culture theories based on the root metaphor of formism are subsumed under the term functionalism. The two varieties of functionalism we shall discuss are those of Malinowski and Firth.

5.2.1 *Functionalism.* Bronislaw Malinowski describes culture as a "vast apparatus" through which human beings are able to cope with the problems facing them—that is, through which they are able to satisfy their organic and social needs (1944:36). Whereas structuralism emphasizes what cultures do not share, functionalism emphasizes what they do share. Thus Malinowski is concerned with universal human needs and the similarities among cultures in fulfilling these needs.

The culture forms which are the units of analysis and the structures through which needs are satisfied are *institutions*. Institutions are defined as the "organization of human beings into permanent groups" (ibid.:39, 43). Maintaining each institution is a set of traditional values, sometimes referred to as the "charter" or "idea of the institution as entertained by its members and defined by the community" (ibid.:48). For Radcliffe-Brown, function is the activity which maintains social structure. For Malinowski, function is "the satisfaction of a need by an activity in which human beings cooperate" (ibid.:39). Or, viewed from the perspective of an institution, the "function is the role of the institution within the total scheme of culture" in satifying organic, instrumental, or integrative needs (ibid.:48). Thus there is a one-to-one mapping of human need and institution.

The dialectic in Malinowski's writings is a subtly stated relationship among institutions. Individuals participate in one or more institutions, binding themselves by sets of rules in exchange for the satisfaction of their physical and social needs. Similarly, institutions organize and coordinate their activities in such a way (at least under ideal circumstances) as to maximize need satisfaction. The only change in such a system is institutional change, for "new devices in technique, in knowledge, or in belief are fitted into the cultural process or an institution" if they are to exist at all (ibid.:41).

5.2.2 *Social Organization.* In contrast to Radcliffe-Brown and Malinowski, Raymond Firth is less interested in the ideal structures of social groups and institutions than in the everyday working out of social relationships. He describes social anthropology as the study of "the operation of the social life" and identifies the unit of analysis as "aggregates of individuals in their relational aspects"—in other words, societies (1951:2). Social structure refers to the "principles"on which the "form" of social relations depends. Function refers to the way in which social relations serve their intended "ends" as defined by the society (ibid.:28). This view is somewhat different from that of Malinowski, for whom function is the satisfaction of a human need.

Firth's central concept is social organization. Social organization is decision making, the "directional activity which maintains" the form of social relations and assures that the functions are also met (ibid.). As with formism in general, we have here no reduction to a single mechanism or form. However, Firth assumes that all human societies have formal, ordered social relations which may be analyzed in terms of social structure, function, and organization.

Like Malinowski, Firth emphasizes the similarities among societies. Despite variation there are "sufficient elements of likeness to allow us to attribute identity, to abstract and generalize into a type of social relation" (ibid.:21). Social relations must be inferred from physical acts. By observing human interaction and activities the social anthropologist abstracts the norms or rules which govern behavior and the social relations which hold in a society. Thus Firth's concern is the form of what people actually do, more than the form of institutional relationships as set out by a "charter." In fact, he defines form as "the persistence or repetition of behavior," "the element of continuity in social life" (ibid.:39).

Implicit in the relationship between norms and interests is a dialectic. "The norms are the rules which govern the conduct of the people; and these must be distinguished from their activities, which may diverge from the norms according as their individual interests pull them" (ibid.:34). Decision making, or the exercise of choice, allows for a resolution of opposing interests and a balancing of means and ends.

Firth's explanation of change is also dialectical. Unlike Lévi-Strauss, who is interested in the seeming "timelessness" of forms, Firth allows for gradual change in social structure. Change is essentially the result of the failure of the structure to meet its functions. Thus change tends to occur where there is an "incompatibility of two structural pinciples" (ibid.:60), a statement on the social level similar to Lévi-Strauss' argument on the cognitive level. Implied is that "there was some imperfection" in the previous "means-ends arrangement" (ibid.:86). Function is therefore predominant, for it is organization and structure which give way through "adjustment" or change.

5.3   Contextualism—Culture History

As indicated in Table 1, anthropological theories of culture which are examples of contextualism are those we shall refer to as "culture history" theories. These include the historical particularism of Boas and the culture historicism of Kroeber.

5.3.1   *Historical Particularism.*   Contextualism is the construction of a map of social phenomena or events. Where the formist works by dialectic, the contextualist works by sequence. Franz Boas, the genitor of historical particularism, equated the study of culture with the study of history (1948:244). He gave as his objective "the attempt to understand the steps by which man has come to be what he is" and argued on that basis that "our material must necessarily be historical material." The overall aim is the "reconstruction of culture" in terms of a "chronological succession of forms" (ibid.). Yet Boas agrees with other contextualists that knowledge of sequence is insufficient without "insight into the conditions under which changes occur" (ibid.)—in other words, insight into the context or situation of development.

Here Boas' pluralism is of significance, for he assumes no general chronological sequence for all cultures but rather emphasizes the uniqueness of contexts and the relativity of cultural outcomes in these contexts (ibid.:286). Unlike the formist who seeks logical laws underlying cultural phenomena, Boas argues that cultural phenomena "are so individualized, so exposed to outer accident that no set of laws could explain them." Although we can arrive at conclusions about an individual culture, "we cannot explain its individuality in the form of laws" (1948: 257). Nor can we expect to arrive at *general* laws for culture. Any conclusions to which we come about culture must be tentative, contingent, and relative only to those cultures we have examined. For tomorrow the discovery of a new culture may completely change our conclusions.

Where formism encourages analytic techniques, contextualism demands synthetic approaches. Boas' emphasis on the uniqueness of cultures and on the careful reconstruction of sequences requires that he study all aspects of human life—physiology, psychology, language, and culture customs and traits. But in order to study all aspects of human life, every available technique of analysis must be employed. Thus, although the sequence of events is the primary focus of anthropological analysis, Boas was highly eclectic methodologically.

Where formism encourages detachment from the data, contextualism encourages subjectivity. Boas emphasized long periods of fieldwork and insisted that his students learn the language of the people they study.

Under his firm hand the techniques of participant observation were designed and tested. Stress was placed on recovering the meaning of cultural characteristics and processes to the people under study themselves—in other words, the inside view of culture.

5.3.2 *Cultural Historicism.*   Alfred L. Kroeber carries the historical approach to culture further than Boas. Criticizing Boas for having no interest in higher-order contexts beyond the immediate context (1952:146), Kroeber argues that the "essential quality" of the historical approach as a method of science is "its integration of phenomena into an ever widening phenomenal context, with as much preservation as possible" (ibid.: 5). For Kroeber as well as for Boas, the "context includes the placing in space and time and therefore, when knowledge allows, in sequence" (ibid.).

Context as history is dominant. "In the historical process of cultural development, an invention is a single act or event and, within a given situation, likely to be more or less inevitable" (ibid.:7). Since culture is the context for human life, culture or "civilization" "transcends" the individual and in this sense is "superorganic." The significant relations to Kroeber are not social relations but the relations among cultural phenomena which resemble, precede, succeed, or occur near each other (ibid.:132). Change, then, is dictated by the growth of the configuration of a culture in its historical context.

Kroeber criticizes Benedict's use of culture configuration as "essentially static and nonhistorical" (ibid.:5). His concern is with cultural "growth configurations—configurations of time, space, and in degree of achievement" (1944:6). If the context changes the culture changes; but where major contextual shifts do not occur, a culture's growth is cumulative directionally, as set by its early choices. In line with contextualism's definition of events in terms of developing acts, Kroeber states that the cultures which anthropology depicts "are summaries or averages of a large number of individual acts" over time (ibid.:5).

In his references to growth configurations, Kroeber combines the temporal dimension of contextualism with a spatial dimension which is directly related to time: "Geographically, a radiating spread of culture growth can usually be traced from a first hearth or focus over the larger area finally occupied" (ibid.:845). This culture subarea of intensity or climax spreading outward over time, as well as its location and degree, could be calculated statistically.

5.4   Contextualism—Diffusionism

A second set of culture theories based in contextualism are those referred to as diffusionism. There have been several schools of diffusionism, but here we shall take as examples the *Kulturkreis* school of Schmidt, the heliocentrism of Perry and Smith, and the multicentrism of Wissler.

5.4.1 *Kulturkreis.* A different kind of contextualism is represented by the diffusionists, among whom a leading figure was Wilhelm Schmidt, a member of the German Kulturkreis school of culture theory. With other anthropological contextualists, Schmidt regards ethnology as "historical": the development of cultures takes place "chronologically in the succession of events and becomes thereby historical science" (1939:9).

With Boas, Schmidt rejects evolutionary theory and the notion of progress (ibid.:11). Ironically, however, when he speaks of sequences he refers to a "succession of stages" which in the case of the development from primitive to modern cultures sounds suspiciously evolutionary (ibid.:9–10).

But Schmidt's main interest is in mapping the diffusion of culture traits and establishing sequences for them. Diffusion is the explanation offered whenever two culture traits are not similar merely because of the material or purposes inherent in them (1939:150). Schmidt envisions a limited number of centers—culture circles—from which culture traits diffused not piecemeal (or trait by trait) but as whole cultures. A culture complex is a culture circle if it "embraces all the essential and necessary categories of human culture," meaning that it is "sufficient unto itself and, hence, also assured its independent existence" (ibid.:176). The culture circle is the unity in time and space for human history. By its emphasis on sequential growth, diffusionism also emphasizes change over permanence.

5.4.2 *Heliocentrism.* If Schmidt was willing to recognize a number of cultural centers, W. J. Perry and Grafton Elliot Smith were considerably less generous. These two British anthropologists argued that there had been only one center of original or "archaic" culture—Egypt (Perry 1923; Smith 1933). Perry describes his method of analysis as the establishment of culture sequences "with the aim of reconstructing, so far as is possible, the past history of the region as a whole" by establishing "relative chronology" rather than absolute chronology (1923:2). Both men reject the notion of independent invention on the basis that no evidence had been produced that independent invention of civilization had taken place; moreover, the invention of civilization was so complex a process that it was linked "by the closest bands of genetic process" and thus highly improbable (Smith 1933:11).

Most of the vast writings of Perry and Smith are detailed attempts to show how all the world's greater and lesser civilizations could be traced back to ancient Egyptian "pioneers." The term *heliocentric* is derived from the sun cult in ancient Egypt, which Perry and Smith argued was associated with "mother right" and which was eventually replaced by the war-god cult associated with "father right" (Perry 1923:471). As "children of the sun" the ancient Egyptian rulers were believed to be descended from the sun and thus gods. As Egyptian culture diffused into the rest of the world, it carried with it the divine rulers and the sophisticated elite who brought culture to the masses and the primitives. Hence we find sun-god cults popping up in North America, Oceania, Indonesia, India, and elsewhere. Lest other civilizations feel inferior to the Egyptians, Smith hastens to add that "in the building up of man's greatest achievement all peoples participated, and thus established its essential unity" (1933:232).

5.4.3   *Multicentrism.*   German and British diffusionism influenced American anthropologists, but few of them carried it to the extremes found in Europe. Clark Wissler is perhaps the best known of the American diffusionists. In a classic contextualist statement, Wissler set out the goal of diffusionist research as the study of "examples of distribution" to "seek objective ways of proving that such distributions do have relations to each other analogous to those of strata in a geological deposit" (1926:xv). The unit of analysis is the culture trait placed in space and time. These traits include not only the material but also the social and biological.

In rejecting the notion that all culture traits diffuse outward from a single center, Wissler postulated the existence of multiple cultural centers. Furthermore, "anthropological traits tend to diffuse in all directions from their centers of origin," overlapping with diffusion from other centers (ibid.:183). One judges the age of a trait by how far it has diffused from its center of origin. That is, "the extent of diffusion is somehow proportional to the time"; but Wissler was unable to be more precise without knowing the rate of diffusion (ibid. :189). The relation of extent of distribution to age was called the "age and area concept" (1938:315).

5.5   Organicism—Systems Theory

Systems theory has organicism as its root metaphor. The leading systems theorist in anthropology has been Bateson, whose work is best described as cybernetic theory. To contrast with cybernetic theory, we shall discuss information theory, selecting the work of R. Rappaport as one example.

5.5.1   *Cybernetic Systems.*   Gregory Bateson's work on systems theory, including his discussion of schismogenesis in *Naven* (1958) and his more recent writings on the ecology of mind (1972), is taken here as the cybernetic systems example of organicism. Although Bateson uses the term cybernetic, his own concept of schismogenesis or mind is in fact a metabolic system and thus based on a life process.

Schismogenesis he defined as "a process of differentiation in the norms of individual behavior resulting from cumulative interaction between individuals" (1958:175). Thus the status quo in a society is described as a "dynamic equilibrium in which changes are continually taking place" (ibid.). Schismogenesis was later expanded to an ecology of mind, by which Bateson means the ecology of ideas, since minds are aggregates of ideas (1972:xvii).

In Bateson's view, there must be an interaction of ideas in the system, but equally there must be an economy which limits ideas. His ecological system is an analogy to the mind of an organism, and he argues that just as an organism has a mind, so the universe has not only a physical determinism but also a mental determinism (ibid.:472). It is not a closed system, as Lévi-Strauss would postulate for the human mind, however, for through technology human beings may "create insanity in the larger system of which we are parts" (ibid.:473).

Metabolism is cyclic in that it seeks to maintain homeostasis through self-correction (ibid.:490). Similarly, the universe operates metabolically, adjusting itself on the basis of differences which make a difference, a sort of dynamic equilibrium. The term *dynamic* is significant here, for the metabolic process is not static. Bateson argues that the unit of evolutionary survival is also the unit of mind: as conditions change, the system makes appropriate adjustments and thus becomes changed and differentiated. If the entire universe is one system, then "ecology, in the widest sense, turns out to be the study of the interaction and survival of ideas and programs (i.e., differences, complexes of differences, etc.) in circuits" (ibid.:491). The universe as a single mind exemplifies the emphasis of organism on integration of all phenomena into a whole, or at least a comprehensive perception of the whole.

5.5.2 *Information Systems.*   Whereas Bateson sees implicit mind in the functioning of the universe, Roy A. Rappaport finds a less abstract regulator for ecology: human ritual. Rappaport's concern is not with the part that ritual plays within culture or within a local society, but rather with how ritual affects relationships between a local group and the entities outside it (1967:1). Ritual is shown to have a regulatory function among the Tsembaga and Maring groups of New Guinea in that it helps to "maintain an undergraded environment, limits fighting to frequencies that do not endanger the existence of the regional population, adjusts man-land ratios, facilitates trade, distributes local surpluses of pig in the form of pork throughout the regional population, and assures the people of high-quality protein when they most need it" (ibid.:224). In short, the ritual cycle ensures that the metabolism of the ecosystem is maintained. The ecosystem is thus characterized as self-regulating and coherent, since "a change in the value of a variable itself initiates a process that either limits further change or returns the values to a former level" (ibid.:4).

The regulation function is sanctified, and the introduction of sanctity into the system is ironically rather close to Bateson's concept of mind, which is in essence an undeified substitute for God. Rappaport argues that sanctification "may enhance the reliability of symbolically communicated information," meaning that sanctified messages are more likely to be maintained the way they are and accepted as valid by the faithful (ibid.:236). In this way the system is assured of continuity over time.

As with other organicists, Rappaport's model provides a comprehensive perception of the human and natural life process so that culture becomes one component in the overall ecology. The focus of interest is the process of change—that is, how one cycle leads to another—and yet the aim is to demonstrate integration of the whole.

5.6   Organicism—Social Evolution

Social evolutionism, taken as a theory of culture, also has organicism as its root metaphor. For the sake of simplicity, we have divided theories of social evolution into a British school (with Tylor as the example) and an American school (with Morgan as the example).

5.6.1   *British Social Evolutionism.*   Edward Tylor's theory of social evolution is an example of the unilinear evolutionary approach. His organicism is implied by his metaphor of the growth of societies and culture. Thus, for example, he argues that in all aspects of life one can show how a culture habit or index "grew or shrank by gradual stages and passed into another," thereby revealing "the nature of change and growth, revival and decay, which go on from year to year" (1971:16). The growth pattern, as in biology, is a cycle of birth, growth, and death—or, as Tylor puts it, "progress, degradation, survival, revival, modification" (ibid.).

Tylor seeks to divide these cycles into clear "stages of development or evolution" (ibid:1), and he assumes that studying culture by the comparative method will reveal the general principles on which this evolution operates. The nature and direction of previous stages are revealed by studying "survivals"—aspects of behavior which continue by force of habit or tradition and stand out in a later stage of culture as proofs of an "older condition . . . out of which a newer has been evolved" (ibid.:15). Ultimately Tylor believes that all human cultures have in fact passed through the same stages of savagery, barbarism, and civilization. His point of view is social rather than technological. Civilization is portrayed as a move toward "man's goodness, power, and happiness," whereas technological evolution is regarded as "one main element in the development of culture" (ibid.:21).

Although Tylor does not refer directly to a struggle in evolution, his imagery in writing about progress is filled with lights and darks, with motions of climbing and stumbling, and thus his tone is one of struggle.

5.6.2 *American Social Evolutionism.* If struggle is explicitly missing from Tylor's writings, it is certainly prominent in the writings of Lewis Henry Morgan. Growth is the underlying metaphor for human development for Morgan as it was for Tylor, and he sets out to show how "mankind commenced their career at the bottom of the scale and worked their way up from savagery to civilization" in a "protracted struggle with opposing obstacles" (1877:3-4). Like Tylor, he is concerned with uncovering the "principal stages of human development," which are savagery, barbarism, and civilization, regarded as standing in a "natural" sequence with each other (ibid.). Thus the tracing of the process of change as though culture were an organism identifies Morgan as an organicist.

Morgan borrows terminology from biological evolution to explain how human civilizations developed. The "germ of government," for example, is to be sought in the "organization into gentes in the status of savagery," which passing through "advancing forms" led to the growth of political society (ibid.:5). Each institution can be followed through various stages from its "nascent and feeble" beginning to its "springing into life" and its gradual "evolution" (ibid.:6). No advance was won easily, and Morgan pays tribute to the early human groups: "We owe our present condition, with its multiplied means of safety and of happiness, to the struggles, the sufferings, the heroic exertions and the patient toil of our barbarous, and more remotely, of our savage ancestors" (ibid.:554).

Thus a culture is seen to have a life cycle, and the stages of social evolution pass from one kind of level to another. With other organicists, Morgan is concerned with integrating human development. He therefore emphasizes the "uniformity of human experience" and the "unity of the origin of Mankind" (ibid.:ix,x). His theory of social evolution thus provides us with a comprehensive explanation for culture.

5.7 Mechanism—Cultural Materialism: Technoeconomics

Technoeconomics is an example of mechanism. Julian Steward's technoeconomics stands opposed to unilinear evolution and holds that human culture evolved along a number of different lines—or multilinear evolution. His approach is "an attempt to learn how the factors in each given type of situation shaped the development of a particular type of society" (1956:74). Lest this sound like contextualism, we should notice that Steward brings his analysis back finally to a single "machine" for an explanation. This is the economy, or, more specifically, the technoeconomy (ibid.:76).

As the fundamental process in culture, the technoeconomic system is a thermodynamic machine which converts resources into energy for the use of human societies. Technology thus becomes the main determinant in culture, and those institutions or behavior patterns which are most closely related to technology—or "subsistence activities and economic arrangements"—constitute the *core* of the culture (1955:37). Steward thus first studies the "interrelationship of exploitative or productive technology and environment," secondarily the "behavior patterns involved in the exploitation of a particular area by means of a particular technology," and thirdly how these patterns "affect other aspects of culture" (ibid.:40–41). While Steward regards technology as the primary factor in shaping cultures, his system is not quite closed: other aspects of culture also influence the development of technology and the utilization of the environment (ibid.).

Like other mechanists, Steward seeks precise measurement in order to eventually arrive at laws. He argues that "multilinear evolution is essentially a methodology based on the assumption that significant regularities in cultural change occur, and it is concerned with the determination of cultural laws" (1955:18). Answers to why cultures develop as they do are to be sought in location and relation—that is, the natural environment to which a group of human beings must adjust and adapt and the "level of sociocultural integration" or cultural interrelationships of a particular time span. Integration of the culture into a whole is continually stressed by Steward, characteristic of mechanism's integrative strain.

5.8   Mechanism—Cultural Materialism: Technoenergism

Where Steward argues for multilinear evolution, Leslie A. White argues for universal evolution. With Steward, White agrees on the primacy of technology over other cultural systems. "Social systems are in a very real sense secondary and subsidiary to technological systems. . . . A social system is a function of a technological system. . . . Social systems are therefore determined by systems of technology" (1949:365). Culture itself is therefore material: "A human being is a material body; the species, a material system. The planet earth is a material body; the cosmos, a material system. Technology is the mechanical means of articulation of these two material systems, man and cosmos" (ibid.:366).

But cultural systems are "dynamic, not static" and so the primary process in evolution and in culture is the conversion of *energy*. "Biological evolution is simply an expression of the thermodynamic process" (ibid.:367). Similarly, the "functioning of culture as a whole therefore rests upon and is determined by the amount of energy harnessed and by the way in which it is put to work" by technology (ibid.:368). From this White derives a law for cultural evolution which is to parallel the second law of thermodynamics: "Other factors remaining constant, culture evolves as the amount of energy harnessed per capita per year is increased, or as the efficiency of the instrumental means of putting the energy to work is increased" (ibid.:369; italics removed). Culture therefore becomes "a mechanism for harnessing energy" (ibid.:369). Since White's law allows for precise measurement of cultural development, and since it is applicable to all societies, he is postulating a kind of universal evolution for culture.

All nontechnological systems in culture are depicted as subsidiary to and based on the technological system, feeding back into technology at the level of "conditioning." Culture is therefore a closed system, as most machines tend to be. White does not deny the existence of other kinds of systems, but all of them are reduced to materiality. In his discussion of symbols, for instance, he argues that symbols are "things" because "all symbols must have a physical form otherwise they could not enter our experience" (ibid.:39). Thus, although "human behavior is symbolic behavior; if it is not symbolic, it is not human" (ibid.), even symbolic and philosophical behavior are ultimately the products of technology and hence ultimately mechanisms: "Philosophy is a mechanism of adjustment of the human animal to his cosmic setting" (ibid.:401)

6.0   CRITIQUE OF CULTURE THEORIES

In Section 3.4 we reviewed the two criteria of conceptual adequacy identified by Pepper as scope and precision. In Section 4.0 we argued that racial determination and Teilhard's theory of the evolution of consciousness failed to satisfy basic requirements for sufficient scope and precision. While we have already labeled the sixteen culture theories surveyed here as "relatively adequate," there remains the specific task of evaluating the eight theory types against Pepper's criteria. That is, as noted in Section 3.5, each root metaphor has a characteristic flaw. The question now is this: How do these flaws, the lack of scope or precision, manifest themselves in culture theory? We shall speak to the theory types rather than to the theories themselves in order to clarify that ours is a metatheoretical and not a textual critique.

6.1   Formism

The generic problem of formism is its tendency to arrive at ultimate forms and thus reduce itself to a sort of dialectic mechanism. In structuralism (Benedict, Radcliffe-Brown, Lévi-Strauss), the reduction of the multiplicity of cultural forms tends to take place through evolution, equilibrium, or neural physiology. Once a single oppositional principle is identified in the dialectic, it is seemingly necessary to specify the overall pattern of culture integration. The uniqueness of cultures initially perceived by formists is replaced by adherence to a general "culture typology." Differences among cultures become differences in destiny, homeostasis, or mind type. In each case, there is the threat that all will be reduced to a single culture form—that is, to mechanism.

In functionalism, the same threat is expressed as a sort of universal social physiology of satisfying needs. The dialectic becomes one of desire/satisfaction. As in structuralism, the cultural forms in functionalism that deal with this dialectic are susceptible to mechanistic reduction. For both Malinowski and Firth, such a potential reduction is implicit in the importance they assign to *rationality*. If all cultures are to be considered rational within their ontological and epistemological assumptions, then at some point we must either accept ontological relativity (Quine 1969) or acknowledge ultimate logical reduction.

Thus built into both structuralism and functionalism is the potential for losing the complexity of types in the cultural typology. It is as if the periodic chart of the elements were reduced to a single atomic equation—which of course it is, and which is why physics supports chemistry. But what is desirable in the natural sciences may be unacceptable in the social sciences. Epistemologically, while most if not all culture formists are positivists, it is the positivism of Comte and not Mach that they support. Given the generally acknowledged state of disrepair in which positivism finds itself as a philosophy of science, formists may be well advised to seek new roots for their culture typologies. A reasonably clear contemporary alternative is the phenomenology of Alfred Schutz (1962) or the ethnomethodological approach of Harold Garfinkel (1967). Of course, no easy importation of new "life form" approaches to ethnology is going to end the threat of mechanistic reduction. Such is a given of formism itself. However, the rethinking of formist culture theory in terms compatible with the underlying root metaphor will prevent confusions regarding types.

6.2 Contextualism

Unlike formism, contextual culture theories (Boas, Kroeber, Schmidt, Wissler) share a single organizing concept: the culture trait. Thus they also share the task of tracing traits either through time or space. Historicism (Boas, Kroeber) stresses the temporal dimension, and diffusionism (Schmidt, Wissler) emphasizes the spatial dimension. In the case of diffusion, heliocentrism itself represents most graphically the potential reduction of contexts to a single fixed network. Rigid philosophies of history with fixed temporal sequences, evident in early twentieth century German historicism, parallel the diffusionist's spatial rigidity. But even in less rigid mappings, the common threat of reduction remains. The key element in contextual theories is the mechanism that ties the subject phenomena together. In the case of ethnology, contextualists use the notion of traits to link discrete bits together into a coherent whole, namely, culture. If the theorist identifies any single trait or list of traits as universal, then his or her mapping in either time or space has become the reduction to a mechanical principle. In such a case, mere correlation is replaced by causation and the indeterminancy of the event is replaced by the certainty of the machine.

Oddly, even as historicism and diffusionism have lapsed into considerable disfavor (primarily because of their "unscientific" image), physicists have at the same time been abandoning deterministic models of reality. In both quantum and relativity physics, for example, there is today a general recognition of noncausal mappings. Equally important, there have been major advances in statistical formulations of spatial and temporal dimensions (Wirsing 1972). Ironically, the early promise of anthropological statistics envisioned by Boas and Kroeber is now possible, but there is no one committed to the contextual paradigm.

6.3 Organicism

If anthropology can be said to have a love/hate relationship with any idea, it is certainly the organic metaphor for culture. Thus we find one of the most popular and one of the most rejected approaches to ethnology resting upon the same root metaphor. The gap between Bateson and Morgan is at once great and small. The narrow unilinear view of evolution, conceived of in raw terms of survival, sharply contrasts with the array of systemic interdependences and neologisms of cybernetics. But underlying the peculiar rhetoric of each is a common assumption of growth. And true to their common roots, both share the tendency to define growth without considering its corollary, decay. Moreover, the dimension of growth that holds the attention of both most clearly is mental development. The great difficulty they confront is that "mind" is not easily rendered as "brain." The biosocial model of organic life, securely founded in genetics, has yet to yield up the part/whole transcendence from body to mind. Without such a bridge, the main features of human culture lie outside the scope of explanation. As it is precisely these features that attract the organicist in the first place, such theorists tend to smooth over their gaps and leaps of faith with conventional wisdom. That is, ethnocentric biases are introduced as entelechies that fit the outcome the theorist projects. Whether the point of view is Christian progressivism or essentially nonreligious ecological determinism, the transcendence from body to mind is spurious in that its source is mind, not mind/body.

Genetics and the expanding field of information theory are promising to converge in the not-so-distant future. If such a synthesis does take place, the organic transcendence may be directly investigated and the scope of analysis expanded to include the key features of culture.

6.4 Mechanism

Like contextualism, both mechanistic perspectives (Steward, White) focus on a single concept: technology. As with historicism and diffusionism, technoeconomics and technoenergism differ on the spatial/temporal dimension. Steward adheres to multilinear evolution, White to unilinear evolution. This difference, which seems perhaps minor at the conceptual level, is highly significant in methodology. For example, multilinear studies may achieve higher degrees of specificity without risking inconsistency with established sequences. Nevertheless, both approaches share nearly total agreement on philosophical premises. These, the premises of cultural materialism, stress the pivotal role of technology in shaping culture and social evolution. It is important to note that technology occupies the logical position in cultural materialism that "control of means of production" has in Marxism. For cultural materialists, technology is essentially passive in human affairs but determinative in the relation between culture and environment. Marx extended the argument to recognize that the logic of technology is control within culture. In fact, there are contemporary theorists now exploring the possibility of a Marxian ethnology. That Marx relied on ethnography written from the standpoint of a social evolutionist has confused the development of cultural materialism with ideological polemics. In general, the recognition that technology is consciously controlled within culture has yet to be meaningfully rejected, but the problem remains to articulate a valid logic for the dynamics of such control. The logic of historical materialism cannot be substituted for a new logic of cultural materialism. Without such a logic capable of analyzing processes in non-Western cultures, materialism loses its comprehensive scope of application. Simply extending the Marxian point of view into non-Western environments leads to a great loss of precision.

7.0 Critique of Meta-Anthropology

Simple parsimony certainly requires that meta-anthropology argue its affirmative case before its critics. We have undertaken that obligation in the preceding sections. Now we wish to defend those efforts against three reasons that might be advanced for rejecting the need to do meta-anthropology: skepticism, dogmatism, and synthesis.

7.1 Skepticism

Perhaps the most obvious criticism of meta-anthropology is the charge that the ascent to meta-anthropology is without foundation. That is, there can be no meta-anthropology because there is no conceptual object (culture theory) on which to ground anthropological metatheorizing. To defend meta-anthropology from skepticism requires a defense of culture theory itself, rather than a defense of metatheory. Moreover, distinctions among metatheoretical perspectives are themselves as irrelevant as saints are to an atheist.

Presumably we need not consider the skeptic who denies a conceptual object called "culture." Such a position, in our view, denies any distinctive object to anthropological studies at all, reducing them to exotic sociology (although the skeptic may deny "society," "polity," and so forth until there is no object to human behavior left). It is the critic who accepts the ethnographic nexus but rejects the ethnological nexus who poses a genuine challenge, and it is to this issue that we turn.

To deny culture theory is to reject second-order abstraction. It is like the bilingual speaker rejecting translation. Each culture, in this view, is like a private language to be fully understood and appreciated only within its own bounds. Perhaps the most notable statement of this position in social theory is attributed to Peter Winch (1958, 1964).

In *The Idea of a Social Science,* Winch advances the rather Kantian notion that "our idea of what belongs to the realm of reality is given for us in the concepts which we use" (1958:15). In place of the Kantian principle of universal transcendence, Winch turns to Wittgenstein's notion of "rules." Thus to understand a cultural phenomenon, the task is "to have mastered the rules governing the usage of the concepts which express it." In contemporary American jargon, all social science becomes an ethnoscience, with a difference.

The difference is that ethnoscience, as now generally conceived, represents the native competency of the informant, not the culture group (unless, of course, the informant is a representative sample). Winch, on the other hand, contends that these "rules" are necessarily expressed in social institutions and not by private motives or purposes. The social contract theory implicit in ethnoscientific explanations of culture is explicitly rejected by Winch. Accordingly, the anthropological task is to inquire after the cultural reality given in the language and institutions of a culture and to be content with that (Winch 1964).

Following the argument against the existence of private languages (Wittgenstein 1969; Pitcher 1966), Winch holds that private rules are impossible. Therefore every social institution articulates shared public rules. Rationality, in this view, must reside within the domain of social institutions. No cross-cultural standards for judging conduct could exist; what distinguishes Azande magic from English science is a matter of culture perspective and not truth. Clearly there can be no ethnology since there are no universal standards of scientific truth to articulate it. Moreover, there cannot be a nomothetic social science because knowledge of the basic rules of life presupposes knowledge of a culturally defined reality. One cannot know reality without a standard of rationality; thus Winch leads us into a vicious circle. To wit, we cannot act meaningfully without cultural institutions, but we cannot ascertain the meaning of our acts without appeal to either personal or universal standards of rationality. To do otherwise is to acknowledge that we are mental captives without hope of escape or independence from our culture. The best we could do as social scientists would be to develop a taxonomy of (prison) cultures. Without the possibility of translation, one might inquire as to why we should even bother. In place of ethnology, Winch offers us ethnocentric solipsism.

Winch's declaration that cross-cultural reasoning is impossible is, in fact, nothing more than an *ignoratio* of the first order solely dependent upon his own reasoning (Hollis 1972:95). To understand the Azande, we must know Zande language and logic and the empirical instantiations thereof which occur to them. Their poison oracle, in their interpretation, becomes understandable to us as a function of random decision making under conditions of high-noise environments. Note that we need not accept Zande beliefs as *true* in order to understand them within the context of Azande society or cross-culturally. (Related arguments are given in Firth's essay on "Problem and Assumption in an Anthropological Study of Religion" in Firth 1964).

It is uniquely the function of metatheory, as it is with metalanguage and language, to provide a way to arrive at adequate standards for discussion across theories. The role of meta-anthropology is not so much to convince anthropologists to think cross-culturally or nomothetically as it is to discipline those thoughts which find formal expression.

7.2   Dogmatism

If the skeptic denies translation, the dogmatist asserts that no one else has anything to say. In a sense, every theorist has the ego of a dogmatist or else very little would get said initially. A perfect silence has yet to be uttered, however, and we must assume that at least a few theorists are listening. The problem with the dogmatic point of view is that it hears only what it wants to hear. All other theories are evaluated by how far they deviate from the dogma. In a virulent form, cultural dogmatism is an intellectual version of ethnocentrism, a cultural Lysenkoism. Such excesses make it an easy target for quiet head-shaking and professional ostracism. The seeds of dogmatism are also the seeds of belief, however, and the *argumentum ad hominem* cuts both ways.

To put the preceding paragraph more simply, a culture theory that did not explain its own status as a cultural product could not be regarded as a general theory of culture. Once a theory is accounted for within a theory, it acquires simultaneous stature as a metatheory, for it explains itself as well as all other culture theories (as culture products).

Actually the dogmatist is not really rejecting meta-anthropology but only the possibility for conceptual pluralism. In the dogmatist's view, the issue is already decided and discussion superfluous.

Just as the skeptic finds that the defense of "private culture" requires the construct of at least a taxonomic ethnology, so the dogmatist ultimately becomes dependent upon the inverse of the original position. When the dogmatist reduces meta-anthropology to a single culture theory in which all other culture theories are identified as culture products, there is an inevitable further reduction to a sociology of knowledge. The culture theory which explains other culture theory must explain itself as a culture product of its own culture. One need not accept a strong "determinist" version of the Mannheimian paradox to acknowledge that this leaves the dogma dependent upon itself. That this position is untenable is best illustrated by reference to a parallel position in mathematics. Note that the paradox of cultural dogmatism is not identical to the paradox of the sociology of knowledge. The sociology of knowledge leads to the social determination of social knowledge and hence a cycle of interdependent reasoning. Cultural dogmatism starts with a gestalt phenomenon, culture, which like language can articulate self-referent explanatory rules without necessarily running into problems. The problem is not simple self-reference.

Mathematics in the early twentieth century undertook the reduction of all mathematics to logical principles. This task, known as the Hilbert program, has had considerable payoffs in abstract mathematics and logic, computer design, and related fields. Less well known is its potential contribution to social theory via the Titanic effect. That is, Kurt Godel's proof in 1931 of the absolute incompleteness of proof involving mathemetical reduction to logic functions as an iceberg in the sea of reductive reasoning (Nagel and Newman 1958). Extension of the proof has created a general theory of proofs (DeLong 1971:56–60).

Stated briefly, current work clearly indicates the impossibility of any consistent proof of any logical system which includes any elementary mathematics as a product. It does not say that mathematics is illogical; rather, it says that proving *everything* requires some inconsistency, or that *complete* consistency entails some incompleteness in demonstration. It should be noted that Godel's proof is not self-defeating: it did not require mathematics.

To examine the implications of Godel's theorem for culture theory, note the following points: (1) mathematics is itself a cultural product; (2) presumably every culture has the potential for the discovery of mathematical reasoning; hence (3) every culture incorporates the theorem. The final step can be illustrated by reference to a problem of culture theory in highly advanced societies projected as "technocracies." In the ideal model of these societies, all decisions are made through cybernetic systems. Of course, it is generally assumed that humans will govern the programming of these systems and thus compensate for logical limitations. However, if at any point the system were to achieve self-control (by design or accident), as is envisioned by contemporary critics and science fiction writers, then the technocracy would be insane. That is, the governance function for the culture would either be unable to make consistent decisions or would make decisions the system did not know to be true or false. We should emphasize that Godel's theorem does not preclude the existence of such systems but only notes their features.

To summarize the dogmatist's position in the light of Godel's theorem only requires us to recall that the dogma ultimately reduces to itself as a culture product. If the dogmatist adopts the strategy for consistency, there must be a recognition that there are cultural phenomena outside explanation. On the other hand, adoption of the requirements of completeness implies inconsistencies within the dogma. In the first case, meta-anthropology provides a bridge to residual phenomena. Godel's proof is no barrier to meta-anthropology. In the second case, the only defense of inconsistency is skepticism. We have dealt with that issue in the preceding section.

7.3   Synthesis

If skepticism and dogmatism are polar types in the argument to reject meta-anthropology, then arguments for direct synthesis are the middle ground. By direct synthesis, we mean arguments which suggest eclectic borrowing among culture theories without regard to theory type. Suggestions for "structural materialism" which do not consider the obvious intervention of the classic mind/body duality as a problem in metatheory illustrate the issue. There is really very little one can say in cautioning against premature or reckless synthesizing that does not sound like trite etiquette to be dismissed by brilliant insight. Certainly genius plays a different game, at least on the surface. But even genius must ultimately diagram, report, explain the foundations of insight. Science does not accept the maxim "Don't ask so long as it works." On the contrary, the fact that something does work automatically focuses our inquiry on it. Meta-anthropology may not help the true genius to get to synthesis but it will be necessary in understanding why the synthesis works.

For the nongenius, of course, and we obviously put ourselves in this category, meta-anthropology is the guide as well as a path. The architectonic displayed in Table 1 clearly indicates productive patterns of synthetic research within and between world hypotheses. It would be the task of *meta-anthropology*, then, to judge which linkages would be most productive.

NOTES

1.   Of course this does not deny the interplay between theory and data but only notes the constructive role played by each; cf. Glaser and Strauss (1967).

2.   Russell's "simple" theory of types has been extended by F. P. Ramsey (1931) as the "ramified" theory of types in order to eliminate some of the remaining paradoxes of self-reference not covered by the original formulation. The debate over the problem of managing statements of self-reference has continued in philosophy; cf. Sommers (1963).

3.   In our view there is no conflict between the existence of tacit or personal knowledge in science and the requirement that scientific knowledge be public. Michael Polanyi's argument for the importance of "feel" in doing science does not deny the standard for reporting scientific findings. Wittgenstein's argument against the existence of private languages simply indicates, as he said in *Tractatus Logico-Philosophicus,* "whereof we cannot speak, thereof we must be silent."

4.   Traditionally, scientists and philosophers of science have stressed the supremacy of deductibility as the principle of coherence. However, as physicists no longer insist on the principle of causality in explanation (stochastic principles are accepted), so social scientists need no epistemological dogmas (Hutten 1970; Quine 1953:19).

5.   An object language is the language under analysis or development. The metalanguage is the language used to characterize the structure of the object language. Both are distinct from the intended interpretation or application of the language (Carnap 1958).

6.   We do not agree with Bateson's conclusion that paradoxes of abstraction are a necessary feature of human communication (ibid.:193). Indeed, the whole point of metatheory is the reduction of metacommunicative problems.

7.   Paul Diesing (1971) makes such an argument about the context of discovery in social scientific theory. The problem remains, however, within the context of verification.

8.   We shall require the *ad hominem* principle in Section 6. The proper role of *ad hominem* agruments is discussed in Fitch (1967:158).

9.   In rejecting the sociology of knowledge argument, we are taking specific exception to S. B. Barnes' essay that presents the "view of Western science which links its growth with the existence of permissive social structural features and minimises the distinctiveness of thought of the individual scientists" (1969:101). Barnes' line of reasoning follows that of Thomas Kuhn's notion of "paradigms" (1962). As far as we know, no one has made an argument for a scientific paradigm in anthropology. The open debate between evolutionists, diffusionists, functionalists, and so forth virtually precludes any reference to a paradigmatic establishment as envisioned by Kuhn. Of course, one might speak of "mini-paradigms" such as functionalism (Gregg and Williams 1948) which do define a form of "normal science" for adherents. However, as far as Kuhn's hypothesis concerning scientific change is concerned, such mini-paradigms would fail to have a truly revolutionary effect, because such an effect can take place only with a major change in paradigm.

REFERENCES CITED

Almond, Gabriel A. and Sidney Verba
1965   *The civic culture.* Boston: Little, Brown.

Barnes, S. B.
1969   Paradigms—scientific and social. *Man* 4 (1):94–102.

Bateson, Gregory
1958   *Naven.* Stanford: Stanford University Press.
1972   *Steps to an ecology of mind.* San Francisco: Chandler.

Benedict, Ruth
1934   *Patterns of culture.* Boston. Houghton Mifflin.

Bertalanffy, Ludwig Von
1967   *Robots, men and minds.* New York: Braziller.

Boas, Franz
1948   *Race, language and culture.* New York: Macmillan.

Boon, James A.
1973   Further operations of "culture" in anthropology: a synthesis of and for debate. In *The idea of culture in the social sciences,* ed. Louis Schneider and Charles Bonjean. Cambridge: Cambridge University Press.

Brace, C. L. and M. F. Ashley Montagu
1965   *Man's evolution: an introduction to physical anthropology.* New York: Macmillan.

Carnap, Rudolf
1958   *Introduction to symbolic logic.* New York: Dover.

DeLong, Howard
1971   Unsolved problems in arithmetic. *Scientific American* 224:50–60.

Diesing, Paul
1971   *Patterns of discovery in the social sciences.* Chicago: Aldine.

Firth, Raymond
1951   *Elements of social organization.* Boston: Beacon Press.
1964   *Essays on social organisation and values.* London School of Economics Monographs on Social Anthropology, no. 28. London: Athlone Press.

Fitch, Frederic B.
1967   *Symbolic logic.* New York: Ronald Press (original 1952).

Garfinkel, Harold
1967   *Essays in ethnomethodology.* Englewood Cliffs, N.J.: Prentice-Hall.

Glaser, B. G. and A. L. Strauss
1967   *The discovery of grounded theory.* Chicago: Aldine.

Gregg, D. and E. Williams
1948   The dismal science of functionalism. *American Anthropologist* 50:594–611.

Harris, Marvin
1968   *The rise of anthropological theory.* New York: Crowell.

Hollis, Martin
1972   Witchcraft and winchcraft. *Philosophy of the Social Sciences* 2 (2):89–103.

Holton, Gerald
1967–   Influences on Einstein's early work in relativity theory. *American Scholar*
1968   37:59–79.

Hutten, Ernest H.
1970   Symmetry physics and information theory. *Diogenes* 72:1–21.

Kaplan, David and Robert A. Manners
1972   *Culture theory.* Englewood Cliffs, N. J.: Prentice-Hall.

Kardiner, Abram and E. Preble
1961   *They studied man.* New York: New American Library.

Kim, Young K.
1964   The concept of political culture in comparative politics. *Journal of Politics*
          26:313–336.

Kroeber, Alfred Louis
1944   *Configurations of culture growth.* Berkeley: University of California Press.
1952   *The nature of culture.* Chicago: University of Chicago Press.

Kroeber, A. L. and Clyde Kluckhohn
1952   *Culture: a critical review of concepts and definitions.* Papers of the Peabody
          Museum of American Archaeology and Ethnology, vol. 47. Cambridge, Mass.:
          Harvard University.

Kubler, George
1963   *The shape of time: remarks on the history of things.* New Haven: Yale Univer-
          sity Press.

Kuhn, Thomas
1962   *The structure of scientific revolutions.* Chicago: University of Chicago Press.

Lévi-Strauss, Claude
1962   *The savage mind.* London: Weidenfeld and Nicholson.
1967   *Totemism.* Boston: Beacon Press.

Malinowski, Bronislaw
1944   *A scientific theory of culture and other essays.* Chapel Hill: University of North
          Carolina Press.

Morgan, Lewis Henry
1877   *Ancient society.* New York: Holt.

Nagel, Ernest and J. R. Newman
1958   *Godel's proof.* New York: New York University Press.

Pepper, Stephen C.
1966   *World hypotheses.* Berkeley: University of California Press (original 1942).

Perry, W. J.
1923   *The children of the sun: a study in the early history of civilisation.* London:
            Methuen.

Pitcher, George
1966   *Wittgenstein: the philosophical investigations: a collection of critical essays.*
            Garden City, N.Y.: Anchor.

Pye, Lucian W.
1973   Culture and political science: problems in the evaluation of the concept of
            political culture. In *The idea of culture in the social sciences*, ed. Louis Schneider
            and Charles Bonjean. Cambridge: Cambridge University Press.

Quine, Willard Van Orman
1953   *From a logical point of view.* Cambridge, Mass. Harvard University Press.
1969   *Ontological relativity and other essays.* New York: Columbia University Press.

Radcliffe-Brown, A. R.
1948   *A natural science of society.* Glencoe, Ill. Free Press.
1952   *Structure and function in primitive society.* Glencoe, Ill. Free Press.
1958   *Method in social anthropology.* Edited by M. N. Srinivas. Chicago: University
            of Chicago Press.

Ramsey, F. P.
1931   *The foundations of mathematics.* New York: Harcourt, Brace.

Rappaport, Roy A.
1967   *Pigs for the ancestors: ritual in the ecology of a New Guinea people.* New Haven:
            Yale University Press.

Russell, Bertrand
1908   Mathematical logic as based on the theory of types. *American Journal of
            Mathematics* 30:222–262. Reprinted in Russell, *Logic and knowledge,* ed.
            Robert Charles Marsh. London: Allen and Unwin, 1956.

Schmidt, Wilhelm
1939   *The cultural historical method of ethnology.* New York: Fortuny.

Schneider, Louis and Charles Bonjean (eds.)
1973   *The idea of culture in the social sciences.* Cambridge: Cambridge University
            Press.

Schutz, Alfred
1962   *The problem of social reality.* The Hague: Martinus Nijhoff.

Smith, Grafton Elliot
1933   *The diffusion of culture.* London: Watts.

Sommers, F.
1963   Types and ontology. *Philosophical Review* 72:327–363.

Stanner, W. E. H.
1967   Reflections on Durkheim and aboriginal religion. In *Social organization: essays
            presented to Raymond Firth,* ed. Maurice Freedman. Chicago: Aldine.

Steward, Julian
1955   *Theory of culture change.* Urbana: University of Illinois Press.
1956   Cultural evolution. *Scientific American* 194 (5):69–76.

Teilhard de Chardin, Pierre
1959   *The phenomenon of man.* Translated by Bernard Wall. New York: Harper.
1964   *The future of man.* Translated by Norman Denny. New York: Harper & Row.

Tylor, Edward B.
1971   *Primitive culture: researches into the development of mythology, philosophy, religion, art, and custom.* London: John Murray.

White, Leslie A.
1949   *The science of culture: a study of man and civilization.* New York: Farrar, Strauss.

Winch, Peter
1958   *The idea of a social science.* New York: Humanities Press.
1964   Understanding a primitive society. *American Philosophical Quarterly* 1:307–324.

Wirsing, Rolf
1972   Measuring diffusion: the Geary method and the Dacey method. Paper presented at the American Anthropological Association meeting in Toronto.

Wissler, Clark
1926   *The relation of nature to man in aboriginal America.* New York: Oxford University Press.
1938   *The American Indian: an introduction to the anthropology of the New World.* New York: Oxford University Press.

Wittgenstein, Ludwig
1969   *Philosophical investigations.* New York: Macmillan.

Index

Ah Long, 103

Ah Tam, 103, 104, 105; business empire of, 112

Aina Pumehana school, 89

Aitape, New Guinea, 102

Alexishafen, New Guinea, 57

Aloha, 93, 96

Ambenob Local Government Council, 65, 66

Angaur, New Guinea, 105

Animism, in anthropological theories, 186–187, 188, 189

Anuta Island

—Chieftains of, 1–7, 8, 9, 28; dual power of, 10, 13; installation of, 7; patrilateral succession of, 2–7. *See also* Ariki i Mua; Ariki i Muri

—Church, Anglican, on, 9, 13, 14, 15, 27, 30; catechists of, 9, 14, 15, 16, 25; companions, function of, 16, 26; Melanesian Brotherhood Mission, 9, 15, 16; St. James Church, 13, 14, 16; St. John Church, 9, 13, 14, 16

—Deities of, 1, 25, 26, 27, 29

—*Kainangas,* 1, 2, 7, 10, 11, 12, 13, 14, 23, 28

—Kinship systems: complex structure of, 18–22, 24, 30; first born, 20, 25; male dominance in, 19, 20, 21, 22; restraints in, 19, 20, 21, 22; status of women in, 17–18, 19, 21, 22, 24, 25, 27

—Language, 9

—*Maru,* 6, 9, 26, 29, 31n13; authority of, 11, 12, 13, 14, 15, 17, 23

—*Pono,* 11, 14, 15, 24; function of, 12, 13

—Social customs of, 8, 9, 13, 14, 18–22

Apollonian culture, 192, 193

Ariki i Mua, 2, 6, 7, 15; powers of, 9–10, 11, 13, 27–28; status of, 8–9

Ariki i Muri, 2, 10. *See also* Ariki Tepuko

Ariki Tepuko, 2, 3, 6, 7, 12, 28; status of, 8–9, 10

Aropa, 28–29, 30

Bagasin area, New Guinea, 57, 60

Bagasin Rebellion, 53

Barth, F., 128, 129, 133, 136

Bateson, G., 175, 181, 201–202, 208

Bay Loo Company, 108–109, 114

Benedict, R., 191–194

Berthoud, G., 131, 133, 137

"Big Man" societies, 33, 36, 41

Bismarck Archipelago, 104; Chinese in, 103, 104, 105

"Black King" (Yali), 55

Blau, P., 127, 128, 130, 136

Boas, Franz, 179, 198, 199, 208

Bogati, New Guinea, 60

Bogia area, New Guinea, 57, 58

Bonjean, C., 176, 177

Boon, J. A., 177–178

Bucca (goblin), 145

Bull-roarers, 34, 35, 36

About the Authors

John J. Attinasi is assistant professor of anthropology at Columbia University. He received his B.A. in linguistics at the University of St. Thomas (Houston) in 1967 and his M.A. and Ph.D. in anthropology at the University of Chicago in 1970 and 1973 respectively. His published fieldwork has been with the Chol in Mexico on Chol Mayan grammar and ritual. His interests include sociolinguistics, symbolism, myth and ritual, and Maya and North American ethnic minorities. Attinasi reports that in 1968, when drafted into the United States Army, he elected to avoid the war in Southeast Asia "constructively by teaching junior high school in Gary, Indiana," through which experience he was made "acutely aware of social and linguistic problems." This led him to enter graduate school in anthropology, where he was a member of Professor Firth's seminar at Chicago in 1970 and 1971.

Stephen T. Boggs is professor of anthropology at the University of Hawaii (Manoa Campus), Honolulu. He received his A.B. in psychology at Harvard in 1947 and his Ph.D. in sociology and anthropology at Washington University (St. Louis) in 1954. His published fieldwork has been personality and socialization among the Ojibwa, community attitudes in a California suburb, values and attitudes of an American occupational group, social structure on Truk, and social structure and speech acts of Hawaiian children. His interests include sociolinguistics and applied anthropology. He has taught at Stanford University and was an NIMH researcher at Bethesda for three years. Boggs states: "I would like to claim to be the oldest graduate student among the contributors to the volume. My first formal study in anthropology was in Professor Firth's seminar at the London School of Economics during the Michaelmas term, 1947, while I was a Shaw traveling fellow of Harvard College." He also participated in Professor Firth's seminars at the University of Hawaii in 1968 and 1969. "I was impressed from the very first by everything of Firth's that I read, and equally impressed by the truly collaborative outcome of his seminars, both then and years later in Hawaii." The insights gained from Firth led Boggs to "studying social structure in the details of daily life."

John J. Cove is assistant professor of sociology and anthropology at Carleton University, Ottawa. He received his B.A. and M.A. in sociology at Dalhousie University in 1967 and 1968, respectively, and his Ph.D. in anthropology at the University of British Columbia in 1971. He has conducted fieldwork in Newfoundland, British Columbia, and Cornwall, England, on fisheries development and production systems and is currently studying the Nishga on the problem of reconstructing traditional culture through mythology. He has also taught at Memorial University. Cove participated in Professor Firth's seminar at the University of British Columbia in 1969.

Richard Feinberg is assistant professor of anthropology at Kent State University, Ohio. He received his A.B. in anthropology at the University of California (Berkeley) in 1969, and his M.A. and Ph.D. in anthropology at the University of Chicago in 1971 and 1974 respectively. His published fieldwork has been on the social structure of Anuta Island, and his interests include kinship and social structure, symbolism, culture theory, culture change, and Western Polynesia and North American Indians. He has also taught at Roosevelt University in Chicago in 1970 and 1971. Feinberg was a member of Professor Firth's seminar at the University of Chicago in 1970 and 1971.

James G. Peoples is a lecturer in anthropology at the University of California (Davis). He received his B.A. in anthropology from Cowell College, University of California (Santa Cruz), in 1970 and his Ph.D. in anthropology from the University of California (Davis), in 1977. His fieldwork on Kusaie in the Eastern Caroline Islands focused on the erosion of traditional sociopolitical structures and the effect of that erosion on government and agricultural development. His other interests are human ecology and economic development. Peoples was a member of Professor Firth's seminar at Davis in 1974.

J. I. Prattis is associate professor of sociology and anthropology at Carleton University, Ottawa. He received his B.A. at London University in 1965, his B. Litt. at Oxford University in 1967, and his Ph.D. in anthropology at the University of British Columbia, Vancouver, in 1970. His published fieldwork has been on economic development among the Northwest Coast Indians, among groups in Arctic Quebec and the Outer Hebrides, and in Greece. He has published on development anthropology, structuralism, methodology in economic anthropology, and exchange theory. Prattis participated in Professor Firth's seminar at the University of British Columbia in 1969.

Dawn Ryan is senior lecturer in anthropology at Monash University, Melbourne. She received her M.A. in anthropology from the University of Sydney in 1965 and her Ph.D. in anthropology from the University of Hawaii in 1970. Her published fieldwork has been on economic development, social change, politics, religion, and urbanization among the Toaripi of Papua New Guinea. She has taught at the University of Sydney, the Administrative Staff College at Port Moresby, the University of Hawaii, and Macquarie University in Sydney and has worked as a researcher in the New Guinea Research Unit of Australian National University. Ryan participated in Professor Firth's seminar at the University of Hawaii in 1968 and 1969.

S. Lee Seaton is an analyst with Vydec, Inc., in New Jersey. He received his B.A. and M.A. in political science from California State University (Fullerton) in 1966 and 1968 respectively, and his Ph.D. in political science from the University of Hawaii in 1971. He has published on philosophy of science, traditional Hawaiian political culture, and cultural symbolism, and is interested in political anthropology and comparative politics. He has taught at the University of California (Berkeley) and at Bowling Green State University, Ohio. Seaton was a member of Professor Firth's seminar at the University of Hawaii in 1968 and 1969.

Karen Ann Watson-Gegeo is assistant professor at Harvard University in the Graduate School of Education's Learning Environments program. She received her B.A. and M.A. in English and literature at California State University (Fullerton) in 1965 and 1967 respectively, and a Ph.D. in anthropology at the University of Hawaii in 1972. Her published fieldwork has been on speech acts of Hawaiian children, Kuarafi culture (Solomon Islands), sociolinguistic theory, and the impact of tourism in the Pacific. Her other interests include myth, ritual, and socialization. Her ethnographic areas are Melanesia (the Solomon Islands), Polynesia, and the United States as a complex society. She has taught at California State University campuses at Fullerton and Hayward, and was a research associate at the East-West Culture Learning Institute, East-West Center, for four years. Watson-Gegeo was a member of Professor Firth's seminar at the University of Hawaii in 1968 and 1969.

David Yen-Ho Wu is a research associate at the East-West Culture Learning Institute, The East-West Center, Honolulu, where he conducts research on interaction and socialization. He received his B.A. in archaeology and anthropology at National Taiwan University, Taipei, in 1963, his M.A. in anthropology at the University of Hawaii in 1969, and his Ph.D. in anthropology at Australian National University, Canberra, in 1974. His published fieldwork has been on socialization, religion, and social organization of Formosan aboriginal tribes and on overseas Chinese communities in Papua New Guinea. Wu has conducted research on social relations in Singapore and on ethnic relations in Hawaii. He is also interested in psychological and economic anthropology. Wu has held research positions at the Institute of Ethnology, Academia Sinica, and at the Research School of Pacific Studies, Australian National University. He has also taught at the University of Hawaii. Wu was a member of Professor Firth's seminar at the University of Hawaii in 1968 and 1969.

Ｘ Production Notes

This book was designed by Roger J. Eggers and
typeset on the Unified Composing System by the
design and production staff of The University
Press of Hawaii.

The text and display typeface is English Times.

Offset presswork and binding were done by
Thomson-Shore, Inc. Text paper is Glatfelter P &
S Offset, basis 55.